PRAISE FOR *SUSTAINABLE ADVERTISING*

"Our industry has long prided itself on driving instrumental change and there has never been a moment in our history where this has been more relevant or needed. Sustainability is complex and nuanced, which is why *Sustainable Advertising* is such an essential text for the advertising industry today. If you have ever asked yourself where to begin in the quest to create a more sustainable tomorrow, this book is without a doubt where you should start."
Dame Annette King DBE, Global Lead, Marketing, Accenture Song and Chair, Advertising Association

"Advertising has a powerful influence on how people behave, and this is as relevant to climate action as it is to consumer trends. This book tells us everything we need to know to make climate action happen."
Dame Carolyn McCall DBE, Chief Executive, ITV

"Essential reading and a necessary check-in on the global industry's drive towards sustainable branded communication. More than that, it's a tool and a resource that will help us all understand how to collectively drive progress through creativity."
Simon Cook, Chief Executive, Lions

"The power of advertising is in its potential to change minds and change the way we live. This paradigm-shifting book demonstrates how that potential can now be harnessed for the better, to change our behaviour and lifestyles before it is too late, so that we can make the greatest change imaginable – to change to save the planet. To transform our economies to become sustainable for the future, the use of the advertising medium is the ultimate message – and this is the ultimate and indispensable guide on how to deliver the message and the change we all need to embark on."
Rt Hon Chris Skidmore OBE, former UK Energy and Clean Growth Minister and Chair, the Independent Net Zero Review

"The transition to a NetZero economy – much like digitization and the rise of AI – is an unstoppable force that firms globally will have to come to terms with, shifting business and operational models, or risk being devaluated into oblivion. In this transition, two factors are undeniable: action is possible and rewarded now; and advertising – our perennial mechanism for demand generation and behaviour change – will need to play a crucial role in every firm's successful transition. In *Sustainable Advertising*, Matt and Sebastian lay out a compelling, clear, and practical path for advertising professionals – in agency, client, or media side – to lead thoughtfully and successfully in this domain."
Felipe Thomaz, Associate Professor of Marketing, University of Oxford's Saïd Business School

"Matt and Sebastian have been at the heart of the advertising industry's drive to become more sustainable since the climate action workstream was first established by the UK's trade bodies. This book brings together all their experience and expertise about how the industry can decarbonize and ensure every campaign makes a positive contribution to a sustainable future. A must-read for every advertising practitioner, with simple and straightforward guidance on how to be effective and impactful."
Alessandra Bellini, President, Advertising Association

"The advertising industry doesn't have a pretty track record, too often shaping demand for a stream of unsustainable products. Now the authors issue a rallying cry for advertisers to become active allies in the big shift to sustainable lifestyles. Packed full of practical tips and guides, based on years' experience, they show how, in the end, every ad could become a green ad, promoting sustainable services and products, and helping us all live with less. It's a total transformation that must happen – and fast."
Harriet Lamb, Chief Executive, WRAP (Waste & Resources Action Programme)

"At Meta, we envision a just and equitable transition to a zero-carbon economy, and we are working with others to scale inclusive solutions that help create a healthier planet for all, ensuring that no one is left behind. It is critical that we are all doing our part and sharing best practices to educate and inspire. *Sustainable Advertising* is an important resource for marketers to share their meaningful progress to the path to decarbonize their operations and drive consumer behaviour change."
Christy Cooper, Global Director, Industry Relations, Meta

"The green economy is the opportunity of a generation for innovators, marketers and their agency partners. Sebastian and Matt have brought together the collective wisdom of those shaping an advertising industry which accelerates a sustainable future. It is full of insights, tips and case studies, designed to help anyone involved in an advertising campaign to make a real difference now."

Keith Weed CBE, President, Royal Horticultural Society and Former Unilever CMCO

"The advertising industry is at a crossroads. Our legitimacy is on the line. Pretending things are greener than they are, that's like farting in public and blaming the person next to you. We have to take responsibility not for our minuscule emissions, but the advertised emissions, if we are to lead the way to a liveable tomorrow. It's time to read."

Thomas Kolster, author of *Mr. Goodvertising* and *The Hero Trap*, marketing and sustainability advisor

"The world is in desperate need of powerful levers to accelerate climate action – advertising, with its unique ability to shape behaviour, can be the next critical lever to engage. *Sustainable Advertising* helps those in the sector not just fulfil their responsibility in reducing their emissions, but more importantly, use their superpower to reduce all emissions. We need the ad sector to be the new hero on the path to net-zero, creating the world we want."

Bill Westcott, Managing Partner, BrainOxygen

"We're saturated with advertising day-in, day-out, and it has long been a force for excessive consumption. This book provides a much-needed review for the industry, shining a light on the marketing techniques and behavioural science theory and evidence we can all use to promote greener consumption. It's a very welcome call to action for all advertisers with a green conscience."

Toby Park, Head of Energy and Sustainability, The Behaviour Insights Team, UK

"Our industry has always used the power of creativity to influence behaviours, drive change and shape society. As *Sustainable Advertising* clearly sets out, the critical role advertising plays in contributing to a more sustainable economy is no different: through our work we have the opportunity and

responsibility to offer more sustainable options for consumers and inspire positive action at the scale needed to safeguard our planet's future."
Mark Read, CEO, WPP

"If we're to truly address the climate and biodiversity crises, we'll need to upend the culture of consumption stoked by the Madison Avenues and High Streets of the world. No amount of green consumerism or values-based shopping can do more than engender incremental change. In their insightful book, Matt Bourn and Sebastian Munden provide the lessons and leadership needed to transform the advertising industry to become a catalyst for positive change, from the industry's own emissions to how it can accelerate more sustainable choices and behaviours. This is a powerful, must-read book for any communicator, marketer or brand seeking to be part of a better future."
Joel Makower, Chairman and Co-founder, GreenBiz Group

Sustainable Advertising

How advertising can support a better future

Matt Bourn and
Sebastian Munden

KoganPage

First published in Great Britain and the United States in 2024 by Kogan Page Limited

2nd Floor, 45 Gee Street	8 W 38th Street, Suite 902	4737/23 Ansari Road
London	New York, NY 10018	Daryaganj
EC1V 3RS	USA	New Delhi 110002
United Kingdom		India

www.koganpage.com

Kogan Page books are printed on paper from sustainable forests.

© Matt Bourn and Sebastian Munden, 2024

The right of Matt Bourn and Sebastian Munden to be identified as the authors of this work has been asserted by them in accordance with the Copyright, Designs and Patents Act 1988.

ISBNs

Hardback	978 1 3986 1385 0
Paperback	978 1 3986 1383 6
Ebook	978 1 3986 1384 3

British Library Cataloguing-in-Publication Data

A CIP record for this book is available from the British Library.

Library of Congress Control Number

2023952597

Typeset by Integra Software Services, Pondicherry
Print production managed by Jellyfish
Printed and bound by CPI Group (UK) Ltd, Croydon CR0 4YY

CONTENTS

07 Quick wins, and long-term success for media plans 100

08 Reducing emissions through awards and events 113

09 The big sustainable behaviour change challenge 126

LIST OF FIGURES AND TABLES

PREFACE

Our book is about how the advertising industry could and should take a pivotal role in accelerating the transition to a sustainable economy. Its main point is that the framing, explaining and desire-creating powers of marketing and advertising should be used to present more sustainable choices to citizens. Marketing and advertising can help people make good choices in service of getting as close as possible to the Paris Agreement targets, formalized in law by many countries, and so help avert the most extreme predictions for climate, and sustainably regenerate our economy.

It appears customary to summarize all the evidence for the severity of the man-made climate catastrophe in any book's first chapter that then seeks to discuss how citizens, governments and businesses should act. We will not spend time explaining why there is a climate emergency. Our starting point is that this is a fact established through peer review and rigorous academic debate by scientists over decades – the question is what to do about it. Please do not assume from the absence of an 'emergency' chapter one, that we do not recognize the severity of the situation.

Our solutions are from the world of marketing and advertising because we have worked for several decades in this world. We believe in what it can (and cannot) do, based on our experiences. We are not proposing that marketing or advertising are the only solutions, just that they can make a significant contribution whenever put to good use. All citizens from every walk of life will need to do their bit. When it comes to other professions, we leave that for others better qualified.

This book is written for now, which is the next best time to act, after a few decades ago. All case studies, research and references to codes and laws are fully up to date today. Our aim is to enlist your help in mobilizing our industry now, as you read this book, to be a force for good. No doubt the codes and laws will change. Progress today, will look like the problem tomorrow. If we succeed, this book will become a hostage to the future. Everything in it will look small, when compared with your achievements that follow.

But we are looking to the future, putting wind in your sails with our review of the efforts being made now and the research available today, so everyone can take a greater number of bolder actions towards a sustainable future.

It is the set of the sails, not the wind's direction, that determines where the ship goes.

London, September 2023

ACKNOWLEDGEMENTS

Firstly, a personal thanks from us to George Grant, editor at Credos, who has been a fantastic support throughout the process of writing and editing this book.

There are many passionate people from across our industry who helped make it all possible. They include James Best who kickstarted the UK advertising industry's climate action initiative and people pushing for action including Ben Essen, and the Purpose Disrupters team led by Rob McFaul, Lisa Merrick-Lawless and Jonathan Wise, Stephen Woodford, the Advertising Association's Chief Executive, for driving Ad Net Zero forward in partnership with the Director Generals of the IPA and ISBA, Paul Bainsfair and Phil Smith, the Ad Net Zero team including Elle Chartres, Anthony Falco, Alex d'Albertanson, John Osborn, Rachel Schnorr, Danielle Willett, Sam Woodman, Jan Sanghera and Amy Nash, the backers of Ad Net Zero to help roll it out in the UK and internationally, namely Alison Pepper and Marla Kaplowitz at 4A's Amy Larm at Amazon, Bob Liodice, Nick Primola and Liz Kneebone at the ANA, Anna Lungley, Stephanie Lambert, Jordan Hunter Powell at dentsu, Liam Brennan and Isabelle Massey at Diageo, Tamara Daltroff of EACA & Voxcomm, Lorraine Twohill, Michael Todd and Yves Schwarzbart at Google, Ben Downing, Patrick Affleck and Rosie Kitson at Havas, Dagmara Szulce at IAA, Andrew Hayward Wright and Lauren Wakefield at IAB Europe, David Cohen at IAB, Charley Stoney at IAPI, Jennifer Oliveras at Indeed, Jemma Gould at IPG, Phil Thomas and Simon Cook at Cannes Lions, Kim Dirckx, L'Oreal, Christy Cooper at Meta, Karen van Bergen at Omnicom, Eve Magnant at Publicis, Johanna Bauman at PubMatic, Fabrice Beaulieu and Maria Shcheglakova at Reckitt, Aline Santos and Dana Cadden at Unilever, Sophie Roosen at Union des Marques, Stephan Loerke, WFA, Mark Read and Hannah Harrison, WPP.

Also, James Craig at the ASA, Rachel Barber-Mack at Media Smart, Felicity McLean and Niken Wresniwiro at WPP, Amanda Forrester at OpenX, Tony Mattson and Rosie Kitson at Havas UK, Derek Moore and Holly Arnold at Coffee&TV, Jo Fenn at AdGreen, Rob Newman at ISBA, Eliot Liss at IPA, Becky Verano at Reckitt, Ian Armstrong at Silverscape, Felipe Thomaz at Saïd Business School, Laura Smith-Roberts at Google,

Christy Cooper at Meta, Maxwell Clarke at Amazon Ads, Tom Patterson at Channel 4, Eva Dvorakova and Martin Corke at Clear Channel, Tim Lumb at Outsmart, Emma Cheshire at Propellor, Rupert Smith and Lewis Boulton at Newsworks, Jo Tomlin at the PPA, Anna Cremin at Pearl & Dean, Michael Ireland at the Radiocentre, Carey Trevill at the BPMA, Carryl Pierre-Drews at IAB, Anthony Katsur at IAB Tech Lab, Rob Rakowitz at GARM, Will Gilroy at the WFA, Gideon Spanier and Jennie Meynell at Campaign, Anna Abdelnoor at isla, Isa Kurata at ACT Responsible, Thomas 'Mr Goodvertising' Kolster, Brett Meyer at the Tony Blair Institute, David Halpern and Toby Park at BIT, Tom Hubbard at Edelman, Jonathan Hall at Kantar, Dagmara Szulce at IAA, Jaclyn Murphy at Edelman, David Hall at Behaviour Change, Harriet Kingaby and Florencia Lujani at Media Bounty, Ryan Uhl at Mail Metro Media, Sarah Jones and Skye Harrison at Sky, Camilla Lambert at Cannes Lions, Claire Shrewsbury at WRAP, Rob McFaul at #ChangeTheBrief, Kate Waters and Jeremy Mathieu at ITV, Emily Olin at IPG, Daniel Pierce at TTG, Leo Rayman at EdenLab, Celine Dallas and team at Tesco, Rachel Arthur at the UN Environment Programme, Kim Johnson at NatWest, Bill Westcott, Julia Ramsay and Sam Tomlinson at PwC, Danika Gregg, Dominic Powers at dentsu, Tim Munden, and Sarah Skinner at Grace Blue.

USEFUL TERMS AND PHRASES

Our industry loves acronyms and technical phrases; the likes of B2B, B2C, KPIs and ROI are ubiquitous and digital technology introduced new terms that we've swiftly adopted – SEO, PPC, CTA, UX, programmatic and more. But now it's essential we fully embrace a new set of terms around sustainability. This next section should help you with them before we start using them throughout the book.

Greenhouse gas (GHG)

Greenhouse gases are gases that raise the earth's temperature. The 'greenhouse' aspect of the term comes from their effect of trapping heat in the atmosphere, similar to a greenhouse. According to the Kyoto Protocol, the key gases which contribute to climate change are carbon dioxide (CO_2), methane (CH_4), nitrous oxide (N_2O), F-gases and sulphur hexafluoride (SF_6). Another group of chlorofluorocarbons (CFCs) were regulated out of existence by the Montreal Protocol (UN, 2012).

Carbon dioxide equivalent (CO_2e)

To simplify the global warming impact of all those different gases, CO_2e calculates the climate impact of each individual gas, and combines it to produce a single figure, equivalent to the climate impact of an amount of CO_2.

One tonne of methane equates to 25 tonnes of CO_2, and nitrous oxide equates to 298 tonnes of CO_2 (European Commission, 2023).

The CO_2e of an action which produced one tonne each of carbon dioxide, methane and nitrous oxide, would be:

Carbon Dioxide: 1 tonne x 1 = 1 tonne CO_2e
Methane: 1 tonne x 25 = 25 tonnes CO_2e
Nitrous Oxide: 1 tonne x 298 = 298 tonnes CO_2e
1 + 25 + 298 = 324 tonnes CO_2e

Many reports are likely to reference GHGs and either CO_2e or tCO_2e, ultimately with the aim of first reporting these and secondly showing a reduction.

Carbon offsets

A carbon offset is a verified reduction or removal of emissions of carbon dioxide or other greenhouse gases to compensate for emissions made elsewhere. Offsets are measured in metric tonnes (a metric tonne is 1000 kg or $3^{1/2}$lbs lighter than a British ton) of CO_2e. Examples include planting trees, energy efficiency, and carbon storage and capture. The SBTi Net Zero Standard specifies carbon credits may only be considered as an option after reducing emissions dramatically (over 90 per cent), and then to use only offsets that remove CO_2 from the atmosphere (vs emitting less via energy efficiency) (Science Based Targets, 2023). Otherwise, offsets can enable companies to continue 'business as usual', just buying their way out of the problem. They are a last resort for any business operating within the advertising eco-system.

Carbon neutral

Any CO_2 released into the atmosphere from a company's activities is matched by an equivalent amount being removed or avoided. Often this is achieved by the purchase of carbon credits or offsets rather than elimination of the company's own emissions. It's important to understand the quality of offsets used; not all deliver the same impact. Better offsets create new and additional carbon storage, are for the long-term and third-party verified to avoid double-counting. Carbon Neutral is not the same as Net Zero (National Grid, 2022).

Net zero emissions

Net zero requires the physical elimination of almost all emissions from a company's activities. The science-based targets initiative (SBTi) requires companies to reduce emissions by over 90 per cent and only *then* use additional *carbon-removing* offsets to neutralize the remainder. The emphasis on reduction before offsetting has a big effect on what a company must actually do.

Energy efficiency

Energy efficiency refers to the relative volume of energy required to power an activity, process or product. Emissions can be decreased by reducing the volume of energy needed to perform the same task.

ESG

This term stands for 'environmental, social and governance', and is a framework that helps stakeholders understand how exposed a company is to environmental, social and governance risks, and what plans they have put in place to address that. This is much broader than just dealing with reduction in GHGs. ESG scores have become important within the world of investment, meaning that companies have become increasingly financially motivated to improve their sustainability credentials. However, they may not truly indicate the sustainability of a company's operations; recently several articles have shown how ESG scores tend to rate the risks of planet and people to profit and not the other way around (Bhagat, 2022).

Renewable energy

Energy derived from natural sources that are replenished at a higher rate than they are consumed (United Nations, 2023). The main sources are solar, wind, geothermal and hydro power. These are used instead of non-renewables such as gas, oil, and coal power.

Sustainable

Responsibly interacting with the planet to maintain natural resources to ensure long-term balance.

Cradle-to-grave

Cradle-to-grave is the measurement of a product or service's carbon impacts, from raw materials and energy all the way through to personal use and disposal. This measurement provides a comprehensive picture of a product or service's lifecycle.

Cradle-to-gate

The carbon impact of a product or service, measured from raw materials to moment of purchase or delivery. Crucially, the measurement doesn't account for carbon impacts related to use or disposal (Clearloop, 2021).

Kuznets curve

An economic theory proposed by Simon Kuznets in the 1950s to explain the progression of income inequality within economies. The theory suggests that a reverse U-shape can be drawn, with undeveloped economies having low levels of inequality, partially developed economies having the highest levels of inequality, and highly developed economies having lower levels again (Halton, 2021).

Environmental Kuznets curve

The same graph can be drawn for the theory of the environmental Kuznets curve. The theory goes that the least developed economies have the least amount of carbon impact, but as these economies start to develop, their carbon impact grows. The most developed economies are then able to reduce emissions and carbon impact (Pettinger, 2019). Both theories have faced criticism but provide a valuable framework for understanding some complex issues (Pettinger, 2019).

Decoupling emissions from growth

In line with the Kuznets environmental theory, decoupling emissions describes the process of a growing economy being accompanied by contracting emissions. The Kuznets theory proposes that this generally happens among more highly developed economies.

Scopes 1, 2 and 3

As you immerse yourself in the topic of sustainability and advertising, you are likely to hear more and more reference to the terms Scope 1, Scope 2 and Scope 3. It is critical that you are clear about what each of these are and how and where they apply to the advertising industry.

Scope 1

These are direct emissions from assets that a company owns, such as factories and vehicles (e.g., owned or leased cars).

Scope 2

These are indirect emissions from the company's business, mostly due to energy use. Although the emissions often occur at the facility where they are generated, they are attributed to the company requiring the energy.

Scope 3

These are indirect emissions that the company does not directly own or produce but are part of the company's business activity through use of product, supply chain, business travel, employee commuting and even working from home (GHG Protocol, 2004).

The Paris Climate Agreement

The Paris Agreement is a legally binding international treaty on climate change. Its goal is to limit global warming to well below 2 – preferably to 1.5 – degrees Celsius, compared to preindustrial levels. To achieve this long-term temperature goal, countries aim to reach global peaking of greenhouse gas emissions as soon as possible to achieve a carbon-neutral world by mid-century. Every year, there is a UN climate conference ('Conference of the

Parties' or COP) to make progress on reducing emissions (United Nations, 2023).

Environmental Reporting Standards

Global sustainability reporting standards. There are several standards and groups that administer the standards for environmental reporting, particularly on climate. One example is CDP (formerly the Carbon Disclosure Project, which is also a founding partner of SBTi; see below). Another option is the Global Reporting Initiative (GRI) Standards, which enable any organization – large or small, private or public – to understand and report on their impacts on the economy, environment and people in a comparable and credible way, thereby increasing transparency on their contribution to sustainable development.

Science Based Targets initiative (SBTi)

Science-based targets provide companies with a clearly defined path to reduce emissions in line with the Paris Agreement goals. More than 3,000 businesses around the world are already working with the Science Based Targets initiative (Science Based Targets, 2023). SBTi was set up in 2014 (a partnership between CDP (formerly known as Carbon Disclosure Project), the United Nations Global Compact, World Resources Institute (WRI) and the World Wide Fund for Nature (WWF)) to help companies adopt climate targets in line with best-practice, and with science.

Financial reporting of environmental impacts

There are several standards that require or encourage companies to report carbon emissions as part of their financial risks including the International Financial Reporting Standards, which created the International Sustainability Standards Board, which is merging a number of reporting standards to make reporting easier. In the US, the Securities and Exchange Commission (SEC) is in the process of finalizing its reporting requirements for all public companies and select others. This is a fast-moving area and the notion of carbon trading as part of the advertising eco-system (particularly in media planning and buying) is a very real prospect. We will look at that more later in this book.

Task Force on Climate-related Financial Disclosures (TCFD)

This is a group of experts convened by the Financial Stability Board (FSB) to develop recommendations for companies and other organizations to report on their climate-related risks and opportunities. Many of the world's largest companies endorse this approach and TCFD reporting has become mandatory for larger companies in countries including UK, France and the Netherlands (i.e., to report in accordance with TCFD recommendations around Governance, Strategy, Risk Management, and Metrics and targets).

References

Bhagat, S. (2022) *An Inconvenient Truth About ESG Investing*. Harvard Business Review. March 2022. [Online] Available at: https://hbr.org/2022/03/an-inconvenient-truth-about-esg-investing (archived at https://perma.cc/G8RH-Q9ZM)

European Commission. (2023) *Glossary: Carbon dioxide equivalent*. [Online] Available at: https://ec.europa.eu/eurostat/statistics-explained/index.php?title=Glossary:Carbon_dioxide_equivalent (archived at https://perma.cc/7JMQ-YV42)

Halton, C. (2021) *Simon Kuznets: Who Was He and What Is the Kuznets Curve?* Investopedia. August 2021. [Online] Available at: https://www.investopedia.com/terms/s/simon-kuznets.asp (archived at https://perma.cc/X9DB-VXVK)]

National Grid. (2022) *Carbon neutral vs net zero – understanding the difference.* [Online] Available from: https://www.nationalgrid.com/stories/energy-explained/carbon-neutral-vs-net-zero-understanding-difference#:~:text=Net%20zero%20is%20similar%20in,2O)%20and%20other%20hydrofluorocarbons (archived at https://perma.cc/FK7X-WDGJ)

Pettinger, T. (2019) *Environmental Kuznets curve*. Economics Help. September 2019. [Online] Available at: https://www.economicshelp.org/blog/14337/environment/environmental-kuznets-curve/ (archived at https://perma.cc/4EWJ-UBGL)

Ranganathan, J; *et al* (2004) *The Greenhouse Gas Protocol: A Corporate Accounting and Reporting Standard*. [Online] Available at: ghgprotocol.org/sites/default/files/standards/ghg-protocol-revised.pdf (archived at https://perma.cc/37QQ-RKDD)

Science Based Targets. (2023) *SBTi Corporate Net Zero Standard*. [Online] Available at: https://sciencebasedtargets.org/resources/files/Net-Zero-Standard.pdf (archived at https://perma.cc/E2UW-WZEP)

TCFD (2023). *Home*. [Online] Available from https://www.fsb-tcfd.org/ (archived at https://perma.cc/PR5P-J9YB)

Team Clearloop. (2021) *Gate vs Grave: What's the Best Way to Measure Your Carbon Footprint?* Clearloop. March 2022. [Online] Available at: https://clearloop.us/2021/03/24/cradle-to-gate-vs-cradle-to-grave/ (archived at https://perma.cc/B2TG-CZ9S)

Tucker, K.P; King, A. (2022) Harvard Business Review, *ESG Investing Isn't Designed to Save the Planet*. Harvard Business Review. August 2022. [Online] Available at: https://hbr.org/2022/08/esg-investing-isnt-designed-to-save-the-planet (archived at https://perma.cc/5JEY-THDD)

United Nations. (2012) *Kyoto Protocol - Targets for the first commitment period*. [Online] Available at: https://unfccc.int/process/the-kyoto-protocol/amendment-to-annex-b (archived at https://perma.cc/2PND-AT4W)

United Nations. (2023) *What is the Paris Agreement?* [Online] Available from: https://unfccc.int/process-and-meetings/the-paris-agreement (archived at https://perma.cc/ZD85-Q9GA)

United Nations. (2023) *What is renewable energy?* [Online] Available at: https://www.un.org/en/climatechange/what-is-renewable-energy (archived at https://perma.cc/CYK4-RKEA)

01

Welcome to sustainable advertising

This book is written for everyone involved in the briefing, creation and distribution of advertising: for advertisers, advertising agencies, advertising production and media. It's both a rallying cry for a vision and a handbook. Our vision of *Sustainable Advertising* is for an industry that shapes demand for the products and services of the sustainable economy, while reinventing its own ways of working and attracting the brightest and most creative minds to the cause. The impact of climate change on humanity, society and the economy is already profound. Human inertia, paralysis or complacency is preventing action: even actions already known to be able to mitigate or adapt the world for climate change.

We are writing this book now because of the sense of urgency to make a big intervention. We believe it will be businesses that will continue to drive change, and the most important questions will be who is leading them, and will they be a force for good? This book is for everyone who wants to be that force for good in business and help shape a more desirable and sustainable way of living. That's where you come in. The power is in your hands, whether you are a formal or informal leader in your organization. This book aims to equip you with everything you need to help be part of the advertising industry's sustainable revolution. The handbook chapters share real examples of how this can be done, and the practical steps required to go beyond aspiration and into action.

We are also reflecting on the first three years of Ad Net Zero: a cross-sector, practical, systematic approach to the climate emergency to 'change the way we work and change the work we make' as an industry. Thanks to the tangible support of a couple of hundred courageous companies and trade bodies around the world, including the very biggest and the very smallest, new tools and measurement frameworks to help businesses decarbonize and become a force for good in the green economy are recently available and in use. Case studies abound, with more to come.

But there is not yet sufficient impact at scale to reach a tipping point, and change the course of the global economy and of history. We are regrouping with a rallying cry – a manifesto for sustainable advertising, backed up by the experiences of those pioneering companies. We are recruiting for the greatest challenge, for marketing and advertising to mobilize all forces to land a positive, desirable, sustainable alternative to consumerism in the world.

As Bill Wescott, Managing Partner at Brain Oxygen LLC, the WRI/WBSCD Greenhouse Gas Protocol subgroup leader on boundaries (which led to the creation of scope 3), and climate science advisor at Ad Net Zero points out, 'advertising is not usually seen as a priority industry for broader climate action. With advertising operational emissions responsible for less than 2 per cent of global greenhouse gas emissions, there seem to be bigger fish to fry — such as circularity and other issues. Yet the advertising industry has a superpower that the climate community lacks: the ability to change behaviour and shape demand. The really big benefit for all climate experts is to have the ad sector as an active ally in changing behaviours'. That's what sustainable advertising is all about – being an active ally in changing behaviours and shaping demand.

And when we asked Bill what is holding the industry back, he answered, 'What has been missing until very recently is building on the vast experience of the climate community and connecting advertising to climate best practices.' Bill lamented the insularity of the ad industry:

> 'in the absence of robust collaboration with sustainability experts, there has been widespread confusion about climate terms, competing and usually opaque ways of estimating carbon emissions, and straight up greenwashing to take advantage of lightly informed decision-makers. Until recently, there has been very little appreciation of the importance of following existing standards, having all methodologies and claims verified by reputable third-parties, and making sure that the focus is on reductions aligned with science-based targets. This situation undermines the trust that all stakeholders will need to have in the actions being taken in the ad sector.'

Our goal for Sustainable Advertising is to put all that straight: best summed up by that phrase we have used from the early days of Ad Net Zero, 'to change the way we work, and change the work we make'. The first part of that goal is to decarbonize the industry process from client brief and agency pitch all the way through production of the ad to it appearing in front of citizens on their screens or on a page, using recognized and scientifically validated frameworks, definitions and calculations. The second part, which is in many ways even more important to the global economy, is to increase the volume and effort behind advertising more sustainable products, services and behaviours. The kind of products, services and behaviours that will help reduce the negative impact of climate change and increase the value and sense of well-being from life.

Put these two parts of the goal back together and, as Matt says, the ambition is that every ad is a green ad. Seb points out that truly green goes beyond carbon alone, as the most sustainable products and services also power biodiversity, regenerative agriculture, the circular economy, respect and fair treatment for people along the entire value chain, as well as decarbonization. That's why we now prefer to use the phrase 'sustainable advertising', to encompass those interconnected aims – again, in both the way to work and the work to make. These amount to a wealth of innovation opportunities for entrepreneurs and their advertising partners. According to a global survey by Nielsen (2015), of 30,000 online consumers surveyed from 60 countries, 66 per cent were prepared to pay more for goods and services from companies showing commitment to positive social and environmental impact.

There is no shortage of voices telling the industry how to improve and how to change. This industry regularly faces challenges; perhaps it always has. Despite (or possibly because of) advertising being a critical component of our economic system, there is often an uneasiness around the role of advertising and its aims. The protest voices cover all kinds of issues, from gambling to alcohol, from high fat, sugar, and salt foods (aka junk food) to children's exposure to any advertising, and now greenwashing (more on that in Chapter 2). The banning of advertising is called for regularly and, while the effectiveness of ad bans continues to be debated, behind this is often a greater goal – an objective of exerting greater pressure on client businesses by taking away their 'social licence to operate' that appearing in mainstream media bestows on them. The effectiveness of advertising is debated – possibly overstated by detractors and understated by advertisers, but everyone knows when it has done well, and not so well. It's death or glory time for advertising.

For sustainable advertising to become a reality, every person working in the industry will need to reflect on these views and ask to what extent the work being created is in the broader interests of every stakeholder in the brand, to do less harm and more good. Marketers can lead from the front here, working with everyone in the advertising industry to make sustainability a reality everywhere. In the adversity of the climate crisis there is the opportunity for advertisers, and their advertising and media partners, to be courageous, give more than they take and solve more problems than they cause. The result will be to disconnect the value of the economy and the value creation of business from the relentless take, make, and waste of natural resources.

They could sign up for and live our Sustainable Advertising Manifesto, created to close the think–do gap and tackle inertia or complacency; and so could you.

THE SUSTAINABLE ADVERTISING MANIFESTO

The people in our company (or our team) will work in support of a sustainable future.

We will become climate aware and sustainability literate (and do what we can through training and peer support to help make this happen).

We will do all we can to avoid greenwash, however unintentional it might be.

We will never seek to delay or confuse the action needed to tackle climate change.

We will make sure that all claims about sustainability are evidenced by the best science available.

We will set targets (scopes 1–3) aligned with the Paris Agreement to help tackle climate change.

We will take every action to decarbonize advertising emissions – operational, production and the media supply chain – as fast as possible.

We will develop expertise in sustainable behaviour change, understanding how best to lead citizen behaviour change at scale.

We will create advertising that helps people live in sustainable ways (and seek to proactively support all regulatory efforts in support of this).

We will redefine creative excellence as the best work in service of a sustainable future.

We will help create and support the jobs and livelihoods which make up a sustainable economy.

We will work to monitor, measure, understand and account for the impact of our work on the planet.

Our motivation for writing this book

Matt first fell in love with the media as a paperboy. He says…

Like many others my age, I had a morning paper round, where I delivered 60 newspapers to houses located in a mile or so radius from the shop. I did it every morning, before school and at the weekends. I tried to do it on a bike, because I was also a gamer and I loved Paperboy, but you couldn't throw papers into people's gardens like you did in the game and there was too much getting off and onto the bike for my liking. So, instead I walked the round.

Now, I can't help reading anything that is put in front of me – I'm so bad, I have to put my hand over the last page of a book because I will, no doubt, scan ahead to the last line. It was inevitable then that I would read, at the very least, the front and back pages of every newspaper I was carrying. My teenage brain soon picked up on how the story on the front page was almost always the same story on every paper, but also how each paper told that story in different ways. Sometimes the differences were subtle and sometimes they were blindingly obvious. At the same time, somewhere in that teenage brain, I was registering that I was putting different numbers of each newspaper through letterboxes; as the people in my hometown woke up, I'd helped more of them to read the most popular version compared to other less popular versions of the story.

All this got me thinking: what if someone (me?) could learn how to convince an editor to put a story on the front page of the newspaper that went through the biggest number of letterboxes in my hometown? That would put me in a pretty influential position, I realized. My interest in the media's power to influence was born.

From there I went on to study media and business, going from school to university, nurturing this thirst for more as I learnt about media business models, communications techniques, and business psychology, before entering the world of PR and communications. I could see how much the business model of media was dependent on different revenue streams, including advertising, and just how much advertising was the bedfellow of my front-page obsession – how it could tell stories through the most incredible use of imagery, text and sound. To my mind, this advertising was a vital part of our world, showing me things I might like, helping to inform ambitions and giving me information which I could use as I built out my life, from a young man into a grown-up. I always believed I had a personal choice to accept or reject the advertising, but I valued the advertising all the same because I valued the media it helped to fund.

There was also a deeper belief that we need the media to act as the Fourth Estate – hold power to account – because when media is at its best, that is what it does, and society is all the better for it. I can hear the brickbats being thrown, with examples of the times media has failed in its role to do that. Worse still, detractors may point to times when the media has abused that position and allowed power to get away with things that have damaged society. But as you read this book, you'll find that my glass is half-full. I like to aim for what I think we can do best, because this is the way we can improve things for everyone.

Fast forward a few decades and here I am, writing this book about how advertising can be a positive force in the fight against climate change. Not much has changed. While mobile phones have joined letterboxes as a means of delivering the news, the principle of getting your story in front of the right audience on the biggest platform holds true.

When I studied media at university, the most famous example of media's power to influence behaviour was Orson Welles' radio broadcast of *The War of the Worlds* to an unsuspecting American public. The news of a Martian invasion prompted many to flee their homes and head for the hills. But I believe we now have a better example.

The government campaign (and the support from the advertising industry) at the outset of the Covid pandemic changed the daily routine of the UK population in just a matter of days. If you'd have told me that this was possible beforehand, I would have dismissed you as delusional. Yet, it happened. If you want evidence that our industry can play a fundamental role in behaviour change, look no further than what happened in March 2020. This wasn't unique to the UK either. It happened around the world and saved many lives in the process. The government had become the UK's number one advertiser during that period. The Advertising Association produced a report studying the impact of the pandemic on ad spend and one of the biggest lessons was the role of government advertising, which stepped forward to show leadership with life-saving messages. It was evident too how advertisers, agencies and media owners helped take that messaging and normalize it, and support people through their own communications campaigns and, by doing so, back the government's efforts to stay safe, to get vaccinated and so forth.

Advertising carrying imagery of climate change devastation won't bring about the change we're looking for. We will see those images and stories in the news, and that's where they are most powerful. The role of advertising running alongside those stories is to show the sustainable solutions which are being developed in every part of our economy. And that advertising must be what all great advertising always is: empathetic, creative, humorous, effective, and thought-provoking, aspirational, functional, useful, and supportive of business objectives to support jobs and help people live their lives.

What we both believe is that more citizens making more sustainable choices won't be the result of one big, amazing campaign. It will be solved by countless campaigns by hundreds of thousands of brands one choice at a time. Those campaigns will be created by advertising and marketing professionals, all striving for better. The world's advertising market was estimated to be some US $880 billion in 2022 and is forecast to cross the $1 trillion mark by 2026 (WARC, 2023). Imagine if every single dollar of that ad spend was directed towards this sustainable economy brief. How powerful could that be?

Seb also reflects on his own motivation.

That scale for making life a little better through everyday products is what motivated me to get into consumer products in the first place. I worked at Unilever for 32 years in many marketing and innovation jobs on many brands in many markets. What mattered most to me was creating the best products – the definition changed and broadened over time – and getting those products to be used and loved in as many homes as possible.

I have been the Chair of Ad Net Zero since it first begun in 2020 while I was chief exec of Unilever's UK and Ireland business as we transformed our business once again, building digital marketing capabilities, a more resilient supply chain, and a brand portfolio for the times, which was responsibly sourced and packaged. At Unilever we wanted to prove that we could deliver outstanding returns to shareholders (think pensioners) by doing the right thing for all our stakeholders: suppliers, customers, employees, the countries in which they live, and the planet they live on.

One of my first projects, some 30 years earlier, as a young brand manager on Persil, the UK's leading detergent brand, was a range of 'eco-refills' for Persil Automatic Liquid. It was far from perfect: filling-line speeds were too slow; the laminated cardboard was an environmental improvement on the big plastic bottles it replaced and refilled, but by how much exactly? And margins were too thin. But it was progress and well received by many shoppers, sold millions of units to people who intuitively recognized its value. I was proud to work on Persil and pleased that the brand team was empowered to address the wider societal context of the early 1990s, and that we took action, however imperfectly, that could be built and improved on.

I learnt many things from that project, and over the years from my time at Unilever. That elusive perfection is always the enemy of progress; it is that persistent focus on the next practical leap that delivers tangible results. Proposals make progress. Leaping takes courage and there will always be colleagues with cogent reasons who don't want to leap at the same time as you. In any decision, there are often many reasons not to, especially if it's choosing the harder, but right thing to do. I felt called to those projects, to be honest. Over the years, I've learnt that this feeling can be summed up in a phrase created after some reflection and discussion. At Unilever we called it 'purpose' – a word that's used a lot these days in many contexts. Today, I'd say my purpose is best summed up in the phrase 'make it better'. This thought explains the kind of work that makes me happiest, my sweet spot, and not surprisingly, the type of work I choose to do.

I believe in the power of people to make progress and make it better. I believe that throughout history there have been people who have done this, responding to the situations in which they find themselves by making it better – not just for them, or their family or their firm, but for everyone. They connect to the unquenchable spirit that is within us all and make the moment better. They bring people together across silos or divides to work for better.

What could be more needed now? As we tackle the consequences of inaction in the face of the climate emergency, and its existential threat to nature, and the wellbeing of humans at a scale we are only just grasping, we need to take stock. While governments around the world must set the framework through laws and taxes to tackle these issues, it will be business that has to deliver the seismic changes in the way humans move around, heat and light homes and offices, the food we eat, and how we spend our leisure time. And those businesses will need to engage and enrol us all as citizens.

This is the opportunity of a lifetime, or an era. For innovation, businesses and for advertising. The chance to invent the future. I believe that the majority of people who work in marketing and advertising want to be part of that positive vision. A mission that specifically calls on their skills. I also believe that this change will not be one epiphany for each citizen but will come one choice at a time. Change isn't an event, it's a process. Advertising that told us we are all doomed doesn't seem to have changed the way most of us live, because we compartmentalize those everyday choices from the big debates.

To change the world, I believe we will need to do it one decision at a time, framing the best options as the most desirable. I know this dismays many people, but my 30 years in marketing tell me that changing behaviours takes focus and requires a lot of things to come together to be successful. Just think of the people in the 1990s who didn't buy those eco-refills despite the fact that they were empirically cheaper and better for the environment than the alternative packages. We will need to make the bigger brands better and the better brands bigger. To quote *Switch* (Heath and Heath, 2011), one of my favourite books on the topic of behaviour change, 'until you can ladder your way down from a change idea to a specific behaviour, you're not ready to lead the switch.' As Chip and Dan Heath write later in their book, 'if you want people to change, you can provide clear direction, or boost their determination and motivation. Alternatively, you can simply make the journey easier'.

So, the rallying cry, and my motivation to write this book, is for marketing and advertising to be a force for good and put those skills in service of a better world, and at the very least, the behaviour changes required to radically decrease greenhouse gas emissions from human activities that cause harmful climate impact. Looking back, I wish we'd called Ad Net Zero something else. Maybe Ad Net Positive, picking up on Paul Polman's reflections on his time at Unilever in his book with Andrew Winston, Net Positive (Polman and Winston, 2021). I love the subtitle (a good piece of marketing) 'how courageous companies thrive by giving more than they take,' and the definition of that, 'when companies solve the biggest challenges, not contribute to them.' If this is all sounding a bit daunting, they make the point very clearly: 'Net Positive is also not about being perfect. It's about fixing the problems that cause negative impacts and going beyond to create positive value for others.'

That's exactly what this book sets out to do, and in that order. We begin by addressing the problems that need fixing in the advertising process and across the sectors of the industry. The second part of the book begins to paint a picture of those advertisers and their agencies who are going beyond to create positive value for all their stakeholders.

In total we set out how marketing and advertising people can change the way they work and change the work they make. What we offer is some practical guidance, and some inspiration, but it's probably also imperfect, the best examples at a point in time, reflecting the best and most sincere effort of all concerned. Like those eco-refills, we will almost certainly look back and see shortcomings, but will nonetheless be pleased that those teams are counted in the number of people who actually did something and made it better.

A leadership moment

All change starts with a moment of leadership: that might be from the formal leadership of an organization or from the informal leadership within an organization. It usually takes the form of a choice or promoting one choice above others. Making choices is determining strategy. It's probably best to acknowledge that and review how these new priorities interlink with the strategy of the business (where to play and how to win). Armed with a clear assessment of the risks and opportunities created by climate change, biodiversity loss, and the consequential disruption of food, agriculture, fresh water, oceans, coasts, forests, and human migration, health and livelihood, they can be integrated into a new version of where to play and how to win. A C-suite understanding of how versions of the future play out for the planet, people and the business. This shapes priorities and creates focus. That's why many advertisers and advertising agencies have already started to definitively tilt their businesses towards addressing these big threats and big opportunities to serve their customers. Whether more follow on because they want to or have to, we see this trend only gaining momentum.

Once a business has reviewed its strategy, risks and opportunities, the result should be one integrated strategy encompassing how to win and where to play in the context of climate change and biodiversity loss. Now attention can turn to how to actually decarbonize up and down the supply chain and accelerate the sustainable economy.

In this section, we outline the Five Action framework of the Ad Net Zero climate action initiative, which breaks down how to decarbonize advertising operations and create advertising that promotes a more sustainable way of life. The genesis of Ad Net Zero was in a conversation begun by UK industry body, the Advertising Association, with the advertiser's representative association, ISBA, and the advertising agency body IPA. They then created a group of industry representatives in a Climate Action Working Group that Matt joined, which commissioned research by the UK advertising think tank, Credos, led by James Best. This working group developed a set of proposals which were then submitted to a Climate Action Steering Group, chaired by Seb, and, finally, to the Advertising Association's Council for sign-off. The Ad Net Zero Plan was born. A set of five simple clear actions which provided the basis of the thinking and work now powering our drive towards a sustainable future.

The five actions

An all-encompassing plan (scopes 1–3) to clean up the environmental impact of each aspect of the process at every single stage from briefing, creation and production of an advert, through to the display of that advert in media was encapsulated into the first four actions.

When we look at the advertising ecosystem, we can break the major players into three major buckets: the advertiser, the agency, and the media owner (including the tech platforms which provide channels and platforms to reach audiences). Within those three buckets sit a whole host of roles, from the client who sets the brief to the strategy lead who considers the response. From the creative team responding to insights that inform the brief to the production professionals involved in making the work and onto the media planners and buyers buying the media space. There are sales teams within media owners, tech services to support the delivery of advertising and many more within this complex eco-system.

Depending on the nature of your business, you may only have control over one or two of these actions. For some readers, there may be power to influence them all.

The original brief to the team tasked to design the framework was to create one that could be addressed at the level of the industry, the company and the individual. This recognized that at a point in time anyone could be the leader, and every one of us has a vital role to play. It is a genuine team effort – hence the original strapline of Ad Net Zero: All For None, created by the team at award-winning advertising agency, adam&eveDDB.

Action 1: Getting our own house in order.
Companies and their employees commit to curtail their carbon emissions by reducing travel, non-sustainable energy use and waste, setting targets and measuring progress against these to be on a pathway to net zero emissions.

Action 2: Reduce emissions from advertising production.
Advertisers, agencies and production companies commit to adopt tools and training to measure, manage and reduce the emissions from advertising production.

Action 3: Reduce emissions from media planning and buying.
Developed through industry collaboration, media agencies commit to use carbon measurement programmes, working with their clients to measure, manage and reduce the emissions from media distribution.

Action 4: Reduce emissions through awards and from events.
Event and awards organizers commit to build sustainability credentials into entry criteria for all awards and plan all industry events to minimize their carbon footprint.

The working team added a fifth action for the second part of the mission, to create advertising that promotes more sustainable products services and behaviours. This action is to inspire advertising that is a force for good (scope 3) as well as delivering on commercial objectives.

Action 5: Harness advertising's power to change behaviour.
Advertisers and their agencies commit to harness the power of their advertising to accelerate more sustainable customer choices and behaviours and drive more sustainable consumption.

One step at a time, quickly

The scale of the challenge means that taking positive action on a day-to-day basis can be overwhelming for any one person working in advertising. One of the concerns in creating the five actions framework, when the team were reviewing the research about our industry's attitudes towards climate change was how to address paralysing fears and turn them into a set of clear, simple, and practical actions. The five actions were the result of a step-by-step plan which reviewed the end-to-end process of advertising and explained what actions were needed at each stage to decarbonize the industry's operations and to harness its power to support the building of a net zero economy, along with all the responsibilities that brings.

The goal of the Ad Net Zero climate action programme – to change the way we work and to change the work we make – is built upon a belief that sustainability will be one of the core competences for every role in the advertising industry. Decisions and behaviours throughout the entire working process need to consider, account for, and reduce carbon emissions.

Developing that job-specific sustainability competence for every advertising professional in their day-to-day role will make sustainability an integral consideration of the advertising work they go on to make. It will generate a fundamental change right at the heart of the industry. That, combined with the shift within every industry to sell products and services that are ever more sustainable, will have a positive multiplier effect.

Welcome: summary

Considering the range of roles across the industry, there's no single easy answer to 'how can I help advertising tackle climate change?'. Motivations are shaped by our individual experience, and opportunities to influence are framed by our specific role, but everyone can take a leading role, with marketers in pole position. We can each do two things: make the decision to sign up for the Sustainable Advertising Manifesto, including the commitment to develop our job-specific sustainability competence, and play a leadership role in our organization to ensure that the business strategy and the sustainability plan are merged into one.

References

Heath, C. and Heath, D. (2011) *Switch: How to change things when change is hard*. 1st edition. London: Random House Business.

Nielsen IQ. (2015) *The Sustainability Imperative, Niselsen IQ*. Available at: https://nielseniq.com/global/en/insights/analysis/2015/the-sustainability-imperative-2/ (archived at https://perma.cc/SF59-ZQ79)

Polman, P. and Winston , A. (2021) *How is your company making the World Better?* Available at: https://hbr.org/2021/09/the-net-positive-manifesto (archived at https://perma.cc/E29H-XLX8)

WARC Media. (2023) *The Ad Spend Outlook 2022/23, WARC An Ascential Company*. Available at: https://www.warc.com/content/feed/warc-adspend-outlook-2022-23-what-you-need-to-know/en-GB/7142 (archived at https://perma.cc/2FES-JJ8M)

02

Greenwashing, and how to avoid it

Greenwashing is advertising that carries misleading environmental claims, and it is a serious issue – an issue that could damage public trust in the genuine sustainable claims that brands make. It is essential that, as an industry, we promote our clients in totally open, honest and transparent ways so that we can preserve the public's trust in our work. Greenwashing not only erodes trust towards advertising (thus, reducing overall advertising effectiveness) but could even discourage companies from promoting their green initiatives, in fear of being labelled 'greenwashers'. This is a topic that we need to get right.

As we will explore further in this book, sustainability can deliver significant commercial value. It might be tempting to overstate claims in advertising or marketing, and it could be easy for a business to fall into the trap of greenwashing, at the expense of integrating sustainable change into their strategies and throughout their operations. An advertising professional could be encouraged to support or even enhance these claims to achieve better sales results.

Greenwashing may be unintentional or well-meaning – a misunderstanding of sustainability, for example, caused by a disconnect (or lack of integration) between the sustainability and marketing departments in a business. Or it can be intentional – overstating sustainability credentials to win business or to divert attention from bigger environmental damage. While intentional greenwashing is clearly more unethical than accidental, the aim of our industry must be to eradicate greenwashing in all its forms; from the audience perspective, a misleading advert is a misleading advert whether intentional or not.

Whatever the motivation, as we all strive to play our part in the net zero transition, and as the regulatory framework around advertising sustainable products and services becomes more rigorous, everyone must up their game to eradicate misleading environmental claims.

Given the scrutiny of our industry around the issue of global warming and in a world where customers increasingly demand transparency and environmental responsibility from brands, being challenged on environmental claims is inevitable.

So, as a responsible advertiser or marketer, what do you do? The answer is that, when making environmental claims, you should prioritize efforts to ensure they are accurate, substantiated and contextualized in accordance with the rules.

The role of the ASA

The Advertising Standards Authority (ASA) is the UK's advertising regulator, enforcing rules on the content, placement and targeting of advertisements. They represent the gold standard of advertising regulation worldwide. The Committee of Advertising Practice (CAP) is the ASA's sister organization. They write the rules that the ASA enforces, produce educational material to explain how the rules apply, and give free advice to advertisers about their copy.

The ASA exist to prevent misleading and irresponsible advertising such as greenwashing, and they do a fantastic job of doing just that. But agencies and production companies must act responsibly of their own accord, without the threat of fines, sanctions and reputational damage. We don't just want to be an industry that avoids scandal, but one that leads the way in the fight against climate change.

Matt can get frustrated with marketers who complain about getting caught out by the ASA. The self-regulatory body is there for good reason, and a particularly good one in the context of climate change. They are funded (just) by the industry to do an incredible job and they need everyone's support. By support, he doesn't just mean funding – he means properly understanding their guidance and, whatever your role in the advertisement's production, making sure that it follows that guidance. If you don't, you will get called out by someone who encounters that ad, it will be reviewed, and it will be highlighted publicly as an ad that wasn't legal, decent, honest or truthful within the realms of the rules and guidance the industry has set.

This chapter will look at the rules and regulations set by the industry's self-regulatory bodies and by governments around the world, to help you understand what is allowed and where you can get the best guidance to avoid greenwashing. We are not outlining these guidelines to show you how to avoid getting caught, though. This is an exercise in understanding the common pitfalls and mistakes made by companies, regardless of sanctions. We should all be motivated to avoid misleading environmental advertising. It's the right thing to do for our businesses, for our customers and for the planet.

Presenting to the ASA and learning lessons from tobacco

Back in February 2020, Matt presented to the ASA who were, at the time, forming a climate action workstream to review their guidance given to advertisers. The following is what he put to the ASA audience as they began formulating the next phase of their work around climate change and setting the standards for environmental claims in advertising.

> In my view, advertising's role in the fight against climate change has precedent. Tobacco was a health issue, and the advertising industry was targeted by a specific set of NGOs and policy decision-makers who ultimately imposed a ban on the advertising of tobacco products. This was part of a range of measures introduced over decades of change to help eradicate smoking as a behaviour. A behaviour that advertising, and wider popular culture, had helped to normalize. Try and find a photo of a classic popular culture icon without a cigarette in hand or somewhere in the scene. It's not easy. In fact, many classic images are intrinsically linked to a cigarette balanced between lips or in a hand.

> If we thought tobacco was bad for our reputation, climate change is tobacco times 100. Why? Because if you believe that advertising promotes consumption, and consumption is directly responsible for global warming, then the criticisms of advertising won't just come from one set of NGOs; they will come from every corner of our society. Everywhere I look, advertising has potential culpability – whether that is through the support it provides to fashion, to travel, to finance, to auto, to supermarkets, to FMCG, to media and entertainment. It is difficult to isolate any category of advertising that couldn't be a possible target. And as the issue of climate change becomes more and more urgent, the potential for complaints by NGOs about ads from all directions will only increase. From where I stand as Director of Communications at the Advertising Association, we need to listen to these criticisms, really understand what we are doing and take action to make sure we are doing the right thing.

> It can be argued that the industry defended the right to advertise tobacco for too long, so we need to make sure that we are ahead of the curve with this issue. We don't want to be looking back in another thirty years, thinking that we should have been quicker to act. The reputation of our industry depends on decisive action across the board.

Our industry at its core is only as good as the people that want to work in it. We need to attract the most talented people – creatives, strategists, tech experts, production, and post-production geniuses, plus all the skills of handling briefs, approval processes, delivering campaigns and evaluating the impact of the work. But no-one wants to work in an industry that is helping to burn the planet. By focusing more of our work on climate-friendly initiatives and products, we will start to attract more talent that want to be a part of the solution. If we sleepwalk down the tobacco-trodden path, my job as Director of Communications will just be about reacting to one attack after another. The more work we do that is on the right side of the climate change battle, the better job I can do to support the reputation of the industry and help people be attracted to the industry as a place where their skills can be put to the best, most responsible use.

Government may intervene, just like they did with tobacco, but wouldn't it be better if we got there first through our own series of self-regulatory messages?

The ASA team truly have an open goal in front of them; to set the standards for the industry to aspire to when it comes to the promotion of products and services that support a net zero economy. And to also set the boundaries of where advertising shouldn't go in promoting claims about a product or service without the evidence to back up those claims. The stronger, the clearer, the firmer those self-regulatory standards are in line with the latest climate science and evidence, the better our industry can be at helping all industries tackle climate change.

The rules and regulations

Let's look at the rules and regulations around greenwashing that are specific to advertising. We're going to cover the fundamental issues around green-washing, including a detailed look at the specific ASA rules that apply to misleading environmental campaigns. The ASA's rules will be the only ones that this section covers, so if you operate outside of the UK, it is worth checking your regional regulator's rules as well. It is also important to note that this is an area which is fast-moving and in constant flux, with regula-tions constantly being reassessed, altered and updated. We wouldn't be surprised if, by the time this book is published, some regulations featured here have been changed, so make sure to check for more recent updates to the regulations as well.

5 ASA principles to follow

The following are five key principles on environmental claims from the UK Code of Non-broadcast Advertising and Direct & Promotional Marketing and the UK Code of Broadcast Advertising (the CAP and BCAP Codes). These could be used as a checklist at an early stage of any campaign you might be working on. The ASA have broader principles outside of environmental claims but, for the purpose of this book, we will focus on those specifically relating to greenwashing.

Principle 1: Is the basis of the claim clearly stated in the copy?

Whenever an ad includes an environmental claim, whether it's implicit or explicit, the basis of the claim needs to be clear to people. In this context, the 'basis' of the claim would be the specific ways in which the environmental benefit is achieved.

Vague, nonspecific, or ambiguous claims about a product being 'green' or somehow good for the environment are only likely to be acceptable if the copy also makes clear what these claims are based on.

SOURCES CAP Code rule 11.1 and BCAP Code rule 9.2.

Principle 2: Is the meaning of the term clearly stated?

This is related but slightly different to principle #1. As well as the basis of the claim being clear to people, the meaning of the terminology should also be clear. Technical jargon is unlikely to be considered acceptable if people can recognize it as an environmental claim, but don't know what it means in relation to the product.

In one case, the ASA investigated a complaint about an ad from Shell that stated consumers could 'drive carbon neutral' if they bought a particular fuel. The ASA considered that consumers would understand the claim to mean that the brand would offset the carbon emissions related to the fuel purchase. However, as the emissions would only be offset if consumers also took part in a loyalty scheme, the ASA ruled that the practical meaning of the claim 'Drive carbon neutral' was not sufficiently clear.

SOURCES CAP Code rule 11.2 and BCAP Code rule 9.3.

Principle 3: Does your evidence support an absolute claim or a comparative claim?

Comparative claims are claims about a particular benefit compared to something else, whether to the brand's products or competitors' products. In contrast, if a product is described in absolute terms (e.g., as 'green' instead of 'greener', or 'sustainable' instead of 'more sustainable') this is considered an absolute claim.

Because these claims refer to a product, brand, or service as a whole, brands would need to hold evidence about the environmental impact of the entire product, brand or service. A specific improvement to one aspect of a service is unlikely to be seen as sufficient evidence to back up an absolute claim.

If the basis of the environmental claim is that there is a relative improvement against the brand's previous practices or competitors, don't make an absolute claim.

SOURCES CAP Code rule 11.3 and BCAP Code rule 9.4.

Principle 4: Are absolute claims backed up by evidence about the entire lifecycle?

Unless the copy states otherwise, the default requirement for environmental claims is that the supporting evidence must relate to the entire lifecycle of the product or service being advertised.

If the copy contains an absolute environmental claim (e.g., 'green', 'sustainable', 'eco-friendly'), it should be clear whether the claim relates to the brand as a whole, to a particular product or service, or a particular aspect of a product or service. If the claim is attributed to the brand as a whole, this would need to be supported by evidence about all aspects of the brand's operations across its entire lifecycle.

If it is attributed to a particular product, it would need to be supported by evidence about the product's entire lifecycle, from production through to transport, use and disposal. If the evidence only relates to a specific part of the product, or a particular subset of the lifecycle (e.g., excluding transport or disposal), the ad should make this clear.

The ASA investigated a complaint about an energy company's claim that their electricity 'contains 0g of CO_2' and considered that consumers would understand this to mean it came from sources that did not produce any net CO_2 over their full lifecycle. The ads were found to have breached the code because the supporting evidence excluded parts of the lifecycle, such as the emissions produced during production and transportation.

SOURCES CAP Code rule 11.4 and BCAP Code rule 9.5.

Principle 5: Does the copy overstate the environmental benefits?

Ads can mislead consumers by implying that environmental benefits are specific to the product, e.g., by indicating or stating that an environmental benefit is specific to the product when it results from a legal obligation that applies to all products in the same category.

Likewise, if a particular type of product doesn't normally involve an environmentally damaging ingredient or process, it could be misleading for an ad to highlight the absence of that ingredient or process.

As more laws and government requirements about CO_2 emissions and other sustainability measures are introduced, brands should ensure they don't misleadingly take credit for following what's required of them by law.

In one case the ASA investigated, an ad described a waste bag as 'biodegradable'. The basis for the claim was that the bags were made of a type of plastic that degrades, like other plastics, over a timescale that can range from several years to hundreds of years. The ASA considered that consumers would expect a product described as 'biodegradable' to have a greater environmental benefit than conventional plastic waste bags, and the ad was considered misleading on this basis.

SOURCES CAP Code rule 11.7 and BCAP Code rule 9.8

Global campaigns: General principles – national rules

When you're planning a big global or regional multi-country campaign, it would be wonderful if there was a single set of rules you could follow to make sure all your environmental claims in your advertising are sound. You'd simply come up with your copy or treatment, run it past this 'central' set of rules with the help of the lawyers, and move on to the next stage of getting that work out there. Unfortunately, things don't work like that when it comes to rules around making environmental claims. While there are broad principles which are useful internationally, the rules are specific to each jurisdiction you're advertising in. This means the approach you take will ultimately be multinational, not international.

The best starting place is to understand the big picture. Several organizations have produced useful global guidance to help people working in our industry navigate this complex area.

For example, the World Federation of Advertisers (WFA) published their 'Global Guidance on Environmental Claims' back in April 2022 which has support from environmental experts from self-regulatory organizations around the world, including the ASA.

Another international source that you might find useful as you think about how to make sure your work is not greenwashing is the Internationals Chamber of Commerce's (ICC) 'Advertising and Marketing Communications Code'. Chapter D of this code covers environmental claims.

The ICC code is a full-length code of practice and is used as the basis for self-regulatory codes in a number of different countries, including France, Belgium and China. But while the ICC code is another useful starting point, we can't say that if an ad follows the code, it will be fine in all countries in the world. You'll also need to look at both self-regulatory codes and local laws in each individual jurisdiction.

The ICC has published a helpful guidance framework to accompany its code, covering complex areas such as general 'sustainability' claims or specific claims about climate, the circular economy, recyclable content, degradability, and 'free-of' claims. This is well worth referring to for practical guidance in these areas.

WPP'S FORMULA FOR EFFECTIVE GREEN CLAIMS

According to *Climate Change 2022: Impacts, Adaptation and Vulnerability*, The Sixth IPCC Report, consumer behaviour change could drive down global carbon emissions by 40–70 per cent by 2050. It's clear effective green claims can help shift opinion and change behaviour at the scale needed to transition to a low-carbon economy. But Ogilvy Consulting identified in its *Sustainability Communications Need to Get Real* report that more than 60 per cent of consumers are cynical about the motivations behind brands' sustainability actions.

In response to this challenge, which is faced by practitioners around the world, WPP launched a new Green Claims Guide in 2022, informed by guidance from regulators such as the UK Competition and Markets Authority and US Federal Trade Commission, and underpinned by legal compliance advice.

The guide is designed to help its people ensure that any environmental claims made on behalf of clients are fair and accurate, and to avoid content that could be misleading in any way. There are 12 principles of the Green Claims Guide which WPP has given permission to share here:

1 Be truthful and accurate

2 Do not omit or hide important information

3 Only make fair and meaningful comparisons

4 Consider the full lifecycle of the product

5 Substantiate the claims

6 Be specific

7 Be clear and unambiguous

8 Use plain language

9 Do not overstate the benefit

10 Avoid sweeping or unqualified claims

11 Carefully consider imagery

12 Be socially responsible

The Green Claims Guide provides practical tips for account managers, strategists, creatives and media planners to use from brief to behaviour change and is supported by training sessions to give employees the chance to explore real case studies and rulings to help them identify and avoid greenwashing. The guide is complemented by a legal toolkit, which has been incorporated into WPP's legal clearance process.

It followed the internal launch with a client version of the guide in 2023 and offers targeted training focusing on green claims in specific sectors or markets to our people and – where requested – to clients.

Individual countries: from self-regulation to the law

When it comes to environmental claims, understanding global guidance is a good start. But you may be working in multiple individual jurisdictions, whose specific rules and processes may differ. This is where things start to get complicated – so it's helpful to have an overview of what to look for in each jurisdiction.

One thing's for sure, regulator awareness about the importance of getting environmental claims right is consistent wherever you advertise.

When advertising in individual countries, there are two different types of regulation to be aware of: self-regulation, and regulation under the law. Practically, this means:

1) *Consult the self-regulatory organizations (SROs)*

In many countries, advertising is regulated by the industry itself – which funds that regulation. So, it's important to consult the specific SRO for your jurisdiction, to find out the rules that should be observed.

To find the SRO you need, take a look at this list of organizations published by the International Council for Ad Self-Regulation (ICAS) – or, for Europe, this list by the European Advertising Standards Alliance.

Consult the SRO before making an environmental claim; many provide guidance notes and most provide a copy advice service. Be aware, too, that in some countries, claims may need to be pre-cleared.

2) *Be aware that statute could apply*

While advertising is typically self-regulated, that's not to say that civil (or in some cases, criminal) law cannot also apply – in particular, laws relating to competition, consumer protection or unfair commercial practices. For example, in July 2022, the UK's Competition and Markets Authority (CMA) said it was investigating 'green' claims of three fashion brands; while in the Netherlands, an activist group sued KLM under EU consumer protection law. The EU is planning to strengthen rules against greenwashing – including its Unfair Commercial Practices Directive, which is transposed into law in individual EU countries, and also reflected in self-regulatory rules across the bloc.

3) *Consider rules for individual industries*

Beyond specific advertising rules, be aware of course that there are sector-specific environmental rules in some sectors, whether self-regulatory or statutory. For example:

- The industry rules of Cosmetics Europe also cover environmental promotion, and are applicable to its members.
- Misleading environmental claims relating to investments are a matter of criminal law, notably in the EU and US, but also elsewhere.
- Emissions data rules for cars are statutory in many jurisdictions.

Tips to avoid greenwashing

Top Tip 1: Consider the specific sections of the CAP and BCAP codes that relate to the rules and regulations around greenwashing. How might you be able to raise the question of awareness of these in your business? Is there a 'greenwash check' put in place across all advertising work? If not, consider how you might put this to your line manager or colleagues.

Top Tip 2: Think of ways that you can make exploring these rules and regulations more engaging. For example, could you hold a session with clients and/or colleagues where you look at examples of your work or work from the wider industry, and debate whether any of it might be subject to greenwashing? Can you spot any common pitfalls and how to avoid them?

Top tip 3: Explore the work you currently have with clients. Are there any potential reputational dangers or over-claims that you can be proactive about – for example, by raising them with your line manager or client lead?

Educating young people about how to spot greenwashing

A sustainable advertising industry also has a responsibility to equip the next generation of young people with the ability to read, interpret and understand the sustainability messages of advertisers. At the same time, it can also inspire young people to join the industry and, through their own creative, technical and strategic skills, help to build a net zero economy.

Media Smart is the non-profit education programme from the advertising industry, established in 2002, and is on a mission is to ensure every 7–16-year-old child in the UK can confidently navigate the media they consume. It provides free teaching resources and parent guides on subjects like social media, body image and influencer marketing.

In March 2023, it launched a new guide called *How to Spot Greenwashing*, designed for 11–17 yrs | Key stage 3, 4 and 5. Its research highlighted that 52 per cent of teenagers are concerned about the lack of action on climate change, and 56 per cent of them feel anxious as a result. Media Smart created a simple five-point guide and short film to be shared in the classroom, assembly or at home explaining what greenwashing is so young people can spot it, report it, and ultimately help to stop it.

How to spot greenwashing – a guide for children and young adults.

1. 'Green' does not always mean green

Some businesses use symbols, like trees and flowers, or green colours to try and seem like they are more eco-friendly than they are.

You can fact-check these claims by reading a company's website and remember to read the small print on product labels and descriptions.

2. Misleading language

Phrases like 'all natural', 'green' and 'eco' sound positive, but they don't necessarily mean a product is environmentally friendly.

Be suspicious of buzzwords – especially when they don't come with evidence.

3. Re-use, swap or resell?

You can reuse, swap, recycle, not only through businesses and organizations, but through your community (which are your friends and family).

You should take the responsibility to always research your purchases.

Some brands encourage you to return used items like clothing, for example. You might think they are being recycled, but double-check the company's website to find out that this is definitely the case.

4. Fact-checking

Do your own research and check a company's claim to see if it stands up. They should provide evidence of how they are being green.

To tell the difference between a fact and greenwashing, you can:

Read the 'sustainability' section on their website.

Look for third-party certification of any 'eco-friendly' claims.

Ask someone whose opinion you trust… go to someone more knowledgeable that you trust, like your teachers, parents or older siblings, to help you navigate the internet around fact-checking and greenwashing.

5. A sustainable purchase?

A business might highlight one 'green' element of a product's supply chain and not mention harmful ones. Its overall lifecycle must be sustainable – or else it isn't.

A product might be 'all natural', but if it was flown halfway across the world in a jet, it probably can't claim to be 'eco-friendly'.

Building on this, Media Smart developed a new education pack in summer 2023 to set students the challenge of creating an advertising campaign for a fashion company that follows the rules around communicating environmental messages and sustainability benefits. Matt spoke with Media Smart's Executive Director, Rachel Barber-Mack about the new pack.

Firstly, please can you tell us about the education pack – what is the brief?

The education pack is a series of three inspirational workshops for young people aged 14–16 years teaching them about the world of advertising and media through an advertising literacy lens, while also highlighting the many and varied roles within ad or media agencies as a career option. The brief component is the exciting bit, where we've adapted a real client brief that came into OMG UK from an iconic clothing brand and the young people get the chance to crack the real-life brief. Essentially the client wanted to start communicating their long-standing sustainability credentials for the first time in way that resonated with a Gen Z audience. This challenges the students to look at the creative ideas that bring the brand's key messages to life, the media used to reach the right demographic, potential partners to work with and the ASA rules around greenwashing.

How does it work practically in the classroom?

It's really simple. Teachers download the pack for free from mediasmart.uk.com – the detailed presentations, notes and films are all there. It's a real 'plug and play' session which doesn't involve too much prep. Importantly, if the young people want to learn more about advertising careers or greenwashing, we signpost ways for them to do this post lesson.

The team is also developing an abridged one-hour session which will see OMG UK agency employees going into their local, inner-city schools from September and deliver the workshop themselves. Of course, then they will talk more from their personal experience, which will be an incredibly powerful thing for the young people, particularly around the sustainability brief.

How important do you think it is that young people can navigate advertising of sustainable products and services?

It's really important. We know that the climate emergency is a real and major concern to young people; it gives them huge anxiety. They are aware of more and more brands promoting their sustainability credentials and offerings and they are distrustful of it – by supporting their advertising literacy in this area it will empower them, help to alleviate their concerns and build trust. In particular, they are generally unaware of the rules for brands around greenwashing and that they can report it when they see it.

What is the ultimate goal of this exercise?

Our mission is two-fold: to inspire young people into creative careers hand-in-hand with increasing their advertising literacy, particularly around greenwashing. Those involved in advertising have a huge responsibility in this area, but it's also an opportunity and gift that can lead to positive change.

Greenwashing, and how to avoid it: summary

Greenwashing must be avoided at all costs. Everyone working in the industry must take responsibility for ensuring the work our industry produces in support of a sustainable future can be trusted to be exactly that. There are clear rules set by self-regulatory bodies like the Advertising Standards Authority in the UK which everybody can familiarize themselves with. Best practice standards and guidelines are being put into place by many organizations, freely available for you to review and understand. Make sure every piece of work which includes a sustainability claim has been made with these in mind and ask questions of any work you see being made that could be construed as greenwashing.

References

ASA. (2010). *The BCAP Code: The UK Code of Broadcast Advertising*. [Online] Available at: https://www.asa.org.uk/static/846f25eb-f474-47c1-ab3ff571e3db5910/BCAP-Code-full.pdf (archived at https://perma.cc/K6PX-Z5YR)

ASA. (2017) *Non-broadcast Code*. [Online] Available at: https://www.asa.org.uk/codes-and-rulings/advertising-codes/non-broadcast-code.html (archived at https://perma.cc/L44C-X2NM)

B Corp Climate Collective. (2021) *The Climate Justice Playbook for Business'* [Online] Available at: https://www.bcorpclimatecollective.org/climate-justice-playbook (archived at https://perma.cc/9BFB-6MUH)

Calcabrini, A; Hamill, J. (2022) *Sustainability Communications Need to Get Real*. Ogilvy. September 2022. [Online] Available from https://www.ogilvy.com/ideas/sustainability-communications-need-get-real (archived at https://perma.cc/M3TG-X7YP)

Carrington, D. (2020) *Hypocrites and Greenwash*. The Guardian. November 2020. Available at: https://www.theguardian.com/environment/2020/nov/09/ hypocrites-and-greenwash-greta-thunberg-climate-crisis (archived at https:// perma.cc/6AZ6-HMVR)

European Commission. (2022) *Circular Economy: Commission proposes new consumer rights and a ban on greenwashing*. [Online] Available at: https:// ec.europa.eu/commission/presscorner/detail/en/ip_22_2098 (archived at https:// perma.cc/5WNX-RCQ5)

ICC. (2018) *ICC Advertising and Marketing Communications Code*. [Online] Available at: https://iccwbo.org/news-publications/policies-reports/icc-advertising-and-marketing-communications-code/ (archived at https://perma. cc/5MUJ-UT4K)

IPCC. (2022) *Climate Change 2022: Impacts, Adaptation and Vulnerability*. [Online] Available at: https://www.ipcc.ch/report/ar6/wg2/ (archived at https:// perma.cc/ZH49-5CCP)

Media Smart. (2023) *How to spot greenwashing*. [Online] Available at: https:// mediasmart.uk.com/greenwashing/ (archived at https://perma.cc/LDG9-67DD)

Nielsen. (2015) *The sustainability imperative*. [Online] Available at: https:// nielseniq.com/global/en/insights/analysis/2015/the-sustainability-imperative-2/ (archived at https://perma.cc/7DEF-8X5Z)

WFA. (2022) *Global Guidance on Environmental Claims*. [Online] Available at: https://wfanet.org/knowledge/item/2022/04/04/Global-Guidance-on-Environmental-Claims-2022 (archived at https://perma.cc/7NB8-WGXY)

WPP. (2023). *Sustainability Report 2022*. [Online] Available at: https://www.wpp. com/-/media/project/wpp/files/sustainability/2023/sustainability-report-2022/ wpp-sustainability-report.pdf (archived at https://perma.cc/4N3T-28MK)

03

Getting our own house in order

Companies and their employees commit to curtail their carbon emissions by reducing travel, non-sustainable energy use and waste, setting targets and measuring progress against these to be on a pathway to net zero emissions.

The road to a sustainable advertising industry is a complex and challenging one, so we have broken it down into five separate actions. Let's begin with the things that can be done immediately; the things that can be described as 'getting our own house in order'. What we're outlining here is the role for every company (and every person) in the advertising industry to proactively take responsibility for reducing their own carbon emissions. This first step is a crucial one, as it will establish a culture of environmental consciousness within each organization.

The importance of setting and reporting a plan with science-based targets

The acceleration of plans based on science-based targets across the advertising eco-system will be critical in building an industry that is sustainable, so the first task is to ask if your organization has a plan with science-based targets in place and, if not, actively push to make this happen. This is possible to do for any organization, large or small. Many have these in place, but there are still those that don't. We suggest it is the responsibility of everybody working in the organization to be aware of the plan, its annual results, and their role in helping to reduce the GHG (Greenhouse Gas) emissions the organization creates. Note that best practice methodology includes the emissions up and down the supply chain your company fits into, as part of scope 3, so for an agency this should include production and media as a minimum.

You will see examples of how and where companies are doing this during this book.

To help, the broad recommendation for every advertising business is to commit to a net zero target of 2030, simultaneously giving a near-term and net zero target. If these are split out, the recommendation is a near-term reduction target for 2030, with a supporting additional long-term target for hitting net zero, which can be 2050 at the latest.

In our view, the best way for all companies to do this is with the Science Based Target Initiative (SBTi), which will help validate that the targets set are consistent with the Paris Agreement, mandates scope 1–3 inclusion, and requires publication of annual progress once targets are set. There are also resources to make commitments at the SME Climate Hub, and The Climate Pledge. Workshops and sessions on target setting and data collection, including recommendations on a reduction plan on how to achieve set targets, are available via the Ad Net Zero initiative (and companies operating in this space). These are freely available online.

Along with science-based targets, your organization will need a plan in place to deliver those emissions reductions every year, and ensure that it is being valued and measured with the same rigour as the annual financial accounts. Every company can put in place expectations of those in their supply chain to also work towards science-based targets. Equally, you can ask that of the companies that you consider as clients and use this as a measure of who you can confidently work with and for in support of a sustainable future. It is even possible to see which companies are more advanced than others along the pathway to net zero, and this will be critical as you consider the type of work you might do for these companies.

Tracking the industry's paths to net zero emissions from operations

In June 2023, Ad Net Zero shared a review of the publicly released plans (Figure 3.1 and Figure 3.2) of its Global Group to establish a more informed view of how and when supporters can be expected to reach net zero for their emissions. The charts show several public commitments by each of the commercial organizations in the Global Group, based on materials found in the public domain as of June 2023.

FIGURE 3.1 Public Net Zero Targets, Ad Net Zero (2023)

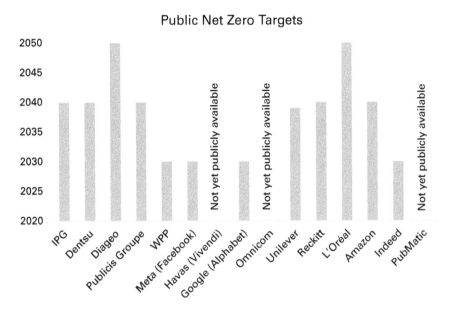

FIGURE 3.2 Targets for scope 3 emissions reductions by 2030, Ad Net Zero (2023)

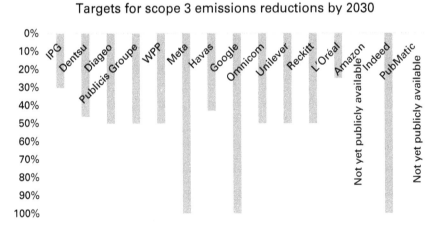

NOTE Scope 3 definition is at the discretion of each company.

This is important because it allows us for the first time to see how the industry can reach net zero for its emissions, and it also provides the opportunity to track the progress being made annually. As a result of this analysis, the initiative introduced the mandatory setting and reporting of science-based targets for global and national supporters.

FIGURE 3.3 100 per cent renewable energy achieved/target dates, Ad Net Zero (2023)

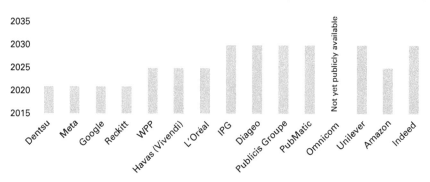

Key points to note, as of June 2023 (Figure 3.3):

- Ad Net Zero is operating in territories collectively representing 45 per cent of the world's ad market by spend.
- Overall Ad Net Zero Global supporters, when weighted by 2022 revenue, have a 2030 scope 3 emissions reduction target of 46.8 per cent by 2030.
- Of the world's ten largest advertising companies, 80 per cent of them are Ad Net Zero supporters through their holding companies.
- Four of these holding companies have net zero targets publicly announced of 2040 or sooner.
- Three of the world's three largest tech companies are *Ad Net Zero* supporters, in 2021 these provided advertising services representing 74 per cent of online advertising spend, and 47 per cent of all money spent on advertising.
- All of them have net zero targets publicly announced of 2040 or sooner.
- Three of the world's largest brand advertisers are Ad Net Zero supporters.
- All of them have net zero targets publicly announced of 2050 or sooner.

Where does the organization you work for feature on a chart like this?

First practical steps you can take to reduce emissions

Getting your house in order begins with three key areas (spanning scopes 1–3): reducing travel (specifically minimizing air travel), reducing fossil energy use, and minimizing waste.

Any company striving for sustainable advertising will need to measure their own carbon footprints, reduce emissions from travel, energy and waste, and account for all of these as part of their own reporting procedures. Finally, where remaining emissions cannot be removed, companies must offset these through renewal schemes.

This principle applies to every company, large and small, and during this chapter we will look at examples of best practice in this area, ranging from an SME employing tens of people, to a global holding agency group.

Individual responsibilities

Everyone, from apprentices to upper management, has a role with responsibility; make sure you're working for a company that is taking a sustainable approach to its own operations. If not, find out why not. It's OK to ask what the plan is to make sure your employer is taking positive steps towards a more sustainable footing, and pressure from employees will be an important part of expediting this change. As you'll see from this chapter, there are good reasons to do this beyond tackling climate change – you could help your company save money and be more attractive to prospective colleagues. Companies are increasingly open to these changes in operations if it means creating a more conscious and attractive workplace, so vigorously champion the mission of sustainability. Don't wait for someone else to call into question your business' sustainability practices. You have the power to effect change at scale. The impacts of your actions may well extend far beyond the walls of your office or production studio, too; by putting sustainability at the heart of your operations, you'll be creating a blueprint for others to follow and setting a new industry standard.

What does the data say?

Let's look at the evidence. From 2017–2019, before Covid-19 changed working habits, UK advertising think tank Credos estimated the average annual operational carbon footprint of a UK advertising agency per employee to be 3.4 tonnes CO_2e (carbon dioxide equivalent). This was worked out by looking at operational carbon footprints for an organization and averaging this across the number of full-time employees and full-time equivalents (Credos, 2020).

When we say 'operational', we mean the energy and water from office buildings along with emissions from business travel. It is possible for any company to access precise information on operational data. From those, people can take practical action to reduce emissions, using their initial results as a base figure to improve upon. Also, by looking at an average for an individual, trade bodies representing an entire industry can scale that amount by the number of people working in an industry.

Interestingly, advertising's operational footprint is comparable to other professional service sectors such as accountancy or law, which have similar office and travel practices. In total, Credos concluded that the annual operational GHG emissions for the whole UK industry, across all its sectors, is more than a million tonnes. Scale that globally and we have a huge number to take responsibility for.

For agencies, the beating heart of the industry, two emissions sources stand out (Credos, 2020):

1 Business travel (especially flights) which, based on the 2017–19 data, was typically just under 60 per cent of emissions.
2 Office energy usage, which is typically just under 40 per cent emissions.

Of course, Covid changed things drastically, for two years at least, but advertising and marketing services professionals still use energy to work, and as lockdowns have been lifted around the world, people are returning to the office. The commute is back, and business travel has returned.

So, what can be done?

Firstly, every advertising and marketing professional should be demanding that the energy they are using comes from a renewable energy source. This applies to the shared office you work in, but also to the office at home where many of us now spend a portion of our week.

One of the biggest single things that you can do is use less energy overall, and switch to renewable energy if you haven't already and urge your colleagues to do the same. If you're met with a no, ask 'why not?' and work out a plan to change that as soon as you can. For those with access to infrastructure decisions, that may include steps within your own control such as investing in solar panels on roofs of offices. Take a top-down approach and do what you can depending on your business' circumstances.

Secondly, if a flight for a meeting is suggested, question it. The Ad Net Zero team has developed an excellent decision tree to help inform a travel policy which actively seeks to limit the number of flights (Ad Net Zero, 2022). One of the upsides of lockdowns was the rapid adoption of video-meeting software, changing the mindset when it comes to demanding in-person meetings without considering the consequences of air travel.

But we do need to meet face-to-face (we are a people industry, after all) and sustainable advertising is not about a complete travel ban. Rather, we are asking for responsible business travel. For example, where possible, people should be encouraged to take the train.

Companies should consider ways to incentivize sustainable forms of business travel, from the use of EVs (electric vehicles) rather than petrol vehicles, opting for renewable energy-powered modes of transport including city buses and trains, and help with cycling.

If, after due consideration, flying is the only option, then there are some golden rules here. Fly economy, rather than business class. The carbon footprint of an economy class flight is 2.9 times smaller than that more expensive business class option. Travelling first class uses four times the amount of carbon. Also, look at your choice of airline; some are making faster progress than others. Make sure you build in a cost to offset the flight.

Employee pressure comes in here, too. Matt knows of one global media planning director who set out with an ambition to prove that the role was possible to do successfully for a year without ever getting on a flight. That's a great example to set, and to follow. If you know a serial flight-taker within your organization, now's the time to ask, in a sensitive way, if that behaviour is necessary and what alternative ways of working might be possible to achieve the same result.

Take this model (Figure 3.4) and adopt in your own organization.

Above and beyond

There are fantastic examples of organizations which have taken these simple principles on board and gone much further, too. While not every company has the financial or resource capacity to overhaul every aspect of their company's operations, these examples should provide inspiration to anyone looking to make meaningful change.

FIGURE 3.4 Ad Net Zero travel decision tree

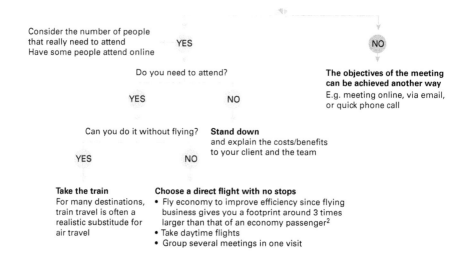

Is the physical meeting necessary?

Consider the number of people that really need to attend / Have some people attend online — YES

NO

The objectives of the meeting can be achieved another way
E.g. meeting online, via email, or quick phone call

Do you need to attend? — YES / NO

Can you do it without flying? — YES / NO

Stand down
and explain the costs/benefits to your client and the team

Take the train
For many destinations, train travel is often a realistic substitute for air travel

Choose a direct flight with no stops
- Fly economy to improve efficiency since flying business gives you a footprint around 3 times larger than that of an economy passenger[2]
- Take daytime flights
- Group several meetings in one visit

CASE STUDY

OpenX

OpenX are the world's leading sell-side platform for data and identity targeting and have made sustainability measures a high priority over the past few years.

Aims

OpenX committed to a 90 per cent reduction in Scopes 1, 2, and 3 from a 2018 base year – the most ambitious Net-Zero target allowed by SBTi at the time for companies with less than 500 employees.

The company set out to not only make meaningful change within OpenX operations, but also bring about major changes from the rest of the advertising industry.

Actions

The mission began in 2018, when OpenX decided to re-platform its business, selecting Google Cloud Platform (GCP) for its efficiency and scalability. Coinciding with pandemic lockdowns, the company pivoted to remote-first working, reduced business travel, downsized office locations from nine to four, and cloud-enabled office infrastructure.

Bringing in Dr Wescott, an internationally recognized expert in innovation, OpenX developed a formal procedure, named 'The OpenX Greenhouse Gas Inventory Management Plan'. The 19-page plan was based on best industry practices and provided guidance for the core team to develop the GHG inventory.

The company addressed Scope 3 activities, including business travel, working from home and commuting, basing their methodologies on best practices and global standards.

Result

The net effect of OpenX's measures reflects the rigorous nature of their approach. From the 2018 base point, the company reduced its carbon emissions for all three scopes from 24,441.4 tCO_2e in 2018 to 909.5 tCO_2e in 2021 – this represents a 96.3 per cent reduction.

As a result of these impressive results, at the time of writing, OpenX is one of less than 1,000 companies in the world to be awarded carbon neutral certification. Additionally, the company is one of fewer than 10 companies to be named a Climate Registered All Star. The company is now regularly hosting events on sustainability, as well as frequently featuring on sustainability panels such as that at Cannes Lions.

In 2021, the OpenX efforts reduced carbon emissions within advertising campaigns on its exchange by 23,531.9 tCO_2e.

CASE STUDY

Havas UK

Havas Group is one of the largest advertising and communications groups in the world, operating in over 100 countries worldwide.

Aims

Havas Group's decarbonization targets align with those set by its parent group Vivendi. The Group's decarbonization targets for scopes 1 and 2 are aligned with the trajectory for limiting climate warming to 1.5°C. They provide for a 71 per cent reduction in these emissions by 2035 (compared to 2018). In addition, the Group has committed to a 43 per cent reduction by 2035 in absolute scope 3 emissions relating to business operations. These targets have been validated by SBTi.

The Havas Global group has set out specific targets for its businesses worldwide to achieve in relation to sustainability. The targets set spanned from 2018–2024 and include:

- 5 per cent decrease in electricity consumption
- 25 per cent of total electricity consumption to come from renewable sources
- 20 per cent decrease of non-hazardous waste generation
- 100 per cent use of recycled and/or certified paper

- 40 per cent decrease in paper consumption
- 100 per cent of agencies implementing recycling programmes.

Actions

While their global business has been making clear moves towards sustainable practice, it is their UK-based business that has been making the biggest steps forward in environmental progress. In 2020, Havas launched Impact+, a CSR (Corporate Social Responsibility) strategy structuring its approach around three key pillars: environment, people, and meaningful communication.

The mission of Havas Impact+ is to:

- Fast-track the decarbonization of the business in line with science-based targets
- Empower our people, build an inclusive culture, and make a difference in our communities
- Harness the power of creative ideas through our communications to bring about positive change in society.

In their London headquarters, all energy comes from REGO-certified renewable sources – a huge achievement that can be taken as inspiration for all companies looking to minimize their footprint while leading their field. Solar panels on the building's roof contribute to this renewable energy.

The building utilizes energy-saving equipment including state-of-the-art lighting systems to further reduce energy usage within the building, while the building also boasts a 'living' roof that captures carbon dioxide from the atmosphere and releases oxygen. The London building's café is over 80 per cent single-use plastic free, uses rainwater to flush the toilets and uses entirely recycled paper.

Result

All of Havas UK's headquarters' actions have led to audited confirmation of a 54 per cent decrease in GHG emissions between 2018 and 2021. A huge reduction figure, and one that has led to BREEAM, the world-leading validation and certification system for assessing building sustainability, rating the building 'outstanding'. This makes it one of the most sustainable buildings in the UK.

Havas London is B-Corp certified and Havas UK is going through the certification process, highlighting the company's commitment to sustainability as well as to ethical decisions for their employees, customers, suppliers and community. This all served to make Havas UK a Campaign Ad Net Zero award winner in 2022.

CASE STUDY

Coffee & TV

Coffee & TV is a London-based independent creative studio whose work and artists-led culture have been recognized by BAFTA, RTS, Ad Net Zero, Campaign, D&AD and more. As the UK's first Certified B Corp creative studio, sustainability and responsibility are at the heart of Coffee & TV's operations, productions, and culture.

Aims

Coffee & TV have made a fantastic discovery. It is that every step they take to be a better company makes them better at their work. Coffee & TV has set an SME Climate Hub Target to halve emissions by 2030 and reach net zero by 2040, this means focusing on engaging their supply chain. Alongside this ambition, Coffee & TV's Conscious Creative Team focus on reducing their work with controversial industries and building relationships with purpose-driven brands and businesses to have a positive impact through the work they do.

Actions

Coffee & TV has been measuring their operational carbon footprint since 2019 with albert and Climate Essentials. Their studio, data centre and over 80 per cent of their team working from home use 100 per cent renewable energy. They use FirstMile and a charity partner for their technology to ensure zero waste goes to landfill. Cabs and courier partners are working towards a zero-emission fleet, and they offer the Octopus EV salary sacrifice scheme for those able to transition. The team are kept engaged around climate action through green onboarding, events, environmental group meet-ups and regular internal communications. Their new studio in Farringdon was refurbished with environmental impact in mind and certified BREEAM 'Excellent'. Coffee & TV are engaging with their suppliers to understand their sustainability targets and ethical practices and provide resources to help them align with the 1.5 ambition.

Result

Using Climate Essentials, Coffee & TV measure their scope 1, 2 and 3 emissions and they have minimized their scope 1 and 2 to near zero. From 2019 to 2021 they reduced their emissions by 75 per cent (from 252 t CO_2e to 114 t CO_2e). In 2022, the growth of the team and new studio meant their emissions rose to 262 t CO_2e.

Coffee & TV have reduced their energy usage each year, 2019 to 2020 53 per cent, 2020 to 2021 95 per cent, 2021 to 2022 25 per cent and have committed to remaining a carbon neutral business (since 2021) by investing in nature-based solutions with Earthly. Coffee & TV releases an annual Sustainability Policy and Impact Report on their website.

Tips for sustainable advertising operations

The Ad Net Zero team gathered examples of best practice from across its supporter base and set these out in a Guide (Ad Net Zero, 2022).

Tip 1: Get company-wide buy in for sustainability plans

This is critical and it involves everyone in the company, not just the sustainability lead, C-suite or your 'green team'. A powerful, practical thing you can do is to update the travel policy so that the principle of sustainable travel is embedded in the company's way of working. Then, map out a target of annual reduction of your operational emissions at an organizational level and make a commitment to track that and publish it regularly over time. Hold yourselves accountable and discuss where improvements can be made. Get used to making that data public too, because this will become a standard part of business practice as carbon accounting is standardized and becomes a legal requirement.

For management, there is a benefit to doing all of this; it shows your team that you are serious about tackling the issue and being a responsible business when it comes to net zero advertising practices. It also means your stakeholders (clients and suppliers) can see what you're doing. Environmental responsibility will be a standard requirement and, if your company falls behind, it will become a reason to actively not work with your business and for people to not work for you.

Tip 2: Harness the sustainability passions of your team members

People working in advertising and marketing services care deeply about this issue. Unlock that passion by creating a cross-discipline green team of individuals that will lead the way with thinking about behaviours which can improve the operations of the company. Encourage those to be regularly shared, not just within the company, but through conversations with your peers. Initiatives such as Green Weeks act as a catalyst for change, with companies regularly inviting speakers to help challenge people's thinking about how they work. It is also possible to put the passions of your employees to effective use by creating space and time for volunteering on environmental projects.

Tip 3: Taking the power of the individual further

It is incredibly important for everyone working in advertising and marketing services to monitor and reduce their own carbon impact, to recognize how behaviours in and out of the office can be supportive of the ambitions of net zero advertising. Generally, people working in the industry believed their benchmark for sustainable living was not high enough, with just 37 per cent of respondents believing the way they live their life is good for the planet (Credos, 2020). If we are to be the people who make the work that supports a sustainable future, we must develop an innate understanding of what that means by living more sustainably.

Examples of support from companies within the Ad Net Zero community include Cycle to Work schemes, staff volunteering days for sustainability projects, pro-bono work for sustainable solutions and flight-free pledges. Companies can offer training to people on how to calculate their own carbon footprint and even introduce technologies that enable competitions between staff to live more sustainability with leaderboards to help provide momentum. People working from home could also be supported to make the transfer to renewable energy at home if they can do so.

Tip 4: Bring in specialist help if you need it

There are specialist consultancies which can help set up ways to track carbon emissions and provide guidance on carbon-cutting initiatives. A specialist can also keep you informed and up to date on new developments and regulatory changes – this is a constantly-moving area. Most businesses should be able to report the basics themselves. There are widely available calculators now to help you not just report your own emissions but also understand how you are performing versus other companies of a similar size and location.

Tip 5: Know the essential data points

Some data points are key for businesses to collect. They are:

- Annual electricity use for the reporting year
- Annual gas usage from grid
- Air travel, origin, destination, and distance travelled
- Annual water usage
- Annual wastewater
- Annual non-recycled paper usage
- Annual recycled paper usage
- Amount of rubbish to landfill.

All of this should be easily collectable from your finance, office management and other internal sources. These data points will form the basis of your annual report, so make sure you're collecting and measuring them accurately.

Carbon offsetting

Carbon offsetting relates to the investment in positive environmental projects to compensate for emissions elsewhere. The practice is a big topic of debate across the sustainability sector. Its detractors have understandably raised concerns regarding its removal of responsibility around carbon emissions. The bottom-line for sustainable advertising is that you must have done absolutely everything you can to remove carbon emissions from your operations before you get to this stage.

There are lists of recommended offsetting schemes you can use if you have done everything you can and are now looking to offset the remainder of your emissions. Our best advice is to only use carbon-reducing offsets verified by a trusted third party which create new and additional storage for the long-term.

Training and development

If you're serious about change, the next step is to get yourself and your team on one of the training schemes offered by the industry. A good starting point is the Ad Net Zero training course which is available to all advertising and marketing services professionals.

This training is a relatively inexpensive entry-level online course for everyone to help make the change towards net zero advertising happen.

Other courses are on offer to practitioners, such as #ChangeTheBrief, which we will go into in more detail about in Chapter 11, as well as courses offered by the likes of Cambridge University through its Institute of Sustainability Leadership.

But much of what you need is in this book, and there are practical tips, actions and case studies all the way through to help you make change happen where you work.

Getting our own house in order: summary

As we have seen in this chapter, there are many simple and practical steps you (and your organization) can take to track, measure and reduce the carbon footprint of your operations. No matter whether your organization is large or small, set a science based target, report on it regularly and make it integral to the way you are working to reduce your emissions as rapidly as possible. Choice of energy source and decisions around travel are particularly important. Share what you're doing and learn from others by supporting initiatives which bring practitioners together. Put the expectation on everyone around you, up and down your supply chain, to be doing the same thing.

References

Ad Net Zero. (2020) *Ad Net Zero, All for None report.* [Online] Available at: https://adnetzero.com/ (archived at https://perma.cc/TRX4-NUMB)

Ad Net Zero. (2022) *Ad Net Zero Guide.* Available at: https://adnetzcro.com/news/ad-net-zero-guide/ (archived at https://perma.cc/SBL7-NPMG)

Ad Net Zero. (2023) *Tracking Ad Net Zero's Global Supporters' Paths to Net Zero.* [Online] Available at: https://adnetzero.com/news/tracking-ad-net-zeros-global-supporters-paths-to-net-zero/ (archived at https://perma.cc/4P8A-UMDH)

IPA. (2023) *Ad Net Zero Essentials Certificate.* Available at: https://ipa.co.uk/courses-qualifications/ad-net-zero-essentials-certificate (archived at https://perma.cc/GE5C-ULPA)

04

Reducing emissions from ad production

Advertisers, agencies, and production companies commit to adopt tools and training to measure, manage and reduce the emissions from advertising production.

Thousands of ads are produced around the world by advertisers, agencies, production companies and media owners every year. There are many ways that the carbon emissions created during this process can be tackled and reduced; this chapter will provide and explain some of these solutions, particularly for adverts which require high quality video production. We will look at where these carbon emissions come from, consider which tools and training are available to support you further, and share examples of learnings and best practice from leaders in this space.

Just as in the previous chapter, the first step is to recognize how and where the carbon emissions are created, and then adopt a tool that allows you to measure, record and track reduction of carbon emissions in ad productions. This will ultimately allow you to eliminate the most negative environmental impacts of advertising production without reducing the quality of the work or its impact.

As with the operational side of businesses, measurement is key to reduce emissions, and is likely to become increasingly important as countries move towards green economies. From 2023, all publicly listed companies in the UK with a premium London Stock Exchange listing will be under more strict requirements to report on climate risk, as part of the Taskforce on Climate-related Financial Disclosures mandate (TCFD, 2022) with the rules likely being tightened and extended in 2025. Reporting on Scope 3 will become mandatory in the EU from 2024, impacting large businesses in the

UK that operate within the EU. In the short-term, this will directly affect a small number of brand advertisers with more to follow. These companies in turn will likely seek clearer emissions reporting from suppliers, increasing pressure on the advertising production supply chain to track, measure, report and reduce carbon emissions from its working practices.

Learning from the film and TV industry

albert, the authority on environmental sustainability for film and TV production, was established in 2011 and hosted by BAFTA. An industry-funded initiative by UK broadcasters, albert provides free tools, training and resources for film and TV productions to measure and reduce their carbon footprints and waste. albert also seeks to encourage and enable the creation of content that will inspire screen audiences to act more sustainably.

Unsurprisingly, there has always been a creative overlap between the talent that works in TV and film, and the talent that works in advertising. Countless people working in front of and behind the cameras have turned their hand to advertising to make great creative ads and vice versa. This is particularly apparent around major cultural events such as the Super Bowl in the US, the World Cup, and gifting seasons such as those seen around Chinese New Year and the Christmas period, when advertisers seek to connect with large audiences of potential customers.

It became clear to the advertising industry that, to achieve similar levels of carbon literacy, similar standards of production talent and equipment would be required. However, while a standard TV or film production produces anywhere from 30 minutes to 3 hours' worth of content, an advert is most often no more than 30 to 60 seconds. This means the relative intensity of carbon emissions involved in ad production vastly outweighs those of TV and film when you consider the total against the length of final output, although – one caveat – this doesn't account for the repeated playout of the ad. It is clear, though, that significant steps need to be made to reduce the impact that the ad production process has on our planet. This means a rapid change in thinking, approach, and skills by hundreds of thousands of professionals involved in ad production around the world.

There are some key considerations that ad production professionals should keep in mind when planning a campaign which broadly fall into four activity areas: travel and transport, how spaces are powered, materials and disposal. These are:

- How locally the work can be produced based on the proposed script
- Whether locations can be changed, virtual production solutions incorporated, or local talent used, to reduce reliance on air and road travel for cast, crew, and client, and/or whether train travel could be considered
- Whether locations can make use of battery powered equipment or clean energy sources
- Whether studios are powered on renewable energy
- Whether lower carbon-footprint, vegetarian or vegan, catering can be provided, with low to no food waste
- Whether props, sets and costumes can be hired instead of purchased
- How any purchases will be repurposed, reused – or disposed of.

All these areas contain their own inherent challenges, all of which are surmountable, from the moment of creative development onwards. Steps can be taken that will not only reduce carbon emissions, but also offer up cost savings and greater efficiencies to the benefit of the businesses involved. As an example, making use of local talent or changing a location to eliminate the need for air travel will save money on flights, hotels and per diems.

Introducing AdGreen

The UK advertising industry's answer to albert launched in September 2020. The initiative, named AdGreen, set out two clear aims:

1 To measure advertising production carbon footprints allowing project teams to understand which activities have the biggest impact
2 To empower the industry to reduce emissions and move to zero carbon/zero waste.

AdGreen seeks to unite the advertising industry to eliminate the negative environmental impact of ad production. To support this ambition, it provides specialist training to help the workforce become carbon literate, a carbon calculator for the industry to measure the proposed and actual impact of advertising projects, and resources to help production teams make reduction decisions – all of which are currently free at the point of use. You can find out more about everything AdGreen offers at: **weareadgreen.org/**

Much of the data, insights and tips in this chapter will be based on AdGreen. We've had the opportunity to work closely with the AdGreen team as it has grown these past three years – they are experts in their field, highly committed to sustainability and driven to help every person involved in ad production to reduce their environmental impact.

AdGreen's origins

AdGreen's founder, Jo Fenn, battled for several years to get the initiative off the ground, before securing backing from a coalition of global advertisers, agencies and media owners. Her story of how this passion project grew into a not-for-profit initiative to embed sustainability in all forms of ad production is an inspiration to anyone looking to bring about positive change.

Matt sat down with Jo to get some insight into the process of setting AdGreen up, her inspiration for the project, and the process of transformation that the programme has gone through so far.

What were the origins of AdGreen?

Prior to running AdGreen, I worked in advertising production for almost ten years. Over many shoots, I saw a huge amount of waste being generated. I wanted to do something, and started by facilitating on-set recycling, and encouraging attendees to bring their own reusable water bottles and mugs to cut down on single use plastic.

The response from those on my shoots was positive, but I wanted to take it further. This is when I reached out to BAFTA's albert team. They support the UK's Film and TV industry to reduce the environmental impacts of their productions. They have over a decade of data at their fingertips, and heaps of interesting insights. For example, did you know that in 2021, the average CO_2 equivalent emissions generated while producing one hour of television content was 5.7 tonnes? Although this is almost half compared to 2019's data – which is likely due to Covid restrictions on travel – 4.4 tonnes is still over a third of the average UK citizen's annual footprint, which is around 12.7 tonnes. During the production of this average 1 hour, most emissions came from people transport, and energy use for the various spaces involved in creating a TV show. A tiny fraction of the total emissions generated were from disposal. What albert's data taught me is that recycling on set was a drop in the ocean. And, if 5.7 tonnes of CO_2 equivalent were being generated per hour of TV, I couldn't imagine what was being generated by each ad break that sat in between. AdGreen began when I started trying to find out.

Did you experience a low point where you thought AdGreen wouldn't get off the ground?

It was probably in 2018 – after bringing together the key trade bodies and trying to find a way of funding the project, the plans fell apart. That was quite draining – trying to keep the momentum going while I was working, trying to organize the right people to come together, trying to keep enthusiasm high and keep the community that had been built engaged. At that point I was moving to Scotland and took a break from it for a while, to focus on my new job. I chipped away at a few things when it was quiet, chatting to brands who had got in touch, trying to get funding for a calculator, but again still nothing happened. With the establishment of the climate action working group at the Advertising Association (AA), I had a couple of the group members get in touch about AdGreen in late 2019, and slowly conversations started to pick up again. The break, the distance and some real enthusiasm from the AA started to give me hope, although it wasn't until it officially launched in September 2020 that I believed it was happening!

What does success look like for you in sustainable advertising production?

For me personally, success would be seeing a fully engaged industry who are making informed choices. We're already seeing this to a degree, but for measurement and reduction to become part of everyday production would be great. I know we're a way off that yet, and a lot of other things would need to change to accommodate this, but that is what I'd love to see.

AdGreen's first annual review

In March 2023, the AdGreen team published their first Annual Review. This is the richest data set yet on ad production where carbon emissions are involved and contains crucial learnings and techniques which can be adopted to reduce these going forward. The team selected a series of stats from the review of the data collected in its first full year of operations that they believe highlight the key issues facing the industry. This data comes with the caveat that the sample size of the 515 projects recorded in the AdGreen carbon calculator was significantly skewed towards smaller sized projects – for the greatest change, we need more of those working on larger projects to measure their impact using the tool.

1 The 515 projects recorded as complete in 2022 emitted a total of 2,446.1 tCO_2e.

2 More than half (56 per cent) of these projects were under 1 tCO_2e – these are those smaller projects mentioned. The combined impact of these was 83.53 tCO_2e, compared to the four projects over 100 tCO_2e, which totalled 459.7 tCO_2e.

3 While the mean size of a completed ad production project was 4.7 tCO_2e, they ranged massively from 1.5 kg to 129.6 tCO_2e.

4 Travel & transport accounted for the most emissions generated because of all activities recorded (62.4 per cent). Energy and fuels used to power spaces accounted for almost a quarter (24.6 per cent) with Materials accounting for 12.4 per cent. The activity area with the least impact was Disposal, at 0.6 per cent.

From this data, it's clear that decisions made about where an ad production takes place has a dramatic impact on the carbon footprint. Unsurprisingly, it also indicates that, the more shoot days required, the higher the tCO_2e impact.

This first set of data from AdGreen is just the tip of the iceberg. As the tool is used more widely, and the practice of properly recording data about the activities which go into a production increases, the recorded carbon footprint of ad production is likely to also increase. However, the opportunities to make decisions that reduce that impact will also grow. This will be particularly true if the tool is used in the early stages of planning an ad campaign, as opposed to at the latter stages when key production decisions have already been made.

We can already see that this data set which has started to provide average tCO_2e for different types of productions is going to be invaluable as it will provide a benchmark for practitioners working on ad production and it will help shape targets for reduction to beat with future productions. It will also help provide proxies for advertisers with large-scale ad production schedules to get to grips with the total carbon footprint of this element of their advertising operations. We will go into campaign measurement in more detail in chapter 14.

Large or small though, now is the time to record the activities and review the carbon footprint data of your ad production, and to adopt techniques advocated by AdGreen to reduce the environmental impact of your work in this area. Now let's look at what each key group involved in the production of advertising can do.

FIGURE 4.1 Which activities have the highest impact? AdGreen Annual Review 2022

Which activities have the highest impact?

You'll see that travel and transport activities emitted the most tCO2e, followed by powering spaces such as studios, locations, hotels, and post production suites.

Materials comes next, and disposal is a very small piece of the pie. This trend follows across all of the different subsets we have looked at, albeit in slightly different proportions, as you can see here. Travel and transport was the highest impact area in 55% of all projects (282 of 515).

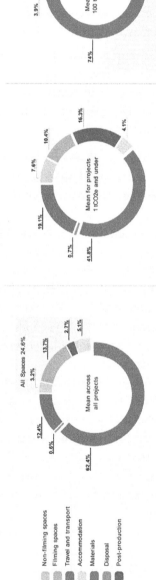

Advice for brands and their partners

Let's start with the most influential player in the mix for reducing the negative environmental impact of ad production – the client and the demands they can place on their supply chain.

Rob Newman, Director of Public Affairs, ISBA, which is the voice of the UK's biggest advertisers, highlights that as follows:

> This is where initiatives like AdGreen come in: enabling brands to make granular, project-by-project judgements on how they can push down carbon emissions in production and improve the sustainability of their marketing operations. Those brands who are already engaged with AdGreen are the early adopters who are reaping the benefits of this analysis, and who consequently are able to think more intelligently about the impact of their production work and the changes that they can make.

Advice for creative agencies

Creative agencies have a different, but still critical, role in the process of considering the environmental impact of an ad production they might be planning. The question for creative agencies is how to take these things into consideration without limiting the creative impact of the resulting ad. For sure, the influence of a creative on the positive/negative environmental impact of the ad production is key. As the IPA's Head of Production, Eliot Liss, says:

> Some of our industry's most creative work has developed in response to constraints and the channelling of evidence and insight, so I know sustainability is another opportunity to be grasped. Only through enhanced viability and visibility of carbon measurement can we galvanize buy-in, change and upstream impacts on the creative dev, planning and pitching phases of projects.

AdGreen's top tips for creatives to consider include:

Travel

- Develop scripts which can be shot locally, or by using CG/VFX, and allow for seasonal weather advantages, to avoid baking air travel activities into the production.

- Take public transport to the shoot and reduce the number of people attending where possible with remote monitoring.
- Consider Visual effects (VFX) before live product shots to avoid the impact of shipping hero items.

Spaces

- If office space is a line item in your production budget, make sure it's renewably powered.
- When selecting other production partners and suppliers, choose those running their spaces on renewable tariffs too.

Materials

- Remove or rework material heavy script elements, such as wet downs, intricate set builds and multiple costume changes.
- Discuss how food shoots can be achieved with as little food waste as possible.
- Encourage those staying in overnight accommodation as part of a production to choose evening meals with less impact.

Disposal

- Ensure client product is returned, rehomed or goes to a food waste collection service.

Advice for production and service companies

Production and service companies can lead the way in adopting best practice in sustainable ad production. The following are tips suggested by the AdGreen team for consideration if you are working within a Production & Services company:

Travel

- Use local talent (cast and crew) and remote monitoring to reduce/remove air travel.

- Hire/use electric and hybrid vehicles over petrol and diesel transport.
- Encourage facilities drivers to avoid fuel waste by having a no idling policy.

Spaces

- Use low-energy lighting to reduce the amount of power required and turn things off when they're not in use.
- Use mains power before diesel generators or see if there are rechargeable battery options.
- Switch off aircon and heating when not in use.

Materials

- Work with creatives and directors/photographers to remove or rework carbon intensive script elements, such as wet downs.
- Use reusable location protection such as mats, rather than disposable items.
- Supply water coolers instead of individual bottles to cut down on plastic.

Disposal

- Discuss reuse and rehoming plans for any set build items such as timber, as well as costume, and food – aim for zero waste in the first place.
- Recycle and compost where possible – landfill should be a last resort.

Green the bid

Another initiative providing excellent resources for any ad production professional looking to work in more sustainable ways is called Green The Bid. It is a grassroots, non-profit industry organization and you can find more about them on their site: https://www.greenthebid.earth/

Green The Bid provides resources to ad production companies for free and encourages them to use these during ad productions. On their site, you can find production checklists, where ad producers can track and report their carbon footprint and environmental impact, but Green The Bid recommends an additional cost for the delivery of that reporting to the client (advertiser or agency).

This makes sense, in that reporting on sustainability is an additional service which needs to be funded, because it requires extra time and new tools to make it happen. There is a challenge here – how our industry recognizes the additional costs of sustainable advertising operations right across the supply chain and the need for this to be funded in one way or another. There is no simple solution to this, but it is a cost that needs to be recognized and considered.

Looking to the future – can virtual production be ad production's silver bullet?

A boom in virtual production is happening, turbo-charged by competition in film and particularly TV, in answer to the demand for high quality content from the world's biggest streaming companies and broadcasters. The UK is growing as a base for investment in this area – just look at the funding going into new facilities at Sky Studios Elstree and the new Sunset Studios in Broxbourne, backed by US investors, Blackstone, and Hudstone Pacific Properties, just a few miles from the Warner Bros Studios in Leavesden and, of course, the ongoing development of neighbouring Pinewood Studios. The Studio Map carries an updated list, showing the scale of building and investment in this area, with many examples of virtual production facilities for film and TV, either in planning or being built in the UK. Meanwhile in the US, Forbes has reported on an 'arms race' taking place, citing the example of Amazon Studios unveiling the nation's largest LED wall stage in December 2022 to support more virtual production of its TV and film content.

As such, the creative industries are preparing the next generation of filmmakers to work in virtual production studios, using the latest technology and techniques, so it seems inevitable that this wave of change will come to the advertising industry too. Leaders in the industry are recognizing the potential of virtual production to transform the production of their advertising content, with Reckitt's Vice President for Marketing Operations and Capabilities, Becky Verano, saying:

> 'For me this is a pivotal moment. Our objective now is to get to a global scale and to produce more than 80% of our production volume in this way in the future. By using a virtual studio, we can leverage the exponential growth of

technology while making our production more sustainable by minimizing wastage and reducing our carbon footprint. At Reckitt we shoot over 250 ads a year and we have also increased the creative ambitions with the work which will be created in virtual studios.'

So virtual production's potential to be a silver bullet when it comes sustainability is clear - it could help facilitate major savings in carbon through reduction of high carbon travel needs and wastage from set builds.

It's not easy to get a precise figure for how much is spent on ad production each year, but the best estimate is around 10 per cent in addition to the total ad spend in the market. For the UK, that means £3.5 billion for 2022, based on the circa £35 billion reported by AA/WARC (2023). Scale that globally, circa $880 billion according to WARC (2022), and that means nearly $90 billion in the pot for ad production. Experts suggest only 1 per cent of ads are currently using Virtual Production (VP) technology and techniques currently, so the market opportunity is huge here – 80 per cent of $90 billion is $72 billlion spend up for grabs from those who can offer VP services to the advertising community as we build a net zero advertising industry.

This is certainly what a new business, Silverscape, is preparing for. It is building the UK's largest dedicated VP studio complex and the 'under one roof' proposition aims to support film makers, including advertisers, decarbonize production and accelerate the essential transition to sustainable ad production, using new and emerging technologies and workflows.

Virtual Production for Silverscape is a catch all for much more than just LED screen first made famous by 'The Mandalorian' and the team at ILM, though. From the company's POV, VP technology includes Green Screen LED Volume, Motion Capture, 360° Cameras, Building Environments, Real-time Rendering, LED Wall/Ceiling, Camera Tracking, Colour Calibration, Unreal Engine Unity, Gaming Engines and Volumetric Capture. The first of its studio complexes will be in Greater Manchester and, aside from studio and production facilities, it will include the Silverscape Academy, helping to upskill production technicians, graduates, and creative talent in film and advertising.

The important point here is the business is aligning with the advertising industry's greater aim to get ad production to net zero as quickly as possible, presenting the business case that VP technologies offer the best solution to significant reductions in carbon impact. Benefits of adopting VP range from travel reduction as a key driver for lower carbon impact to reduced waste from set build, digital multi-reuse of sets and components, reduced shoots days and no disruption by pesky weather conditions, as well as accurate and consistent measurement of carbon in studio. All this at an estimated 20–30 per cent lower cost of production, with an unlimited range of creative possibilities. Ah, that magic combination of quality content, cost savings and a potential 70 per cent carbon reduction, according to the Silverscape team.

However, the Silverscape team acknowledge the widespread adoption of VP across the UK's biggest advertisers' productions will not be straightforward. Matt spoke with the founders about the change they anticipate coming to the ad production industry and what advertising professionals need to prepare for. Ian Armstrong was previously Global Marketing Director at Jaguar Land Rover, and is a Fellow of The Marketing Society, the Marketing Group of Great Britain, and a consultant to the Advertisers Producers Association, while Simon Binns was previously a Board member of BBH, Ogilvy, WPP/BlueHive and Spark44 and Exec Director/Chief Commercial Officer in fintech.

Why will adoption of VP be tricky?

The 'half-life' of technology is arguably shorter than the 'half-life' of culture and this type of change requires people to accept, understand and embrace it. It's often seen as a restrictor of creativity when in fact, it frees up creative thought. It's therefore important that the industry learns about VP in all its forms, uses it and engages with it so that talent can create in new and different ways.

What are the implications for the creative process?

The fundamental change is that those workflows and processes often described as post-production now have to be considered much earlier in the process. The technology is so good that once you start shooting it's at a much higher standard and finished version than in a conventional shoot process. Therefore, the pre-production process is much more like a live broadcast. You need to align and prepare everything so that once you turn the camera on, you're in effect as live.

What are the pitfalls currently in the way VP is planned into ad production?

Due to its nascent status, especially in the advertising industry, VP solutions are often thought of as either an afterthought (and therefore too late to realize any real benefits) or it's included in a treatment pitch as a methodology because it's felt it better be on the list.

As more and more people use and embrace its benefits, its inclusion should become much more relevant and appropriate.

What sort of targets should advertisers and their ad production partners be setting to drive this transition?

VP should only be used for positive reasons such as it adds value, provides incremental creative opportunities, allows for solutions that were, up until now, not practically possible. Due to potential reductions in air travel, materials needed for set builds and the associated disposal, it is also a real option to reduce the amount of carbon used in asset production. Therefore, if a client has a particular strategy as part of their ESG framework to reduce their own corporate carbon footprint then VP technologies can play a real part. If advertisers and their production partners declare carbon reduction targets, then this will force the whole system to innovate and find ways of hitting those targets.

What are your goals beyond the ad production process when it comes to advertising and sustainability reporting?

SilverScape is broader than just a studio or production business. We believe it's critical to grow the next generation of skilled people to continue to fuel the growth of the ad industry. This means we also have an Academy business to educate and train people in a range of skills and competencies spanning ideation, game engine software, production workflows, technology, craft, immersive technologies and post-production. These skills are transferable across not only advertising but also film/tv and other creative industries providing people with a much wider range of career opportunities.

The purpose of SilverScape is to help content makers accelerate the transition to net zero using innovative technologies and workflows and so reporting of carbon usage is critical to that purpose. The SilverScape carbon tracker will calculate the carbon cost of any asset produced and provide a management report to each client avoiding cumbersome manual data collection. Ultimately, the advertising industry needs data and reporting systems to rapidly reduce its emissions.

Another company helping the advertising industry prepare for the growth in virtual production is ARRI Rental, part of ARRI, a German-owned global company which has been supporting the motion picture industry since 1917. Matt spoke with their Commercial Marketing Executive, Ed Jones, who explained how short-form content costs are prohibitive currently. However, with the right understanding of the new technology and its capabilities, plus a shift in the creative development where the production process is accounted for much earlier on, VP will become a fantastic creative tool for advertisers, with the byproduct of less travel and less consumption. He cited the example of car advertisers who, with a limited number of proto-type models, won't face the same challenge of flying them around the world, instead shooting multiple locations from one stage. His view was the industry will increasingly embrace VP, that clients will set the standards in terms of how much VP is used, and that advertising professionals involved in the creative and production process should follow this fierce curve of technological development and be ready to create accordingly. To that end, ARRI Rental, ran a session for over 150 ad production professionals at the ARRI London Stage in January 2023, designed to show how simple it is for a director to change the time of day, different textual effects added to a scene, or the light bouncing off the face of the actor. The demo underlined the role of virtual environments and extended reality in production, with all the benefits it brings – budget management, time efficiency, sustainability-tracking, but most importantly the creative opportunity to create something out of this world.

One final point to consider is from the Chief Executive of the Advertising Producers Association, Steve Davies, who talked to Matt about the role of clients in setting annual targets for VP, reducing their scope 3 emission and helping the production community fully realize the creative, cost-efficiency and sustainable capabilities of this exciting new technology.

It seems planning for the how and when of VP in the ad production process will be critical in achieving its fullest potential.

Reducing emissions from ad production: summary

Knowledge is rapidly growing about how to track, measure and reduce the environmental impact of ad production, thanks in many ways to the progress made already in film and TV production and the passion of teams like AdGreen. There is training available, tools you can access and best practice guidelines like those outlined in this chapter from organizations like AdGreen and Green The Bid. The traditional way of producing ads is changing, with expectations of a much smarter management of resources, so reduction in emissions are growing. The world's biggest advertisers are looking at different ways to make the best ads with a lower production footprint, including exploring the possibilities offered up by virtual production. It is difficult to picture an ad being made in the near future without due consideration of its environmental impact including credible, supporting data.

References

Adgreen. (2023) *Home*. [Online] Available at: https://weareadgreen.org/ (archived at https://perma.cc/WJ4V-BG8V)

Adgreen. (2023) *The AdGreen 2022 Annual Review*. [Online] Available at: https://weareadgreen.org/adgreen-annual-review-2022/ (archived at https://perma.cc/ZL7B-JJ46)

Advertising Association. (2023) *UK ad spend grew 8.8% in 2022 to reach £34.8bn*. [Online] Available at: https://adassoc.org.uk/our-work/uk-ad-spend-grew-8-8-in-2022-to-reach-34-8bn-inflationary-pressures-persist-with-minimal-growth-forecast-for-2023/ (archived at https://perma.cc/G977-JVB7)

albert. (2023) *Home*. [Online] Available at: https://wearealbert.org/ (archived at https://perma.cc/M995-UXZS) [Accessed August 2023]

Aldrick, P. (2021) *You want La La Land? Head to Hertfordshire with plans for film studio*. The Times. August 2021. Available from https://www.thetimes.co.uk/article/la-la-land-hertfordshire-plans-film-studio-investment-oliver-dowden-fw8dmqh35 (archived at https://perma.cc/C9TP-NHMR)

Berners-Lee, Mike. (2010). *How Bad Are Bananas? The Carbon Footprint of Everything*. Profile Books Ltd. London.

Bloom, D. (2022) *Amazon Studios Unveils Biggest LED Wall Virtual Production Stage In U.S.* Forbes. December 2022. [Online] Available at: https://www.forbes.com/sites/dbloom/2022/12/06/amazon-studios-unveils-biggest-led-wall-virtual-production-stage-in-us/?sh=5145e39a2caf (archived at https://perma.cc/7K6P-Y28A)

Echochain. (2023) *CSRD – Guide: What to report & How to comply*. [Online] Available at: https://ecochain.com/blog/complying-with-the-csrd-frequently-asked-questions/ (archived at https://perma.cc/4KU3-73MA)

ICAEW. (2023) *TCFD and related UK reporting regulations*. [Online] Available at: https://www.icaew.com/technical/corporate-reporting/non-financial-reporting/tcfd-and-related-uk-reporting-regulations (archived at https://perma.cc/VZ9G-5PM7)

Newman, J. (2022). *Streaming giants open door to new UK studios*. The Times. April 2022. [Online] Available at: https://www.thetimes.co.uk/article/rise-of-streaming-drives-spending-on-uk-studios-f6h35x2m8 (archived at https://perma.cc/Z45M-ACGP)

Studio Map. (2023) *Home*. [Online] Available at: https://thestudiomap.com/uk/ (archived at https://perma.cc/BV4P-WEMK)

WARC. (2022) *The Ad Spend Outlook 2022/23*. [Online] Available at: https://www.warc.com/content/feed/warc-adspend-outlook-2022-23-what-you-need-to-know/en-GB/7142 (archived at https://perma.cc/7X7W-PYQP)

05

Reducing emissions from ad distribution

So, we've got our house in order, and we've tackled how to produce that ad in a more sustainable way. Now we need to think about how we are going to deliver that ad to our target audience(s) and what carbon emissions might be caused by that choice of distribution.

This is a big challenge. Especially when you consider just how many distribution channels are available to an advertising and marketing professional and just how many times that ad might be served up to people each minute of every day around the world.

If you think there is the possibility of a carbon footprint made by the single act of serving an ad each time to an individual, it throws up a big question at the heart of the advertising industry and the responsibility it must ensure that major, significant steps are taken to remove that footprint from any ad it serves.

The ultimate answer is a simple one in principle: a carbon budget which sits on a media plan, right alongside the financial budget, the audience size, and the frequency of the ad visibility.

But the rapid proliferation of digital advertising opportunities, not just through the tech platforms which have entered the advertising market during the first two decades of the 21st century, but also the transformational changes within established media channels, from out-of-home to news brands, from cinema chains to radio and from streaming TV services to direct mail.

In this chapter, we will look at the role and needs of each part of the advertising ecosystem as the industry works to develop and settle on a solution that is practical and actionable for all parties – advertiser, agency and media – and we will explore the thinking that is developing to help inform this solution.

In the next chapter (Chapter 6), we will look at the innovations and tools being developed across the media landscape which can provide inspiration and impetus for action to others and how marketers can encourage competition around sustainability between media owners in their supply chain.

Then, in the final chapter on the topic of media distribution (Chapter 7), we will look at quick wins which anyone can adopt now to decarbonize their media plan and point to what success looks like in the longer-term for a system where the emissions of a media plan are tracked, reduced, and properly accounted for.

Our goal in these three chapters is two-fold – to quickly understand how and where carbon emissions are created through the distribution of ads so these can be tracked and reported and for everyone to understand their role in helping all media channels to decarbonize as rapidly as possible.

The advertiser POV

What's the end goal here? From the advertiser point of view, it is to be able to put a carbon emissions measurement against their media plan and reduce it to zero, which requires full visibility of how much carbon is created through their investment in promoting their product or service through their choice of media plan.

For a global advertiser with a portfolio of brands that allow it to differentiate and compete for customers, the requirement is a way of reporting carbon emissions as a standard metric, year-on-year, to be able to include this in their overall carbon accounts. As mentioned in Chapter 4, this will become a legal requirement for many of the world's largest companies, all of whom are heavily dependent on advertising as a means of supporting their businesses. While the total carbon emissions of their advertising's media plan may represent a small percentage of the total responsibility across this supply chain, it will be an important metric all the same to ensure accurate and consistent carbon reporting as part of scope 3.

For those global advertisers, a solution which differs by type of media or country is not going to work. This requires a solution which works at a pre-competition level, an industry standard that all parts of the advertising eco-system can agree on and implement and one that is consistently evolving to reflect the decarbonization efforts of media owners.

The agency POV

What is the role of the agency in this? It's fair to say, views differ across agency holding groups as to where the responsibility for the carbon emissions created by media plans lies. Some would say it lies with the media agency, others that it belongs to the advertiser, or that it should be counted by the media owners, but all agree on the fundamental point that the carbon emissions of a media plan must be tracked and reported to aid reduction.

Requests for information about carbon emissions from ad inventory have already become more regular from agency to media owner, but there are a variety of data requests, and the information is changing all the time as media owners implement their own plans to decarbonize.

One thing's for sure: this is an area of competition for agencies who provide specialist services to help advertisers optimize their media plans, an extra edge for who can provide the greenest plans with the same reach and impact.

The media owner POV

The opportunity for a media owner is to demonstrate their competitive credentials when it comes to reducing carbon emissions from their own ad inventory. Each media channel has its own unique set of challenges. Some carry more intensive carbon emissions than others, but they also have greater potential to support the transition to a net zero world with the right investment and support. In Chapter 6, we will take a closer look at media channels and their efforts to decarbonize.

The academic view on advertising emissions

Before we go further, let's dig into where these emissions might be coming from to understand the problem the industry needs to address here.

Professor of Marketing, Dr Felipe Thomaz of Saïd Business School, part of the University of Oxford, conducted a review of the advertising industry's emissions during 2022 and published a detailed paper in January 2023 called *Ad Net Zero: Conceptual Framework for Integrating Advertising and Advertised Emissions*. Much of the paper sets out how the industry needs to account for its advertising emissions in preparation for a world where carbon reporting and accounting will be standard. The requirement, as we know, will be for the industry to be able to record and provide accurate data from the production and distribution of ads by advertisers. This will allow the advertising industry to transact with other industries when it comes to the reporting of carbon emissions for scope 3. We will look at this in the context of the full lifecycle of an ad in different media, but right now, our focus is on the emissions that arise from distribution. There'll be further discussion of the other responsibilities advertisers, agencies and the media supply chain have in Chapter 14.

The following is the definition of 'Advertising Emissions' provided by Professor Thomaz:

> We use "Advertising Emissions" to refer to the carbon footprint of a specific advertisement or campaign. The emissions are calculated by aggregating the smallest unit within each sub-process and channel, starting with channel-specific functional units. The process involves multiplying the intensity of the allocatable process by the size of the ad, then multiplying the number of ads and impressions by the emissions of a single ad to calculate the channel's emissions. The 11 media channels and 25 sub-channels will be described according to their value chains, with a focus on identifying the "cradle to gate" boundary and the sub-processes that make up the channel lifecycles. Detailed calculations for emissions from each component activity are provided.

The Saïd Business School paper references a selection of channels:

1 TV

2 Video On Demand (VOD)

3 Cinema

4 Social Media

5 Digital

6 Print

7 Out of Home

8 Digital Out of Home

9 Radio

10 Digital Audio

11 Transient

Let's review some examples of how and where carbon emissions are created depending on the choices of media channels in the plan. We're going to show how TV, video-on-demand (VOD), social media and print can be considered in what the paper's author describes as a cradle-to-gate responsibility which sits with the advertiser/agency when it comes to the carbon emissions created during the production and distribution of an ad.

TV

For example, the Saïd Business School paper defines TV as the linear 'traditional' playout service that delivers live media on a planned schedule. There are three subtype channels, namely broadcast, cable and addressable TV. Figure 5.1 shows the full lifecycle, and we are interested in the cradle-to-gate element which includes production development (dealt with in the previous chapter), playout services and network transmission.

VOD

The cradle-to-gate responsibility changes for VOD to become production development (again, dealt with in our earlier chapter), cloud (and data centre) and network transmission, with factors to consider including programmatic delivery, and resolution of the ad on the user device as per Figure 5.2.

Social media

Turning to social media, the Saïd Business School paper defines this as a multiplatform mobile application that delivers ads to end users via cloud (and data centre) services and network transmission infrastructure, across mobile and web-based platforms. Cradle-to-gate here includes production development, cloud (and data centre) services and network transmission. Factors here include programmatic delivery and ad resolution/quality as seen in Figure 5.3.

FIGURE 5.1 Full lifecycle of Broadcast TV, Saïd Business School (2023)

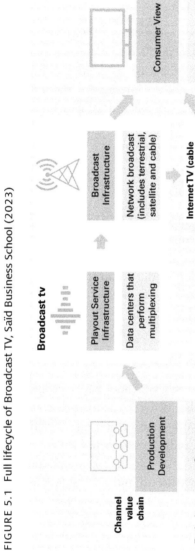

FIGURE 5.2 Full lifecycle of VOD, Saïd Business School (2023)

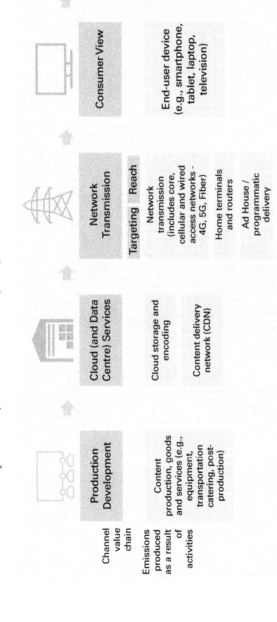

FIGURE 5.3   Full lifecycle of Social Media, Saïd Business School (2023)

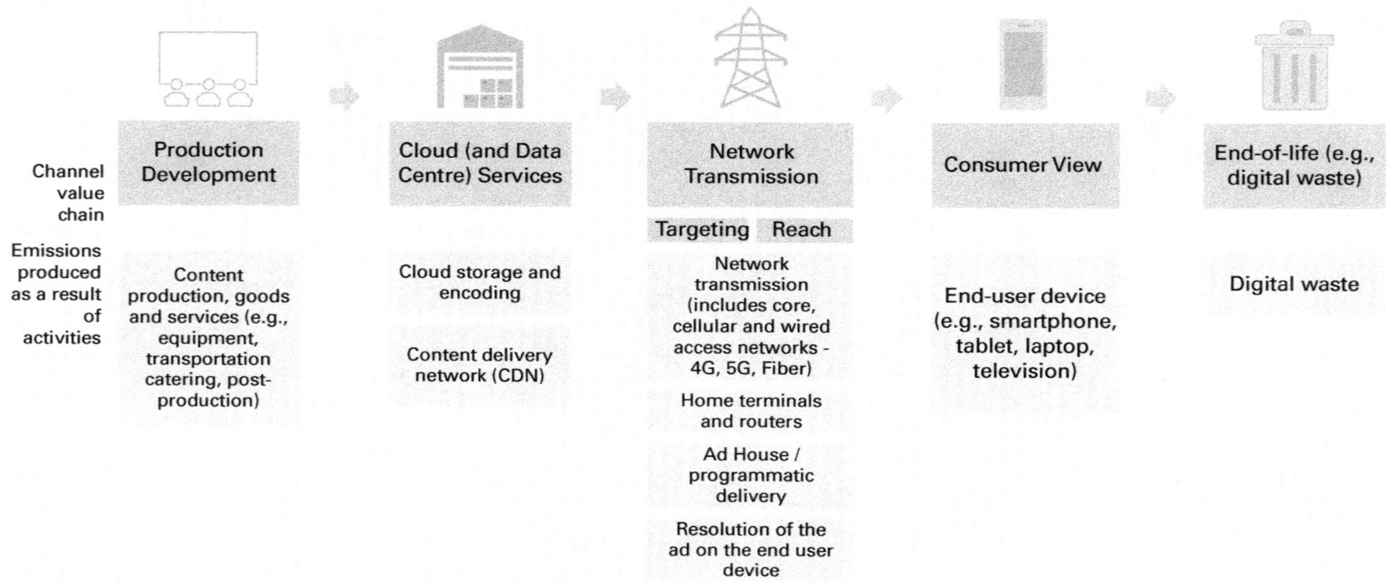

	Production Development	Cloud (and Data Centre) Services	Network Transmission	Consumer View	End-of-life (e.g., digital waste)
			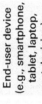		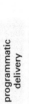
Channel value chain					
Emissions produced as a result of activities	Content production, goods and services (e.g., equipment, transportation, catering, post-production)	Cloud storage and encoding Content delivery network (CDN)	**Targeting Reach** Network transmission (includes core, cellular and wired access networks - 4G, 5G, Fiber) Home terminals and routers Ad House / programmatic delivery Resolution of the ad on the end user device	End-user device (e.g., smartphone, tablet, laptop, television)	Digital waste

FIGURE 5.4 Full lifecycle of Print, Saïd Business School (2023)

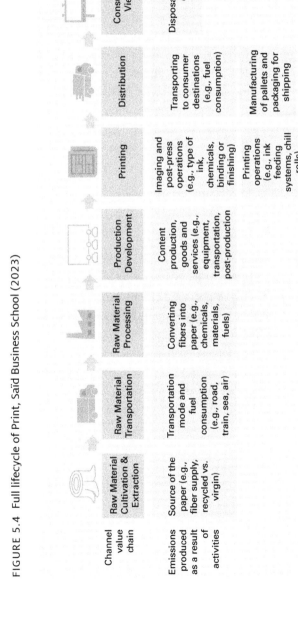

Channel value chain	Raw Material Cultivation & Extraction	Raw Material Transportation	Raw Material Processing	Production Development	Printing	Distribution	Consumer View	End-of-life (e.g., landfill, recycling)
Emissions produced as a result of activities	Source of the paper (e.g., fiber supply, recycled vs. virgin)	Transportation mode and fuel consumption (e.g., road, train, sea, air)	Converting fibers into paper (e.g., chemicals, materials, fuels)	Content production, goods and services (e.g., equipment, transportation, post-production)	Imaging and post-press operations (e.g., type of ink, chemicals, binding or finishing) / Printing operations (e.g., ink feeding systems, chill rolls)	Transporting to consumer destinations (e.g., fuel consumption) / Manufacturing of pallets and packaging for shipping		Disposal, recycling and landfill operations fuels

Print

Finally, for this example of how and where carbon emissions are involved in a choice of media channel, let's look at print, which for Saïd Business School's paper defines the physical advertisement planed in a magazine or newspaper outlet. Cradle-to-gate boundary for advertiser/agency here includes raw material cultivation and extraction, raw materials transportation, raw material processing, printing and distribution as seen in Figure 5.4.

These diagrams will hopefully demonstrate how and where we can take responsibility for the emissions associated with the media planning work of our industry during the provision of advertising services for clients.

We can begin to see the types of things we need to know, what we need to account for and how complex it could be once you start to consider the carbon emissions from different competing media owners within different sectors in different geographical locations. This isn't simple and it will need a solution that works for everyone – advertisers, agencies, and media owners...

A plan to decarbonize media rapidly

Accounting for carbon emissions in a media plan and encouraging media to rapidly decarbonize is of particular interest to the businesses that buy media space globally on behalf of portfolios of advertisers.

One example of that type of company is GroupM, which describes itself as 'the world's leading media investment company with a mission to create a new era of media where advertising works better for people.' According to Comvergence (2022), it is responsible for more than $60 billion in media investments each year. So, rightly it wants to know what the carbon footprint is of this spend so it can help its clients (and media partners) to tackle how to track, report and ultimately reduce this footprint.

In July 2022, it published a report: Calculating A Cleaner Future Now: A Unified Methodology For Accelerated Media Decarbonization. Oliver Joyce, Global Chief Transformation Officer at GroupM agency Mindshare explained the goal of the report:

> If we all continue to work on this problem independently, we're going to have a very limited impact on carbon emission reductions. This framework and the research behind it is our attempt to consolidate the industry around a unified

vision of decarbonization, starting with defining consistent parameters around boundaries, then agreeing on what data is required and coming together on a calculation methodology. It took us ten to fifteen years to get meaningful progress on privacy, and five to eight years to get meaningful progress on harmful content. We simply do not have that much time to align around what carbon measurement and carbon reduction look like.

The global carbon measurement framework launched by GroupM comprises a set of measurement methodologies designed to break down the media value chain and define the necessary data inputs to measure carbon emissions across all five stages of the advertising lifecycle for all formats, channels and markets in accordance with the Greenhouse Gas Protocol's standards.

The GroupM team described the problem it faces through Figure 5.5 which showed how the emissions from their annual media investments is equivalent to 7.3bn petrol car miles.

The report authors argued that the creation of a robust methodology which could inform any carbon calculator was important because existing media carbon calculators use inconsistent parameters, meaning emissions

FIGURE 5.5 Emissions from annual media investments, GroupM (2022)

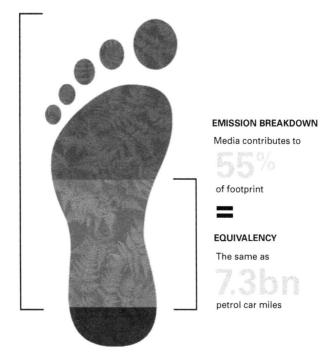

EMISSION BREAKDOWN

Media contributes to

55%

of footprint

=

EQUIVALENCY

The same as

7.3bn

petrol car miles

EMISSION FOOTPRINT

98.3%

are **scope 3 supply** chain outputs

from one channel to another cannot be compared. Consistent methodology across all channels in line with GHGP will be critical.

They also reasoned that better data would mean advertisers move their investments to lower-emissions media owners, in turn encouraging greater decarbonization efforts across the media supply chain.

This latter point is key – media has always competed for advertiser spend; it is inherent in the way the companies work across the media sector. They compete in many ways, for example by demonstrating the quality of their audience reach and engagement, their influence on sales, their status as a credible media brand in the eyes of their audience. Introducing decarbonization as a competitive factor will certainly accelerate as companies in the media sector transition as fast as they can to be confident of securing ad spend from companies like GroupM and advertisers working to reduce their scope 3 emissions.

Reducing emissions from ad distribution: summary

Everyone has a vested interest in seeing their media plan decarbonize as rapidly as possible, whether you are an advertiser, an agency or a media owner. The fact that every ad which is served to a target customer has a carbon footprint is clear, and there is much which can be done to take responsibility for this and so take significant steps to account for the carbon impact of a media plan. We're going to spend some more time in the next chapter looking at how this competition for media to decarbonize is already happening and where there could even be benefits emerging that support a more sustainable way of life. Then in Chapter 7 we're going to look at how the efforts to settle on one central robust methodology will be key to the advertising industry understanding its carbon footprint when it comes to ad distribution and the media plan.

References

GroupM. (2022) *Comvergence Report: Comvergence Certifies GroupM As World's Leading Media Agency Group In 2021 Full Year Global Billings Report.* [Online] Available at: https://www.groupm.com/newsroom/largest-media-agency-groupm-comvergence/ (archived at https://perma.cc/7BAB-TFFV)

GroupM. (2022) *GroupM Report: Calculating A Cleaner Future Now: A Unified Methodology For Accelerated Media Decarbonization.* [Online] Available at: https://www.groupm.com/media-decarbonization-framework-groupm/ (archived at https://perma.cc/5UNC-65K6)

Thomaz, F. (2023) *Ad Net Zero. Conceptual Framework for Integrating Advertising and Advertised Emissions.* University of Oxford. January 2023. [Online] Available at: https://papers.ssrn.com/sol3/papers.cfm?abstract_id=4337355 (archived at https://perma.cc/A38M-6896)

06

A sustainable media supply chain

In this chapter we review the media and tech landscape, see how key players are taking responsibility for their carbon emissions, the influential role they can play in positive behaviour change, and the way advertiser expectation and media plan choices can help foster this change. While there is work going on to agree standard measurement conventions within the industry (more on this in Chapter 7), there is still lot of opportunity for increasing the sustainability of every medium.

Global tech platforms

Firstly, we're going to consider the global tech platforms. The decarbonization conversation for this sector is dominated by data storage and the plans to handle the power requirements of the world's data demands. Google, Meta and Amazon have published a lot of information about their plans to make sure their data storage is net zero.

Our way of life is increasingly built on data, and a net zero economy which must account for carbon emissions (and other important environmental measures like biodiversity and water) means even more data will need to be recorded, tracked and reported. This section will reference the work by these companies to decarbonize and explore how they are using their positions to support others to do the same.

Google

Google reports that it aims to reduce its emissions (across its operations and value chain) with the goal of reaching net zero by 2030. It states its goal is to continuously create products and share information that will help everyone make more sustainable choices.

As part of these goals, the company plans to operate on 24/7 carbon-free energy, everywhere, by 2030.

As one of the biggest businesses in the search advertising sector, Google aims to play a helpful role in accelerating progress in climate information and action. Here are three recent examples of that in practice: new APIs from Google Maps Platform help businesses and cities map solar, air quality and pollen information (Google, 2023), working with the airline industry to use AI and satellite imagery to reduce the warming effects of contrails (Google, 2023), and using AI to help address the climate crisis (Google, 2022).

We know that people use Google to ask questions and the company's latest search data shows a growing global interest in learning about and adopting sustainable practices. Awareness and understanding are central to the transition.

Let's take a look at what Google can share about the trends it's seeing in its search data when it comes to sustainability…

For example, and as we'll go onto look at later in this book, transportation is one of the largest sources of CO_2 emissions. Google's data shows that search for electric vehicles reached a worldwide high in March 2022, while Google Trends data reveals electric vehicle and electric car are 'breakout' search topics in the UK in the first quarter of 2023.

Another area of focus is fashion and Google Trends data shows fast fashion is the top trending topic related to environmental issues for the period March 2022–2023. In the UK again, Google Trends data for March 2023 shows 'zero waste' is another breakout search topic, and search for 'environmentally friendly' has doubled in the first three months of the year.

Meanwhile, global search interest in renewable energy hit its highest level in March 2022 and the UK's search interest doubled for energy crisis, while efficient energy use is another breakout topic for 2023.

Returning to Google's plans around sustainability, it sets out its strategy as follows:

• Empowering individuals to take action
• Working together with its partners and customers
• Operating its business sustainably.

What Matt finds most interesting is how Google is working to help others be more sustainable, with the aim of helping individuals, partners and customers to collectively reduce 1 gigaton of their carbon equivalent emissions annually by 2030. It offers a raft of information about what it does on its site.

Meanwhile, its ambition for people is bold, and last year Google reached its goal to help one billion people make more sustainable choices through its products. We'll look more closely at that later on in this book.

For now, we conclude that Google will play an important role in the achievement of a net zero economy – anyone working in the advertising industry needs to consider how the insights its search data offers can inform plans for their own business and the businesses they produce work for. Also, how the products Google develop can be used to help billions of people make more sustainable decisions, adding up to have a meaningful impact.

Meta

Meta, owner of Facebook, Instagram and WhatsApp, has a section on its corporate site dedicated to sustainability. It covers what Meta is doing to operate in more sustainable ways, and how it is working to support communities and make a positive impact on the world.

Meta says it works with external partners to encourage and embody sustainability, and list partners including the United Nations Framework Convention on Climate Change, the United Nations Environment Programme, the We Mean Business Coalition and the EU Climate Pact as well as academic institutions, local companies, sustainability industry experts and NGOs.

Meta records its success around sustainability with metrics including:

- Net zero emissions achieved for operations in 2020
- 100 per cent renewable energy across global operations
- 5.8mn m^3 water restored to high water-stress regions
- 145,000 tonnes CO_2 removed through forestry projects in East Africa and the Mississippi River Valley.

It has three reports well worth a closer look. These are the Culture Rising report, the Sustainability Advertising research report, and the Sustainability Advertising Playbook, all of which we will explore in more detail in Chapters 9 and 10.

Amazon Advertising

Amazon Ads, Amazon's advertising business, joined the Ad Net Zero Global Group in June 2023 as part of the industry's efforts to decarbonize and support the promotion of more-sustainable products, services, and behaviours.

Its advertising business has continued to grow over recent years, and its Amazon DSP (Demand Side Platform) allows advertisers to programmatically buy display and online video advertising to reach relevant audiences wherever they spend their time, whether that be on the Amazon store and Prime Video, or across thousands of apps and websites.

The ads, which can be bought directly as well as programmatically, come in a variety of formats and placements including sponsored products, sponsored brands, sponsored display ads, video and audio ads, as well as custom and out-of-home ads.

Amazon has committed to reaching net-zero carbon across its operations by 2040, and is on a path to powering 100 per cent of its operations with renewable energy by 2025, five years ahead of its original target of 2030. Amazon co-founded and was the first signatory of The Climate Pledge in 2019 with Global Optimism, a purpose-driven organization led by Christiana Figueres and Tom Rivett-Carnac, who oversaw the delivery of the Paris Agreement. The Climate Pledge is a commitment to reach net-zero carbon emissions by 2040 – 10 years ahead of the Paris Agreement. The goal of The Climate Pledge is to build a cross-sector community of companies, working together to address the climate crisis and solve the challenge of decarbonizing our economy.

Any business, large or small, can sign up to The Climate Pledge and, by doing so, they agree to three key areas of action:

1 Regular reporting – to measure and report greenhouse gas emissions on a regular basis.

2 Carbon Elimination – implement decarbonization strategies in line with the Paris Agreement through real business changes and innovations, including efficiency improvements, renewable energy, material reductions, and other carbon-emission-elimination strategies.

3 Credible Offsets – neutralize any remaining emissions with additional, quantifiable, real, permanent and socially beneficial offsets to achieve net-zero annual carbon emissions by 2040.

However, people may also ask what Amazon is doing to help reduce the environmental impact of the products that are sold on its marketplace.

In 2020, it introduced a new badge to appear alongside products in Amazon's store, indicating that the product is part of Amazon's Climate Pledge Friendly programme. Climate Pledge Friendly helps customers discover and shop for more-sustainable products. Amazon partnered with trusted third-party certifications, and the company created its own certifications, to highlight products that meet sustainability standards and help preserve the natural world.

The Climate Pledge Friendly programme is one to track and consider how and where it figures in the advertising of more-sustainable products you may be involved in promoting.

There's no doubt a business the size and scale of Amazon has a huge, central role to play in making a net zero economy a reality, facilitating people to take part in an economy where products are renewed, recycled, and presented in ways that support a more sustainable way of life.

The online advertising eco-system

Alongside the global tech players, there's the online advertising market – a highly complex environment, layered with different service providers, each providing critical elements to support an advertiser's engagement and interactive opportunities with audiences. But what if you consider that every single time an ad is served on any device anywhere, it generates a carbon footprint, that your decision to place that ad helps to raise the temperature of our planet a tiny bit more?

There is an urgent need to account for this within the digital advertising supply chain and great efforts are being made in this space. Equally, there are big asks of the tech platforms which provide a multitude of advertising opportunities to all kinds of businesses, large and small. Then there are the many media owners who have moved much of the content they produce (and the advertising around it) online. Plus, the emergence of the retail media channel, much of which itself is online.

In the UK, online advertising spend accounts for 75p in every £1 spent (WARC, 2023) and that share is expected to grow further still in the coming years (AA/WARC, 2022). So, accounting for the carbon footprint of this vast array of online advertising units will require a concerted and collaborative effort.

If you scale that up, which IAB Europe's Sustainability Standards Committee did when it formed in October 2022, the Internet's estimated overall environmental impact is around 2–4 per cent of global carbon emissions, with a typical ad campaign emitting around 5.4 tonnes of CO_2. If you're interested in working out the emissions of a typical campaign, the Good-Loop carbon calculator is free and easy to use.

When you consider the number of ad impressions transacted on a regular basis multiplies over time, it is easy to see how this has become a must-solve problem for the industry.

So, IAB Europe's Sustainability Standards Committee was set up to create standards for the delivery of digital advertising and help all industry participants reduce the amount of energy consumed and carbon emissions produced using digital media.

The committee published its State of Readiness – Sustainability in Digital Advertising survey in February 2023 to set benchmarks for the digital advertising industry in tackling sustainability and record the measures individual companies have in place. It contains the views of 256 respondents in 29 European markets from across the digital advertising ecosystem, whether Ad Tech, Agency, and Publisher businesses, as well as Advertisers.

The survey revealed a series of interesting findings. For example, over half (55 per cent) of respondents replied that they believe their company has either begun or has made significant progress on its journey towards CO_2e reduction. However, 18 per cent said their companies had either not started or even thought about it yet. Of those companies that were already acting, 50 per cent had done or were doing a sustainability audit, a natural starting place for companies, with 46 per cent nominating a sustainability lead, and 46 per cent creating a checklist. Sustainability was ranked as one of the top 3 challenges, coming in just below cookieless targeting and measurement, showing how important this issue is for the whole advertising ecosystem.

Respondents selected CO_2e measurement as the top action required to drive CO_2e reduction in advertising, with 35 per cent of respondents choosing this as *the* most important focus. When asked if their companies currently measured the emissions produced by the delivery of digital ads, 51 per cent of respondents said they currently did not, highlighting a big gap to address. After measurement, the next most vital action was the creation of consistent standards (chosen by 33 per cent of respondents), followed by the provision of tools and solutions to reduce CO_2 emissions from digital ads now (chosen by 25 per cent of respondents).

Given the size of the industry, the size of the problem it creates and the need for urgent action, the search for quick wins has rapidly picked up pace. There is now focus on agreeing a data framework standard to include digital advertising, with other key players getting involved. Overall there is a significant amount of work to be done in this sector.

We'll review IAB Tech Lab's quick wins in the next chapter.

TV

Much of the work to decarbonize the broadcast supply chain will be reliant on a shift to renewable energy, powering broadcast systems and devices which people use to watch TV.

In the meantime, broadcasters are working to ensure their medium plays its fullest role in decarbonizing. The major broadcasters have made significant steps in production, firstly with their own programming through support for albert, and now, in the advertising they carry through AdGreen. They have set their own targets to reduce their operational emissions – for example, ITV has a target to reduce all emissions by 90 per cent by 2050, aligned to SBTis (ITV, 2023). The industry certainly isn't there yet, but we've seen first-hand the improvements that have been made. Legacy media has probably also come under the most scrutiny when it comes to sustainability – the actions that have been taken are a lesson in what can be achieved when addressing these issues becomes a priority.

It is worth reflecting for a moment on how the ad spend funds efforts by commercial broadcasters to help people understand the climate issue and inspire positive action and behaviour change.

For example, at COP26, 12 UK and Irish broadcasters including Channel 4, ITV, Sky and the BBC signed a Climate Content Pledge to actively educate their audiences about the climate crisis. They continue to build on that with updates each year on the progress being made as the climate crisis features in all kinds of programming content, not just news.

So, let's look at what that means for programme commissions by a UK commercial broadcaster like Channel 4. It has issued a brief to independent production companies for new shows that inspire people to connect with the climate emergency and make positive steps, through hopeful, provocative and irreverent ways.

This is built on insights the Channel 4 team shared about its audience for this book as part of its sustainability plans for 2023. It highlights that:

- 58 per cent of respondents named television programmes as a key source of inspiration for environmental change
- 78 per cent of adults think TV advertisers should be doing more
- 75 per cent of adults think TV programmes should be doing more to resolve the climate crisis.

In August 2023, it scheduled programming across Channel 4 and All 4 in a Climate Matters special strand. Programmes include The Great Climate Fight, a three-part event fronted by C4 talent which hoped to cause real change to government regulation and real action. All of this is funded by the spend of advertisers. What's interesting is how this climate programming can be served by more and more 'green' ad spend when you consider the 4Sales (Channel 4's commercial arm) 2023 Sustainability Plan on a Page, which states that it seeks to 'supercharge the growth of green brands through meaningful partnerships'.

Meanwhile, back in June 2020, the broadcaster launched a temporary solution to help SMEs seeking growth as the UK emerged from lockdown. This was a £3 million initiative to support small- and medium-sized businesses that have never advertised on TV before through match funded commercial airtime across Channel 4's portfolio. The first advertiser to benefit from this scheme was TENZING, which is powered purely by plants and claims to be 'the world's first carbon negative energy drink' (TENZING, 2023).

A broadcaster like Channel 4 can really contextualize and explain the actions needed to counter climate change, and instil a sense of effectiveness by acting together, and help to increase confidence and pride in systemic change.

We will explore more of what other broadcasters are doing later in this book when we look at the role of TV advertising to help drive behaviour change and support the building of a net zero economy.

Out of home

The out of home sector is rising to the challenge of how its advertisers and media agency partners account for the carbon emissions involved in building and running infrastructure as well as the paper used and energy sources required to power the digital screens being built in urban environments around the world.

It is estimated that over 30 per cent of the advertising revenue in out of home reaches the public purse through social infrastructure such as bus stops, as well as rates, rents and revenue shares to public landlords (i.e., local councils (Outsmart/PwC, 2023)). If we are to decarbonize our urban environments and build better public transport systems, it could be argued that spend on out of home advertising is also a good, social investment.

Innovations are appearing which provide advertising and marketing professionals with a glimpse of what a truly sustainable out of home advertising eco-system might look like…

For example, six-sheet posters with recycled and recyclable paper have been in the market since 2021 and more challenging 48-sheet and 96-sheet larger formats have been introduced in 2023. Enzymes are used for de-inking and less water is required in the process, according to Posterscope (Ethical Marketing News, 2023).

Many companies are installing solar panels to power equipment. Asian media specialist Moving Walls cite examples including an Indian agency which has integrated the tech into digital billboards in the city to give free electricity to Indian railways. Meanwhile PG&E have launched a solar-powered billboard, storing the sun's energy during the day to power the billboard's lights at night. Or Toyota's campaign for its hydrogen-fuelled zero-emission electric cars, where billboards were clad in vinyl coated with titanium dioxide to purify the air (WARC, 2023).

Out of home property site owner and manager Wildstone has been making progress in this area too, recently acquiring the Netherlands' most sustainable highway digital advertising mast. Positioned on the A28 in Assen, it consists of two 100m^2 LED panels fully powered by the solar panels around it (Wildstone, 2022).

Meanwhile in Spain, Naturgy, Clear Channel and Arena Media have recently partnered in Madrid to offer people mobile chargers, powered by renewable energy, and installed in street furniture, as part of its 'Naturgy Solar. El Sol a un solo clic' campaign.

Clear Channel is one example of an out of home company taking responsibility for its carbon emissions and environmental impact, with a publicly available plan to transition to Net Zero (Figure 6.1). Advertisers in out of home can be confident of this partner in their supply chain taking action to decarbonize as they look for this right across the sector.

FIGURE 6.1 Roadmap to Carbon Net Zero, Clear Channel Europe (2023)

Short-term

- ISO certification in all markets by 2023
- CDP submission & SBTi for whole of CCE
- Renewable energy for all new supply contracts
- Low and zero emission fleets in all markets
- Low energy lighting as standard for all products and premises + retrofit programme
- Increase recycled content of new products

By 2030

Net Zero for Scope 1 and 2

- Zero emission fleet
- 90% reduction in carbon emissions from premise fuel (from a 2021 baseline)
- 100% renewable energy

Scope 3:

- Rainwater harvesting in all European markets
- Reduce landfill waste by 50%
- Remove virgin material
- Introduce low carbon glass & concrete
- Employ Carbon Pricing to create incentives for low-carbon investments and innovations
- Implement 'Pathway to Carbon Net zero' for CCE asset portfolio & decrease the use of new assets/materials

By 2045

Net Zero for Scope 3

- Transition to ultra-low carbon, ultra-low energy products at scale
- Expand Environmental Impact Assessments
- Increase available data collection

Let's take a moment to picture a net zero economy where all out of home sites and infrastructure give back to their surroundings in one or more sustainable ways. Be that through renewable energy, (not just to power their own screens but to go further still and put power back into the grid) or to provide natural habitats for pollinators, or pleasurable environments for people to enjoy shade, flowers, fruit, or vegetables.

This role of a media channel actively supporting and rewarding investment in a more sustainable future is a reason to believe all media can compete for increased spend and investment. Not just for effectiveness, but because of their sustainable contribution too.

Direct mail

The direct mail industry is facing a challenge, a broadly held perception that print is bad (which incidentally also impacts other media channels including magazines and newsbrands). Surely the less paper we use in media plans, the better? Managed plantations replacing ancient wild forests reduce biodiversity. Also, what about the carbon emissions involved in distributing all that paper up and down countries around the world? It makes sense, doesn't it, to take as much paper and print out of a media plan and replace it with digital options?

Or does it? We have already seen the challenges of the digital media carbon footprint, and the massive efforts required to reduce that. Print media started earlier with decades of work by publishers around the world to build sustainable paper and print supply chains, planting trees and recycling paper for reuse. Publishers are also investing in distribution systems that use EV vehicles and even, in the case of postal services, the oldest form of transport itself, the power of people walking 'the last mile' door-to-door in towns and cities.

More research will need to be done to establish the relative carbon footprints of paper versus digital in all media channels that use them. However, the point is less the comparison between the two and more the urgent need for all media to decarbonize, and in the case of paper production to help tackle biodiversity and not create new plantations at the expense of wild forests.

In April 2023, Marketreach, part of the Royal Mail Group, released the first lifecycle study of mail and its contribution to a circular economy. This included an interactive online tool which helps marketers to determine the carbon impact of different formats across the supply chain. This is the first time the organization has looked in-depth at every element of the process when a business chooses to use direct mail as part of its marketing activity, from forest source to end-of-life, via the processing, design, production and delivery stages. It advocates using every opportunity to regenerate, reinvent, reduce, reuse and recycle, to ensure direct mail is contributing to a circular economy, and remains part of an effective marketing mix.

Its goal is to help marketers make their campaigns carbon smart. Its calculator provides data on the carbon footprint of each stage in the supply chain of 10 of the most used commercial mail formats. The tool then lets you compare the average carbon emissions of formats across the lifecycle of mail and compares with everyday products to provide context of its impact. As an example, the current overall carbon impact for one standard postcard is 43.61 gCO_2e, less than the impact of an orange. The carbon impact of an A4 or C5 Large Catalogue is 445.29 gCO_2e, only slightly more than the one 15g cup of coffee (Marketreach, 2023). The Marketreach tool is complemented by a checklist of points to consider when planning a mail campaign. More information is available in its guide, *Using Mail More Sustainably*. Marketers need to make sure they don't only narrowly focus on carbon, however, in thinking about sustainable advertising but consider its impact on nature too.

Royal Mail has also run TV advertising campaign to make the case to businesses and the public for including the greenest form of delivery in its system – the workforce of postal staff who bring letters and packages to the door on foot.

It's an example of a media owner promoting its USP when it comes to sustainability versus its competitive set. If comparisons are inevitable then a race to decarbonize and ultimately increase the sustainability of all media may be helpful.

The question when you choose a media partner in the direct channel is what do you know about them and how can they make a positive contribution to your own sustainability efforts?

Newsbrands

In the UK, the national newsbrands collaborate on a digital advertising platform called Ozone, providing a means for advertisers to access audiences at broadcast scale across the premium web. Ozone offers advertising solutions across more than 250 domains from brands including The Times, The Telegraph, The Guardian, The Independent, The Mirror, Evening Standard, The Sun, HELLO!, Stylist and Time Out. This means Ozone covers 1,200 different topics, from sport to politics and from travel to fashion, and delivers 1.4 billion page views a month and 1bn+ individual proprietary data signals a day, all to inform its contextual and behavioural targeting capabilities.

That's quite a big digital footprint, so what are the newsbrands doing to drive environmental sustainability? Ozone has been working since July 2021 on how to support sustainable growth through emission reduction and in a recent report outlined steps taking place across five key areas:

1 Firstly, Ozone works with publishers to remove ad tech code on their sites while providing proprietary tools to help them manage buyer connections server side through the Ozone pre-bid adaptor. Both actions have significantly reduced the bandwidth needed to process bids between the user and their ad platform. This has saved on energy consumption and has ultimately reduced emissions for Ozone, publishers and advertisers' supply chains.

2 Next, Ozone employed machine learning – powered by edge computing – to filter out low value bids based on Ozone's predicted ability to monetize them. This strategy was the key driver of reduction in server usage they saw in 2021 at a time of significant traffic growth. The approach continued to pay dividends throughout 2022 when their traffic increased a further three-fold on the year prior.

3 Ozone's third tactic involved a full review of data storage and archiving capabilities. Ozone restructured and optimized their data pipeline to determine the optimal period for data storage based on need at any specific time. This meant they were able to reduce processing requirements, as the remainder of data was archived and placed in cold storage.

4 Fourth involved the scoping and shift to private bandwidth with Ozone's biggest ad partners. This workstream is still in its early stages but it works on the premise that by taking the shortest and fastest route to connect with the biggest ad vendors it is possible to bypass the open internet and use far less bandwidth, thus creating fewer greenhouse gas emissions.

5 Finally, Ozone has invested in direct integrations with DSPs such as The Trade Desk. These partnerships create a more direct and transparent path that connects agencies with publishers, without any unnecessary hops and eliminating the broadcast behaviour created in the open web when using SSPs.

The result of this focus? The average emissions per billion bid requests have reduced by 68 per cent since the programme began. In 2022, Ozone managed to reduce the emissions from its advertising solutions by 52 per cent while the total bid requests grew three-fold.

Ozone's publicly stated aim is to reduce scope 1 and 2 emissions in excess of 40 per cent by 2030 and to reduce scope 3 emissions in excess of 50 per cent by 2030. In addition, and subject to the publicly stated aims of its cloud partners, Ozone has committed to its proprietary ad platform being carbon net zero by 2030. Ozone's goal is a sustainable future for ad-funded journalism, supporting diverse voices, a free information economy and helping the fourth estate hold power to account.

Personal views will differ depending on the editorial voice you feel speaks most for you, but across the newsbrands represented by Ozone, there have been campaigns focused on helping readers to change behaviours and improve the environment.

One of the biggest newsbrands publishers, Mail Metro Media, has assessed its carbon footprint for over 10 years. In 2023 it is updating its approach to sustainability, looking at climate-related governance procedures, strategy, risk management and metrics in line with UK regulations. This initiative comprises a working group of Mail Metro Media's parent Group, Daily Mail and General Trust (DMGT) operating companies, which will support the DMGT Board to comply with the regulations. At the time of writing, disclosures regarding how DMGT is moving to become more sustainable will be included in the 2023 Annual Report and published on the DMGT website.

It cites examples of its work with brands around sustainability including Metro Earth – a four-page special feature focusing on retail, travel, food, tech and more, spotlighting environmental content, educating readers and providing a space for brands to set out their sustainability credentials in a highly contextual editorial setting. *YOU*, a magazine which comes with *The Mail on Sunday*, features a Green Guide.

Print production faces all the carbon and nature issues of any paper-based medium and is undeniably an energy-intensive process which is a challenge for all news brand publishers but there are clear examples of steps being taken to tackle this. For example, Reach, the publisher of titles including the *Daily Mirror*, *OK!* and *Manchester Evening News*, installed 9000m^2 of solar panels at its print sites in Watford, Manchester and Glasgow with the plan for any excess solar energy to be sent back to the grid.

Magazine media

Magazine media brands are enjoyed by millions of people around the world, many engaged through not just the print versions of the titles, but also their online versions and via brand extensions such as events and brand partnership activations. It is also a broad church when you consider the reach of the types of companies in this sector which cater, not just for so many different readers' tastes and interests, but also for business customers in pretty much every sector of the economy, as well as the public sector, government, charities and NGOs.

For context, in the UK alone, the magazine sector employs around 55,000 people, with more than 40 million adults in the UK reading a magazine each month contributing £3.74 billion to the UK economy (Professional Publishers Association, 2023).

So, there are a few key areas of focus for the sector as it tackles how best to rapidly decarbonize and provide advertisers with a more sustainable way of engaging with audiences through their brands.

Most people think first of print when they consider magazine media and the challenges around print are similar for those faced by the direct mail and marketing sector, newsbrands and to some extent, out of home.

When we consider the systemic changes underway in this sector it begins with print and paper, with steps being made in three core areas:

1 To make printing presses more sustainable, principally through the shift to renewable energy and updates to machinery involved, when long-term leases allow

2 To make the paper industry more sustainable through use of paper sourced from managed forests while tackling the challenge of how to maintain biodiversity

3 To make paper mills more sustainable through geographical location to reduce transportation costs and again increased use of renewable energy throughout the process, whether recycling paper or creating virgin paper.

In August 2023, the UK trade association for magazine media, the Professional Publishers Association (PPA), which has been synonymous with magazines for over 100 years, published its Action Net Zero Sustainability Pathway. This covers key action points and tools for addressing emissions, target setting and solutions for tackling the climate emergency.

Members of the PPA's Sustainability Action Group include leaders in the drive to sustainable operations. What does good look like, and what will become a standard expectation of successful businesses operating in the sector?

Bauer Media's Sustainability Report 2023 is full of information about the steps it has taken to shift its operations towards a net zero future. From an operational point-of view, this includes how the business:

- Switched to renewable electricity across all publishing offices.
- Mandated their audio offices to only renew contracts with renewable electricity.
- Consolidated all London offices into one, reducing emissions footprint.
- Reduced gas use by switching to alternative sustainable heating options.
- Reduced size of fleets and continuing to transition fleet to hybrid and electric.

It has a detailed explanation of how its magazine paper is 100 per cent sustainably sourced through its work with UPM and sustainably accredited paper suppliers. It also cites the progress it has made with Frontline, its distribution partner to switch the packaging of all magazine subscription titles from plastic coverings to paper wrap. This move, which is near final completion, will save an estimated 37 tonnes of plastic every year, according to Bauer (2023).

Also worth noting is how Bauer, which reaches over 25 million UK consumers, is using its media brands to encourage more sustainable behaviours in its audiences, specifically:

- Elevating sustainable hobbies to be greener
- Forming sustainable communities and educating on sustainable living
- Trusted sustainable automotive coverage on transitioning to EVs
- Showcasing sustainable fashion behaviours, products, and brands.

The company cites editorial efforts to make sustainable living more accessible by educating on financial and carbon benefits of sustainable cooking and sharing planet-friendly recipes and trending sustainable products through titles like *Take a Break*, *That's Life* and *Bella*. At the same time, it is sharing information about how consumers' hobbies and passions can be more sustainable, for example, practical ways readers can become more eco-conscious in their gardening through *Modern Gardens* and *Garden Answers*, while also championing progress in sporting hobbies through initiatives like *Today's Golfer* 'Green Golf Awards'.

Meanwhile, another leader in the PPA's Sustainability Action Group, Haymarket Media Group, a privately-owned media, data, and information company with offices in the UK, US, Hong Kong, Singapore, India and Germany, has a portfolio of over 70 brands and, in March 2023, it launched Haymarket Impact. This is a new ESG framework aligning all its previous ESG initiatives to the United Nations Sustainable Development Goals (SDGs) helping it to unify action and accelerate progress globally, against which it will measure and report progress. Specifically, these are:

- Global Goal 4: Quality Education – all Haymarket employees globally will receive training on the UN Sustainable Development Goals to help ensure its work aligns with its Purpose: Shaping a better future with remarkable outcome.

- Global Goal 5: Gender Equality – Haymarket commits to publishing a global gender balance audit, annually.

- Global Goal 13: Climate Action – Haymarket has created a climate action dashboard, with a clear set of ambitious divisional targets which has led to its first Global Environment Policy. Its UK offices have shifted to 100 per cent renewable energy and recently became ISO 20121 accredited.

Haymarket Impact is underpinned by Goal 17: Partnerships for the Goals.

Haymarket's portfolio carries a wide range of influence when you look at the types of audiences and communities it connects, ranging from the likes of What Car?, ENDS Report, Asian Investor to Campaign and PR Week and into events like its C&IT Sustainability Forum.

Leaders of magazine media businesses are aware of the importance of decarbonization – driven by audience needs and interests, advertiser expectations and talent ambitions.

Cinema

Cinema advertising is working back to pre-Covid levels of spend, with millions of movie lovers returning to watch box office hits like *Top Gun: Maverick*, Bond's latest outing, *A Time To Die* and *Barbie*.

Like the broadcast media, much of the work to decarbonize will be in the use of renewable energy at the thousands of cinemas around the world.

Let's review what's happening to support a more sustainable advertising industry in one of the cinema advertising houses. Pearl & Dean, probably most famous for its 'pa-pa, pa-pa, pahhh...pah' theme tune, was established in 1953 and it represents cinema chains like Empire and Everyman as well as many independent cinemas in the UK, ranging from the likes of the BFI Max at London Waterloo to the Newquay Lighthouse (Pearl & Dean, 2023).

It has its own sustainability working group, made up of representatives from across the business and is a supporter of Ad Net Zero. It has worked with carbon removal marketplace, Supercritical, to produce a carbon footprint starting point. In the 12 months to 31st Oct 2022, the company's scope 1 and 2 emissions were 0 tonnes and scope 3 emissions were 1648 tonnes. 85 per cent of its scope 3 emissions were from Cinema Exhibitors – the cinema chains and the independent cinema owners they represent. Reduction here is a major focus for the company in the years ahead (Pearl & Dean, 2023).

It has made some useful and interesting steps to note within its own operations including a card-based system to reduce unnecessary printing and investment in plants to improve office air quality. It has a company policy in place to plant trees as an alternative to sending out thank you gifts which it does via The National Forest. No adverts are played during private screenings but a copy of UNDP 'ban fossil fuel subsidies' – 'Don't Choose Extinction' is shown.

The ad originated from the global partnership between the United Nations Development Programme (UNDP) and SAWA Global Cinema Advertising Association, the global trade body for Cinema Advertising Companies, who have been working together to promote the UN's SDGs since 2015. SAWA's President, Kathryn Jacob, is also the Chief Executive of Pearl & Dean.

Together, they launched an eight-week international cinema advertising and social media campaign in summer 2022 aimed at raising awareness of the climate emergency, using advertising to encourage cinema audiences to take urgent action to address it (SAWA, 2022). The 60-second cinema ad created by Activista with production by Framestore shows one of the most iconic figures in cinema (and climate change) history, a dinosaur, speaking from the podium to shock the dignitaries of the United Nations General Assembly into make changes to tackle the climate crisis. The ad conjures memories of the *Jurassic Park* and *Jurassic World* films which have entertained millions for decades, but this dinosaur delivers the most powerful message yet, urging people not to choose the fate that led to the destruction of the creatures we know only from fossils.

Like its fellow UK cinema advertising sales house, Digital Cinema Media, P&D works with its national trade body, the UK Cinema Association (UKCA), itself a member of SAWA, to share best practice among members, to reduce outgoings from energy consumption and to promote the BFI's Green Cinema Toolkit (DCM, 2023). The work by the cinema owners to decarbonize their premises will be central to the cinema advertising channel reaching net zero in the coming years – much of that is dependent on the energy choices they make and the ways they provide food and drink to their customers.

Perhaps most critically, though, will be how the medium of cinema advertising can be used to land powerful campaigns to encourage behaviour change, just like the one featuring Frankie the Dinosaur that Pearl & Dean plays out in every private screening. That campaign reached an audience of 1.5 billion and generated 3000 media mentions. It was voiced in 39 languages, featured world-famous actors, including Jack Black (English), Eiza González (Spanish), Nikolaj Coster-Waldau (Danish), and Aïssa Maïga (French) and went on to be translated into more than 60 languages (UNDP, 2022). Cinema advertising's reach and engagement power is huge, and it can be a key part of any campaign promoting positive behaviour change.

Radio

Decarbonizing radio (and audio in general) will be driven by the shift to renewable energy and the saving of energy at all stages of the process, just like TV.

In the UK, there are two major commercial radio companies with audio assets including national, regional and local radio stations, as well as podcasts. Complementing these broadcasters is a range of smaller radio groups and independent stations.

The UK's biggest commercial radio broadcaster is Global, which is also an out of home media owner. Its audio portfolio includes radio brands: Heart, Capital, LBC, Smooth, Classic FM and Radio X, and podcasts like The News Agents. Like the best examples of media owners leading on decarbonization, Global publicly publishes its plans to drive towards a net zero future.

Its Global Environmental Impact Report 2021–22 shares how 100 per cent of its managed outdoor estate, Global offices, broadcast centres and warehouses now use renewable energy and 99 per cent of its radio transmitters are powered by renewable energy sources.

It has a special initiative called Green@Global and has been working with sustainability consultants Planet Mark for over a decade to put in place sustainability business measures in line with the UN's Sustainability Development Goals. In the report, Global records that its total carbon emissions fell by 20 per cent, as independently verified for its annual SECR report. It continues to invest in carbon and energy reduction strategies and identifying key emission reduction initiatives in a drive to reach net zero.

The company also shares examples of how advertising spend supports the promotion of more sustainable behaviours. For example, Heart and Smooth worked with financial services company, Aviva, in support of its 'What does your brighter future look like' campaign, on a special content series. Heart presenter James Stewart, a climate expert, provided simple tips to help people be more sustainable, Smooth showcased Aviva's services to help people be more sustainable, while presenters from both brands spoke with a 'champion' on different lifestyle topics over a 12-week period.

There are more examples where commercial radio and podcasts have been used to highlight the climate crisis. Bauer Media Audio is the second largest commercial radio operator in the UK, with brands including Kiss, Absolute Radio, Scala, Magic, Hits Radio and Greatest Hits Radio. During the energy crisis, GOV UK partnered with Kiss to help people understand how to get smarter with their energy usage and cut waste. One of Absolute Radio's biggest programmes, The Frank Skinner show, featured a climate change interview with former US Vice President Al Gore, while classical music station Scala Radio programmed a series of nature-themed shows, led by science and wildlife broadcaster Liz Bonnin.

Radiocentre, the industry body for commercial radio, operates a clearance service that ensures that advertising messages on commercial radio stations comply with the necessary content rules and standards laid out in the BCAP Code of Broadcast Advertising and the Ofcom Broadcasting Code. As a result, listeners can trust the advertisements they hear on commercial radio to be honest and accurate. The Clearance team takes into consideration not just the specific initiative or environmental benefit mentioned in an advertisement, but also the overall environmental credentials of advertisers' products and services.

To approve advertisements including environmental claims, the Clearance team uses an environmental consultant for guidance on specific campaigns and bases decisions on interpretation and application of both the Advertising Standards Authority's 'Guidance on Misleading Environmental Claims and Social Responsibility' and the Competition and Market's Authority's guidance 'Making Environmental Claims on Goods and Services'.

It's apparent that these companies are committed to decarbonizing and using their content to promote information and advice around better, more sustainable ways of living. The opportunities for advertisers to engage with radio as part of a transition to a sustainable advertising industry are clear.

Promotional merchandise

In March 2023, Matt attended a debate in Committee Room 9 at the Palace of Westminster, home of the UK's political leaders. The Debating Group, which was founded by the Advertising Association in 1975, regularly holds debates on topics of interest to the advertising and marketing community, using it to raise these with MPs, Lords and their policy advisers.

This debate was hosted by the British Promotional Merchandise Association and the motion was in support of the role of promotional merchandise as the most effective and long-lasting way of creating emotional engagement between a brand and their customer. You know the sort of thing that a marketer might consider for customers – if you're B2B, a pen, a branded water bottle, a tote bag or a notepad for a delegate. A much wider range of options exists in B2C, across toys and fashion apparel to household goods and NFTs. The debate was a lively one, the case for and against, an interesting one. The debate format allowed for an opportunity to make a point or pose a question from the floor to the speakers. Matt had listened intently but there was no mention of sustainability. He suggested to everyone that, given the long-term ambitions of the industry, and the issue of climate change, the industry had to take responsibility for all the merchandise it was producing to ensure that it was sustainable.

The response was a positive one, stories from numerous attendees of transformation in sourcing organic, recycled and upcycled products for client briefs. The opportunity for branded merchandise to be a positive, sustainable contribution to a company's relationship with customers was acknowledged as something which had to grow in importance in the next few years.

We hope that the industry will also take steps to address end-of-life waste issues for merchandise, ensure there is no over-production, or production of unnecessary or single-use items which would be bad for both the environment and brands with their names on such items.

Matt followed up with the BPMA's chief executive, Carey Trevill, who gave some recent examples of better sourcing.

This is an industry worth around £1.5bn to the UK economy and it is driven by demand and creative ideas. We work some 18 months ahead in consumer trends, and we're seeing a revolution in materials and manufacturing, whether that's apparel made from traceable cotton or products dedicated to lower impact materials through meeting the Recycled Claim Standard (RCS).

The world's biggest brands are using their branding in physical form to talk to consumers, customers and employees, creating amazing opportunities to reuse, reduce and recycle and take advantage of manufacturing progress from UK-based businesses. For example, Global tech giants Google stepped into upcycling with 34,000 pairs of socks to say thank you to employees, with a GOTS-approved manufacturer to use a recycled textile yarn.

The process saved 24 million litres of water, reduced energy consumption by 90.168kWH of electricity and avoided the use of 1826kg of possible pollutants. Another example is how a well-known media business sourced a bottle made of 98 per cent sugar cane biomass waste, designed, and produced using carbon negative renewable energy as part of its brief to remove all single use plastic (SUP) from an experiential campaign.

The sustainability brief must consider every aspect of the campaign and rethink repurposing; excess and waste are never the aim but are sometimes the outcome. Our industry is delivering solutions to repurpose left over goods for charitable organizations, or return unwanted apparel for certified recycling, or to show the carbon and wastewater reduction process. A sustainable brand merchandise solution – whether a premium for a promotion, apparel for a brand launch or a simple thank you to a customer – can be simple to achieve.

Imagine if a company could use its promotional merchandise in a way that supported and made a positive contribution to the planet? How are you going to influence any budget you see allocated to merchandise?

A sustainable media supply chain: summary

How and where advertising spend is committed can drive competition around sustainability within a media channel. Many media owners have set out on a path to make their business more sustainable, and more competitive in this way, and a lot depends on reaching 100 per cent renewable energy. But there is more than energy alone to consider. As we neared the final stages of writing this book, Omnicom Media Group announced the launch of OMG Impact, measuring media owners on their environmental, social and governance to help advertisers better understand the ESG impact of their ad spend decisions. Its first client to use the tool is the UK government. It's precisely this type of shift in advertiser expectation that will be a powerful catalyst in helping to shape a Sustainable Advertising industry.

References

Aiman, I., Amalore, Q., Mandalia, M. (2022) *OOH media has a growing role in promoting sustainability*. WARC. August 2022. [Online] Available at: https://www.warc.com/newsandopinion/opinion/ooh-media-has-a-growing-role-in-promoting-sustainability/en-gb/5860 (archived at https://perma.cc/UWN3-MQND)

albert (2021) *Broadcasters and streamers sign up to the Climate Content Pledge*. [Online] Available at: https://wearealbert.org/2021/11/03/broadcasters-and-streamers-sign-up-to-the-climate-content-pledge/ (archived at https://perma.cc/YX65-2JP2)

Amazon. (2023) *2022 Sustainability Report*. [Online] Available at: https://sustainability.aboutamazon.co.uk/2022-sustainability-executive-summary.pdf (archived at https://perma.cc/AE4R-KQCR)

Amazon. (2023) *Driving Climate Solutions*. [Online] Available at: https://sustainability.aboutamazon.co.uk/environment/the-climate-pledge (archived at https://perma.cc/733M-4AZH)

Amazon. (2023) *Sustainability at Amazon*. [Online] Available at: https://sustainability.aboutamazon.co.uk/ (archived at https://perma.cc/6DYY-Q5RT)

Bauer Media. (2023) *Sustainability Annual Report 2023*. [Online] Available at: https://www.bauermedia.co.uk/wordpress/wp-content/uploads/2023/04/Sustainability-Annual-Report-2023.pdf (archived at https://perma.cc/DPQ6-SAB6)

Bauer Media. (2023). *Cultural Impact – Sustainability*. [Online] Available at: https://www.bauermedia.co.uk/cultural-impact/sustainability/ (archived at https://perma.cc/6ANQ-6R9L)

Blakeney, M. (2023) *Greening The Big Screen Experience*. Digital Cinema Media. March 2023. [Online] Available at: https://www.dcm.co.uk/news/uk-cinema-association-2023-conference (archived at https://perma.cc/B4RK-SA37)

Channel 4. (2020) *4Sales launches £3m airtime fund for new-to-TV advertisers.* [Online] Available at: https://www.4sales.com/latest/2020-06/press-releases/4sales-launches-ps3m-airtime-fund-new-tv-advertisers (archived at https://perma.cc/5N2J-8QWT)

Channel 4. (2021) *Tenzing case study.* [Online] Available at: https://www.4sales.com/our-work/tenzing (archived at https://perma.cc/MW69-GU92)

Channel 4. (2023a). 2023 Sustainability Plan on a Page.

Channel 4. (2023b). Core4 and 4Youth survey.

Elkin, C., Sanekommu, D. (2023) *How AI is helping airlines mitigate the climate impact of contrails.* Google Blog. August 2023. Available at: https://blog.google/technology/ai/ai-airlines-contrails-climate-change/ (archived at https://perma.cc/W58Z-DME6)

Global. (2023) *Global Goodness.* [Online] Available at: https://global.com/global-goodness/ (archived at https://perma.cc/K235-455B)

Good-Loop. (2023) *Is Your Advert A Load Of Hot Air? Find Out With Our Carbon Calculator.* [Online] Available at: https://good-loop.com/resources/carbon-calculator (archived at https://perma.cc/A7DH-LW2H)

Google. (2023) *Google Environmental Report 2023.* July 2023. [Online] Available at: https://www.gstatic.com/gumdrop/sustainability/google-2023-environmental-report.pdf (archived at https://perma.cc/G6GQ-9LTQ)

Google. (2023) *Operating on 24/7 Carbon-Free Energy by 2030.* [Online] Available at: https://sustainability.google/progress/energy/ (archived at https://perma.cc/GB4R-AVF6)

Google. (2023) *Sustainability for Partners.* [Online] Available at: https://sustainability.google/for-partners/ (archived at https://perma.cc/2LYN-AB9F)

Google. (2023) *Sustainability Trends data.* [Online] Available at: https://sustainability.google/trends/ (archived at https://perma.cc/JSR6-G9U3)

Google. (2023) *Sustainability.* [Online] Available at: https://sustainability.google/ (archived at https://perma.cc/5Y22-D95U)

Haymarket. (2023) *Welcome to Haymarket Impact.* [Online] Available at: https://haymarket.com/impact/ (archived at https://perma.cc/6BBC-F2SC)

ITV. (2023) *Climate Action.* [Online] Available at: https://www.itvplc.com/socialpurpose/climate-action (archived at https://perma.cc/H6C5-DVX8)

Lloyd-Smith, S, et al (2023) Global. *The Global Goodness Report 2022.* Global Goodness. Available at: https://global.com/wp-content/uploads/2022/12/Global-Goodness-Report_2022.pdf (archived at https://perma.cc/6AQR-98C8)

Maguire, Y. (2023) *New sustainability tools help businesses and cities map environmental information.* Google Blog. August 2023. [Online] Available at: https://blog.google/products/maps/google-maps-apis-environment-sustainability/ (archived at https://perma.cc/4M6P-54C5)

Mail Metro Media. (2023) *Sustainability.* [Online] Available at: https://www.mailmetromedia.co.uk/about/sustainability/ (archived at https://perma.cc/HK4U-HEHV)

Mail Metro Media. (2023) *Satisfying the need to know. Sustainability Report 2020.* Available at: https://flipbooks.mailmetromedia.co.uk/books/qbwt/#p=1 (archived at https://perma.cc/PC77-VLWJ)

Marketreach. (2023) *Discover the circular advantage of mail.* [Online] Available at: https://www.marketreach.co.uk/mail-sustainability (archived at https://perma.cc/NQ2Y-QGUX)

Marketreach. (2023) *Using mail more sustainably.* [Online] Available at: https://www.marketreach.co.uk/resource/using-mail-more-sustainably (archived at https://perma.cc/334W-GGQT)

Matias, Y. (2022) *How we're using AI to help address the climate crisis.* Google Blog. November 2022. [Online] Available at: https://blog.google/outreach-initiatives/sustainability/cop27-adaptation-efforts/ (archived at https://perma.cc/83XF-D3QX)

Meta. (2023) *Transforming our shared responsibility into shared opportunity.* [Online] Available at: https://www.facebook.com/business/resource/sustainability-for-business (archived at https://perma.cc/F7U4-AKR5)

Mitchell, S. (2023) *Posterscope debut 100% recycled and recyclable 48- and 96-sheets.* Ethical Marketing News. August 2023. [Online] Available at: https://ethicalmarketingnews.com/posterscope-debut-100-recycled-and-recyclable-48-and-96-sheets (archived at https://perma.cc/7HEQ-TZXL)

Oakes, O. (2023) *Omnicom offers brands sustainability ratings for media owners.* The Media Leader. August 2023. Available at: https://the-media-leader.com/omnicom-offers-brands-sustainability-ratings-for-media-owners/ (archived at https://perma.cc/2Z7A-WZLA) [Accessed August 2023]

Pearl & Dean. (2023) *Sustainability Policy/ESG Framework.* [Online] Available at: https://business.pearlanddean.com/sustainability-policy/ (archived at https://perma.cc/U3TP-BWKT)

PPA. (2023) *About the PPA.* [Online] Available at: https://ppa.co.uk/about-the-ppa (archived at https://perma.cc/A7SA-QFH5)

Radiocentre. (2023) *Clearance Services.* [Online] Available at: https://www.radiocentre.org/clearance/fast-track-trustmark/ (archived at https://perma.cc/62BN-YJW5) [Accessed August 2023]

Reach. (2023) *Protecting the environment.* [Online] Available at: https://www.reachplc.com/Responsible_business/Protecting-The-Environment (archived at https://perma.cc/V7QC-A8KY)

SAWA. (2022) *United Nations Development Programme (@Undp) And Sawa Global Cinema Advertising Association Launch "Don't Choose Extinction" Global Cinema Advertising Campaign.* Global Cinema Advertising Association. May 2022. [Online] Available at: https://www.sawa.com/document/united-nations-development-programme-undp-and-sawa-global-cinema-advertising-association-launch-dont-choose-extinction-global-cinema-advertising-campaign (archived at https://perma.cc/ZUR7-RFR3)

Sky. (2023) *Royal Mail Is Walking on Air in Carbon Conscious Spot from AMV BBDO*. Little Black Book. February 2023. [Online] Available at: https://www.lbbonline.com/news/royal-mail-is-walking-on-air-in-carbon-conscious-spot-from-amv-bbdo (archived at https://perma.cc/EA8K-S3GK)

The Debating Group. (2023) *Home*. [Online] Available at: https://www.debatinggroup.co.uk/ (archived at https://perma.cc/RSV2-2626)

Townsend, M. (2022) *Environmental sustainability at Ozone*. Ozone Project. May 2022. [Online] Available at: https://www.ozoneproject.com/blog/our-latest-steps-towards-a-greener-ozone (archived at https://perma.cc/T8YH-WKFT)

UNDP. (2022) *"Don't Choose Extinction" global cinema ad aims to inspire movie theater audiences to join fight against climate change*. May 2022. [Online] Available at: https://www.undp.org/press-releases/dont-choose-extinction-global-cinema-ad-aims-inspire-movie-theater-audiences-join (archived at https://perma.cc/N7Y9-WXRG)

Wildstone. (2022) *Wildstone acquires the most sustainable highway digital advertising mast in the Netherlands*. [Online] Available at: https://www.wildstone.co.uk/wildstone-acquires-the-most-sustainable-highway-digital-advertising-mast-in-the-netherlands (archived at https://perma.cc/T2A6-H4QX)

07

Quick wins, and long-term success for media plans

The final part of this section is going to look at how we can decarbonize the distribution of ads around the world. Firstly, we discuss the quick wins that everyone can benefit from right away. We draw on recommendations from two key authorities: IAB Tech Lab and GARM (Global Alliance for Responsible Media). Secondly, we cover the establishment of an industry standard – where data for different media channels around the globe could be measured fairly, accurately, and proportionately, considering the differing attributes of each channel – as a platform for decarbonization.

IAB Tech Lab and the Green Initiative

The IAB Technology Laboratory (Tech Lab) was created in 2014 as a non-profit consortium that engages a member community globally to develop foundational technology and standards that enable growth and trust in the digital media ecosystem. In January 2023 it launched the Green Initiative 'to assist the advertising industry in meaningfully lowering carbon emissions' with a clear focus on setting standards to encourage the digital advertising eco-system to reduce waste in the Programmatic Supply Chain. It is complicated and complex, but it is also essential if the ad industry is to decarbonize.

Anthony Katsur is the CEO of IAB Tech Lab and said of the launch, 'Programmatic advertising, like any other economic activity, contributes to global carbon emissions, which many brands have committed to reducing but lack meaningful ways to benchmark or enforce programmatically. As the global technical standard-setting body for the digital advertising ecosystem, Tech Lab's goal is to provide the information and mechanism to send and receive signals pertaining to carbon emissions programmatically.'

The objectives at launch were:

- Creating a working group open to all Tech Lab members to collaborate on different avenues to lower carbon emissions in the programmatic supply chain
- Collating and re-publishing programmatic best practices and the quantified carbon emissions wasted by not following the guidance
- Expanding into topics that create waste within the programmatic supply chain but have lacked official specification
- Iteratively adding benchmarks to the Tools Portal, starting with information already available from ads.txt/app-ads.txt and sellers.json entries and expanding to carbon emissions and more based on input from the working group.

Following the launch, the focus was on quick wins to eliminate unnecessary duplication of signals, which cause waste. In simple terms, the fewer the signals involved in a programmatic ad buy, the lower the level of energy used and so carbon emissions created. When you consider there are trillions of signals involved in daily ad requests, there is a massive opportunity to remove duplicate signals and save carbon in the process.

In June 2023, IAB Tech Lab published its Sustainability Playbook, covering examples of best practices aimed at making programmatic advertising more sustainable. It is a tool to guide and assist industry professionals to proactively reduce the carbon emissions of their Programmatic Supply Chains.

The playbook places a strong emphasis on practical recommendations and the use of existing best practices enabling buyers and sellers in the advertising industry to simultaneously minimize environmental impact and uphold responsible economic principles.

The playbook breaks recommended actions into two parts:

1 Sell-side – for the people involved in the selling of advertising space on the open internet, primarily publishers which have ad opportunities and the ad tech partners who support them.

Actions include:

- Limit multi-hop resellers to reduce transactions in the bid stream for a direct impact on lowering energy consumption
- Use managerdomain and inventorypartnerdomain to help with visibility and transparency of paths to selling and reselling

- Implement Global Placement Id (gpid) to optimize performance through distinct, unique identifiers of ad slots
- Use preferred paths to create a single integration path, rather multiple paths to the same exchange
- Lazy load pages to embrace UX best practice and delay loading of non-essential resources, all to reduce the amount of energy needed to run a website
- Limit cookie syncs to those that best optimize revenue generation and benefit from better performance and lower emissions
- Always include bid floors to avoid wasted energy for bids in auctions that will not qualify and can never win
- Multi-format ad request is a new area for development to reduce sending separate ad requests for each format
- Use compression, minification and modularization, all serving a purpose to reduce energy consumption (as well as positive impacts on engagement, usability and rankings).

2 Buy-side – for the people involved buying as space on the open internet, primarily agencies, advertisers and DSPs

Actions include:

- Reduce duplicate bid requests using Global Placement Id (gpid) to limit activity to the most optimal path
- Limit purchases of multi-hop impressions to reduce the computational load in auctions and reduce emissions
- Use managerdomain and inventorypartnerdomain to prioritize the best reseller paths
- Support pot bidding helps to lower the amount of video ad requests and support the entire ad break holistically
- Avoid 'Made for Advertising' inventory in a drive to remove clutter which is greener for brands and the environment
- Leverage interoperable IDs where possible to reduce the number of identifiers and significantly reduce resource
- Implement ad management API to stop bidding for inventory that can never be won
- Consider leaner ad creatives to render as small on the page as possible to result in less energy consumption.

The final point in the playbook is one for everyone and that is around the use (and reporting) of sustainable energy sources for every company involved in the advertising ecosystem.

The playbook also acknowledges a growing industry consensus around the need to have a singular, holistic standard for measuring carbon activities informed by Greenhouse Gases Protocols. It references the work by Ad Net Zero, WFA and GARM to design this standard. In the meantime, IAB Tech Lab recommends these actions be taken today and evolved/expanded as measurement becomes more standardized.

'Cleaning up' the programmatic advertising industry's emissions

There's more work being done to put a number on the programmatic advertising industry's emissions. A company called Scope3, which provides a supply chain emissions data standard for any company in the digital ecosystem to use in an emissions model, released its State of Sustainable Advertising report in April 2023. The report was a global study on ad emissions that provided global benchmarking data and shared a total emission estimation for five leading economies – the USA, the UK, Australia, Germany and France – in what Scope3 described as first-of-its-kind.

It showed:

- 215,000 metric tons of carbon emissions are produced every month across the US, UK, France, Germany and Australia, equivalent to more than 24 million gallons of gas consumption or more than 2.5 million metric tons a year for just those five regions.
- 'Climate Risk' websites are those which have been identified as having emissions as much as twice the industry average — eliminating spend on these sites can save 33,500 metric tons of CO_2e monthly (equivalent to 3,449 road trips around the planet).
- The majority (60 per cent) of carbon generated by the programmatic advertising comes from 'ad selection emissions' and can be attributed to the complex supply chain.

The company's team suggested if the industry were to eliminate spending across the highest emitting domains for carbon emissions in the five regions, more than 33,500 metric tons of carbon could be removed every month. It described this as a dramatic reduction in energy consumption in the programmatic advertising supply chain, all without reducing the advertising's commercial impact.

So, how did Scope3 work this out? Its sample was data from players in the programmatic space, large and small, representing billions of impressions across tens of thousands of domains/apps on desktop and mobile, including video and banner ads. It used that data to understand overall ad tech market emissions trends across three emission categories (ad selection, media distribution and creative distribution), with benchmark values from weighted averages of emissions activity on domains and apps active in a given market. That's then validated by a third-party data source – BIScience – which provides all impression activity data for the top websites and apps (Scope3, 2023).

Complex? A little, yes. But essentially they're using their tech to follow the ad and the number of transactions involved, depending on where and how it appears on all kinds of online sites across desktop and mobile, then assigning a number to that and recommending the volume of transactions involved can be dramatically reduced to make carbon-savings, without lessening advertising effectiveness.

Scope3 is certainly on a mission…

In supporting interviews about the report, Scope3 recommended companies shift spend away from high emitter domains, for publishers to turn off reselling and for advertisers to actively avoid the 10 per cent worst-emitting media properties, most of which happen to be fraud, Made For Advertising (MFA) sites, and low value inventory. It discovered removing these worst-emitting domains did not negatively impact advertising results, and that there was a positive revenue reason too for reducing the number of ad tech partners publishers work with and running fewer ads.

There are specific recommendations to reduce carbon emissions in its report.

For advertisers:

- Get baseline measurement for campaigns
- Identify high emitting partners. Ask preferred partners to review their supply paths. Shift spend
- Buy low emissions solutions (segments, optimization and green marketplaces)

For publishers:

- Measure emissions from an ad impression on your site

- Review high emitting partners in supply chain and weigh costs versus SSPs and other partners. Ensure site's ads.txt configuration reflects existing tech stack and keep it updated
- Showcase your low emitting inventory to attract advertisers who want to spend on green options.

In April 2023, Scope3 announced that it had been working with Insider, a global news publisher (formerly Business Insider), to be its first publisher to complete a carbon footprint assessment the company. For context, Insider runs a newsroom of nearly 600 journalists and has more than 176 million unique monthly visitors across the globe with hundreds of millions of video views each month (Insider, 2023). That's quite a big digital reach, supported by advertisers. Scope3 audited Insider's ad tech setup and conducted an analysis of carbon vs. revenue throughout its ad stack. What it described as a 'systemic reduction' led to a 20 per cent drop in carbon footprint in the first quarter of 2023. Insider announced it will work on making more significant reductions to its carbon footprint and announced plans for Green Media Products, allowing partners to measure and compensate for carbon emissions linked to ad spend.

Then in the following month, Scope3's founder and CEO, Brian O'Kelley, published a post called The AdTech Greenscape (Figure 7.1), a market map for ad tech companies that offer sustainable advertising solutions (BOKonAds, 2023). It is modelled on the highly successful LUMAscapes which were established to help people see how various companies in the digital ecosystem fit together.

O'Kelley said in his post accompanying the 'Greenscape' that the categories are 'an attempt to describe "what does this company do" from a buyer's lens. For instance, if you are running a programmatic media campaign, you might be interested in campaign reporting and campaign optimization. Whether these companies are trading desks or DSPs or custom algorithm providers or verification vendors or media auditors matters – but in this context, they all fit into these two categories.'

Creative production measurement:

- Track and measure the carbon footprint of a creative production, generally focusing on the crew, set, materials, travel and post-production emissions
- Carbon Calculators and Planning Tools
- Estimate the carbon footprint of a media plan by channel or media vendor. Ideal for comparing scenarios prior to making buying decisions

FIGURE 7.1 The AdTech Greenscape, BOKonAds (2023)

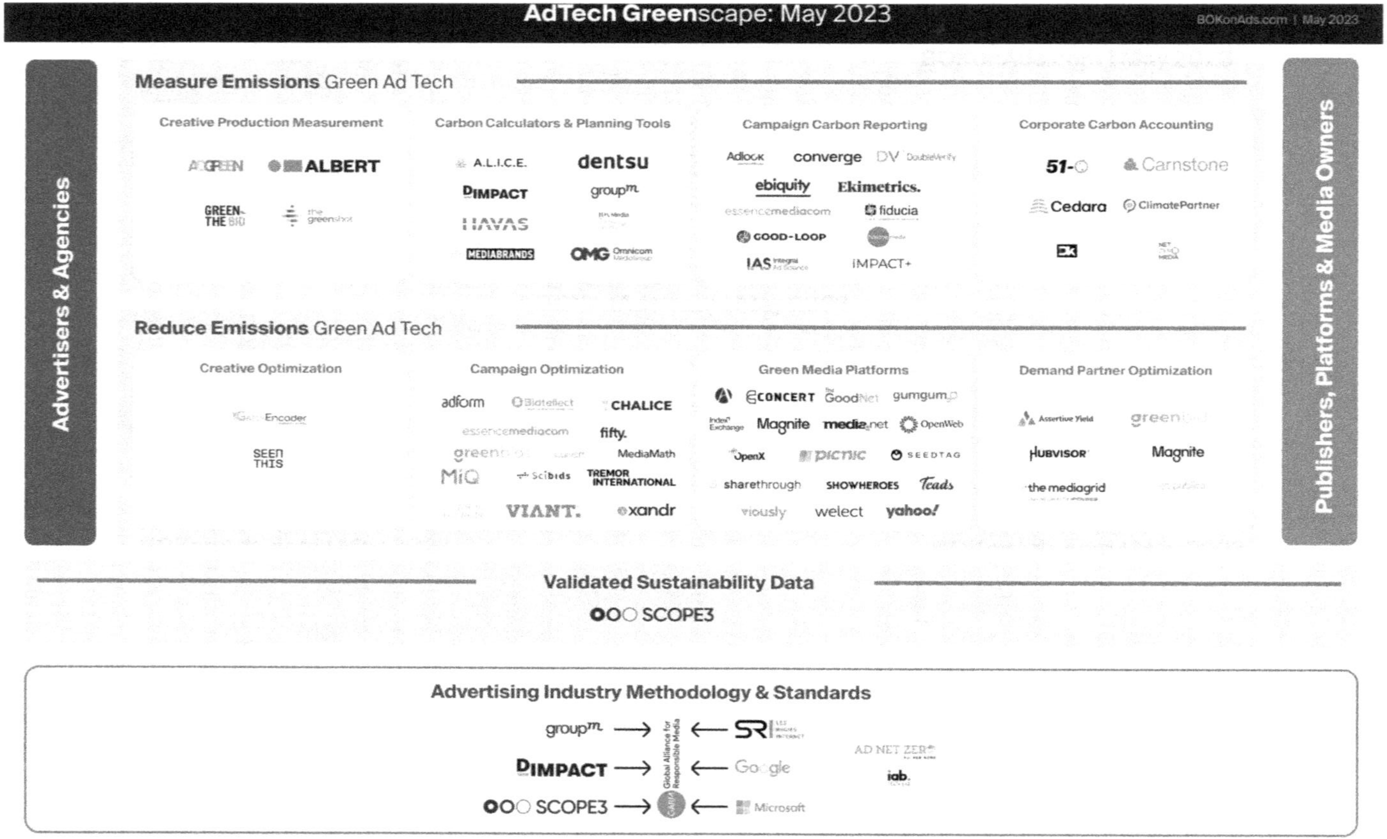
AdTech Greenscape: May 2023
BOKonAds.com | May 2023
Advertisers & Agencies
Publishers, Platforms & Media Owners
Measure Emissions Green Ad Tech
Creative Production Measurement
ALBERT
Carbon Calculators & Planning Tools
A.L.I.C.E.
dentsu
DIMPACT
groupm
HAVAS
MEDIABRANDS
OMG Omnicom
Campaign Carbon Reporting
Adlook
converge
DV DoubleVerify
ebiquity
Ekimetrics.
essencemediacom
fiducia
GOOD-LOOP
IAS
IMPACT+
Corporate Carbon Accounting
Carnstone
Cedara
ClimatePartner
Reduce Emissions Green Ad Tech
Creative Optimization
SEEN THIS
Campaign Optimization
adform
CHALICE
essencemediacom
fifty.
MediaMath
MiQ
Scibids
TREMOR INTERNATIONAL
VIANT.
xandr
Green Media Platforms
CONCERT
gumgum
Magnite
OpenWeb
OpenX
SEEDTAG
sharethrough
SHOWHEROES
Teads
welect
yahoo!
Demand Partner Optimization
Assertive Yield
HUBVISOR
Magnite
the mediagrid
Validated Sustainability Data
SCOPE3
Advertising Industry Methodology & Standards
groupm
DIMPACT
SCOPE3
Global Alliance for Responsible Media
Google
Microsoft
AD NET ZERO
iab.

Campaign carbon reporting

- Measure the carbon footprint of campaigns based on impression-level data. May be real-time or executed post-campaign

Corporate carbon accounting

- Use financial and activity data to calculate the carbon footprint of an organization, generally for inclusion in a sustainability or impact report

Creative optimization

- Minimize the data transfer and CPU usage of a creative

Campaign optimization

- Optimize the targeting of a campaign to minimize its carbon footprint relative to reach and performance metrics

Green Media Platforms

- Curate and package private marketplaces to minimize their carbon footprint

Demand partner optimization

- Optimize distribution of programmatic bid requests to minimize carbon footprint per unit of revenue

Validated sustainability data

- Collate public and private sustainability data to create an 'apples to apples' dataset aligned to scientific, regulatory, and industry standards

Advertising Industry Methodology and Standards

- Organizations working to create a common methodology and standards for measuring the carbon footprint of advertising-related activities

This 'Greenscape' has the potential to become as ubiquitous as other LUMAscapes and prove to be a highly useful visual stimulus for people going forward. Businesses like these are shaking up the digital advertising eco-system, making a strong case that the result will be a cleaner, better system for advertisers and publishers alike, by removing those elements which suck up energy and ad spend with no discernible benefit.

Sustainable media – actions to take now

In June 2023, the WFA's Global Alliance for Responsible Media (GARM) and Ad Net Zero launched a guide to sustainable media during Cannes Lions. This is the first guide of its kind to help advertisers take immediate action to reduce the direct carbon emissions from their advertising activity. Called *GARM Sustainability: Action Guide to Reduce Media Greenhouse Gas Emissions*, the goal is to ensure that advertisers and the agencies and tech partners they work with help meet the Paris Climate Goals and limit temperature rises to 1.5 degrees by the end of the century.

The guide was produced by the GARM Sustainability Steer Team, which brought together brands and industry bodies such as Diageo, Unilever, Procter & Gamble, Mars, L'Oréal, Reckitt, Mastercard, 4A's, Ad Net Zero, ANA, ISBA, WFA and the Responsible Marketing Agency. Agency holding companies, publishers, data and technology providers also helped create the guide. GARM also created a Climate Science Expert Group, featuring Brain Oxygen, BSI Group and brand-side chief sustainability officers from Mastercard, Reckitt and Unilever, who reviewed all suggestions to ensure they make a genuine difference.

The guide consolidates current best practice on media sustainability and has identified 10 Action Points To Decarbonize Media for advertisers across planning, buying and activation. These are split into different areas, as follows:

Sustainable supplier selection and infrastructure

1. Build a Sustainability-Assured Media Partner List

Advertisers are urged to focus efforts on the use of sustainable suppliers in the media supply chain – the single biggest decarbonization effort that can be achieved for the media industry. Brand teams are encouraged to establish an additional filter based on environmental actions and commitments that partners in the media ecosystem are taking.

2. Streamline Your Media Value Chain & Technology

Advertisers are asked to be selective in technologies used to support digital media campaigns and streamline wherever possible. This is because digital runs on significant data and server infrastructures that require energy to power them, producing heat and generating GHG.

Optimize assets for media decarbonization

3. Drive asset sustainability based on media sufficiency

Advertisers are requested to consider how they reduce, reuse, and recycle creative assets. Most advertisers create more assets than they use, and rarely are they over-used, based on available media budgets.

4. Shorten and compress digital creative formats

Longer form assets and heavy file sizes inevitably generate greater GHG output. Advertisers are asked to compress digital creative files and consider shorter formats to help lower carbon footprints.

5. Stream content and landing destinations versus preload

When an advertiser chooses to preload landing pages and/or advertising creatives in digital, this puts greater demand on server energy. Streaming solutions should only show assets as and when they are needed to be seen by the end consumer and auto-play as a default setting should be avoided.

Sustainable media planning and buying best practice

6. Optimize Flighting To Include Off-Peak Energy Periods

The time of day or night that an advertiser chooses to run their campaigns can be optimized around energy use, whether based on network stress or energy source used. The more an advertiser can understand how and where there is a greater intensity of emissions, using location-specific data, the better.

7. Streamline and Optimize Data Usage

Advertisers rely on large amounts of data, frequently used to improve targeting. A review of how data is handled and applied to campaigns, how it is stored and transacted, can ensure it is as energy efficient as possible.

8. Look for Sustainability in Print

As we've looked at earlier in this section, select print publishers have been making strides in sustainability. This includes the use of responsibly sourced paper, PEFC / FSC certified paper, recycled and recyclable materials in the printing process including non-toxic and biodegradable inks, all of which allows for sustainable use of print as part of a media campaign.

9. Look for Sustainability in Outdoor

Similarly, advances in Out of Home media channels range from recycled materials to sustainable energy use to regenerative structures. We have seen that the more sustainably they are built and maintained, the more impact they can have in long term GHG reduction. The guide advises advertisers to consider this when prioritizing campaign executions and site selections, all to reduce environmental impact.

10. Consider Emissions Data in Media Measurement Models

The final recommendation is a very interesting one. Ad buyers should consider a balanced scorecard in evaluating media investment choices against an array of metrics including media sustainability. The guide concludes that advertisers and media agencies will increasingly weigh channel tactics based on media emissions data as it becomes more reliable.

In closing this 'quick wins' section, the leaders behind the guide highlight how there is much that advertisers and their colleagues and partners in procurement and sustainability can do now to ensure the media function can deliver real reduction of direct emissions.

As you can see, anyone involved in the media planning and buying of advertising campaigns can take immediate steps to remove carbon emissions from day-to-day media plans. This is about a reduction of the negative impact while retaining the full effectiveness from your ad spend. There is no excuse for inaction by anybody involved in this part of the advertising industry.

One set of data to rule them all

Where is all this headed? If we go back to the goals of advertisers, agencies, and media at the outset of this chapter, we're aiming for a campaign media plan for any advertiser that allows all involved to track, measure, report, reduce and account for the plan's carbon emissions.

In late 2022, Ad Net Zero's Global Group established a Media Working Group comprising representatives from across the global advertising ecosystem. The group included voices from agencies, every media channel, many of the tech platforms and some advertisers. Its objective was to review the options in development to inform a data set which could become the chassis – the core data source – for any organization to then build out their own tools to calculate the carbon footprint of a media plan. The goal was to establish an industry standard for carbon measurement – where data for different media channels could be measured fairly, accurately and proportionately. Once the set of data is established, the data within it for any channel could then be updated regularly to reflect the steps being taken by vendors towards decarbonization.

This was taken on by GARM, with the agreement of the WFA, in Spring 2023, with a commitment to identify a standard for the data for measuring media campaign carbon emissions and taking it to wider industry consultation before end 2023.

Quick wins, and long-term success for media plans: summary

As we have seen through Chapters 5, 6 and 7, there are many actions possible today to reduce the carbon emissions without impacting negatively upon the efficiency of the spend committed to distributing ads. In fact, there are a growing number of opportunities to meaningfully help accelerate decarbonization of the media supply chain through healthy competition, alongside the usual metrics applied to the selection of media partners in any media plan. We must also keep an eye out for updates on the data set – it is coming, it is the single biggest priority in this area, but in the meantime, note just how much can be done through the series of 'quick wins' offered up by experts in the industry.

References

IAB Tech Lab. (2023) *IAB Tech Lab Unveils Multi-Year Green Initiative To Reduce Carbon Impact Of Digital Ads*. IAB Tech Lab Blog. January 2023. [Online] Available at: https://iabtechlab.com/press-releases/iab-tech-lab-unveils-multi-year-green-supply-path-initiative/ (archived at https://perma.cc/BW78-83UZ)

IAB Tech Lab. (2023) *Sustainability Playbook*. IAB Tech Lab Blog. June 2023. Available at: https://iabtechlab.com/press-releases/iab-tech-lab-releases-the-sustainability-playbook-to-achieve-a-sustainable-programmatic-marketplace/ (archived at https://perma.cc/J4KY-N5HV) [Accessed August 2023]

Insider. (2023) *Insider becomes the first publisher to complete Scope3 carbon footprint assessment*. [Online] Available at: https://www.insider-inc.com/news/archive/2023/insider-first-publisher-scope3-assessment (archived at https://perma.cc/FK62-2MC9)

O'Kelley, Brian. (2023) *The AdTech Greenscape 2023*. NOKonAdes. May 2023.
[Online] Available at: https://bokonads.com/the-greenscape/ (archived at https://perma.cc/SRV3-G33Z)

Scope3. (2023) *Scope3 Report: Programmatic advertising generates 215,000 metric tons of carbon emissions each month across five major global economies*.
Scope3 Blog. April 2023. Available at: https://scope3.com/news/scope3-report-programmatic-advertising-generates-215-000-metric-tons-of-carbon-emissions-each-month-across-five-major-global-economies.md (archived at https://perma.cc/8FT6-5BTW)

WFA. (2023) *GARM Sustainability Quick Action Guide*. [Online] Available at:
https://wfanet.org/leadership/garm/garm-resource-directory-(weblog-detail-page)/2023/06/22/GARM-Sustainability-Quick-Action-Guide (archived at https://perma.cc/CW39-H2XC)

08

Reducing emissions through awards and events

If, as an industry, we are to achieve our Sustainable Advertising ambitions, we must completely reappraise what we consider to be 'creative excellence'.

We cannot imagine being able to celebrate work, with awards held aloft and winners cheered, unless the work has been made in the most sustainable way possible. And that the resulting campaign has accounted for its real-world impact, demonstrating that the results have helped in the battle to tackle climate change.

That's the vision. The question is: how do we get there quickly? The answer is complex because widespread changes will have implications for successful business models that have been built up around our industry.

Who doesn't want to win an award? They're a brilliant way of a company demonstrating it is a leader in its field, as well as a way of attracting talent, investment and new business. Being an award-winner in advertising, particularly of a coveted Cannes LION, D&AD Pencil or IPA Effectiveness Award, has always been an integral part of success and the way we work.

We don't want to lose that (we shouldn't lose that) but we must reflect hard on what we're awarding, why we're awarding it and what impact that lauded work has had on our planet, given the reality of climate change.

So, how do you judge work for its sustainability credentials? Short answer: it's not easy.

When we reviewed our industry's awards back in 2022, the absence of sustainability criteria was conspicuous. Yes, sure there was an award category or two that looked at ESG, Purpose or Planet, but no awards had sustainability at the heart of every entry.

That led the Advertising Association, in partnership with Campaign, to establish the Campaign Ad Net Zero Awards – an awards competition with a single-minded focus: to seek out the work across every category that is helping build a net zero economy and support more sustainable ways of life.

We set an expectation that work being entered should clearly demonstrate two things:

1 There had been clear efforts to track, measure and reduce the carbon emissions during the operational process of producing and distributing the work.

2 There was a clear way of proving that the campaign had achieved a more sustainable outcome, with evidence that backed the submission, for example a record of the reduced levels of GHGs.

We wanted to find the best work out there that was helping industries to reshape our economy, from one that relies on intensive carbon emissions to a sustainable alternative that could still support jobs and livelihoods, encourage competition and innovation, and bring joy and satisfaction to people's lives. We also wanted to help our colleagues in government and fellow industries see the best work in support of net zero goals and discuss ways to accelerate that.

Seb often quotes the phrase 'don't let perfection be the enemy of progress', reminding us at every stage that we need to take steps forward each year. Certainly, when it came to the first year of the awards in 2021/2022, we were reviewing the best of what good looked like. We've no doubt we will look back on those examples in 3–5 years with slight embarrassment but that will be a good thing, because that is when you know progress has been made. This is a continuous process – we are all on the path to understanding what creative excellence really means for advertising in a sustainable world, celebrating blueprints for others to follow.

In short, let's use the power of awards to drive the wholesale change we are looking for. Imagine a world where every awards event in the advertising industry asks entrants for sustainability information. Where every award form requires you to submit your measurement data around the work as it was made and the results of that work. In every category.

A template for sustainable advertising awards

The following is a template example, based on the original Campaign Ad Net Zero awards, of how you might think about embedding the principles of sustainability in any awards you are involved in or thinking of creating.

Firstly, there should be basic evidence of a client company's consistently good or improving track record in sustainability.

Questions to ask in this opening section include:

- Does the client/brand measure and report its annual emissions and set targets in line with the Paris Agreement/SBTi? Do their agency partners? Do the media owners who were also involved in the campaign?
- What sustainability credentials do the entrant companies (brand/agencies/media) have? Examples might include B-Corp, Ad Net Zero Supporter, Race to Zero Supporter etc.

Secondly, there is the Process. These are the sorts of things which could be considered:

- How were processes adapted to achieve a brilliant result for less impact?
- How did you measure carbon emissions and what steps were taken to reduce these emissions from your operations and from your production of the work?
- Have you attempted to track the carbon involved in the media planning? Were any planning choices informed by data that allowed you to reduce carbon emissions?
- Was there any experiential element of the work and, if so, was a carbon calculator tool used? What efforts were made to reduce carbon emissions?

Thirdly, there is the work. Entrants could be encouraged to submit information on areas such as:

- What efforts were made to limit the risk of any work making misleading environmental claims to ensure any possibility of greenwashing was avoided? For example, has the team completed relevant training?
- Did you challenge the client to do something different with this campaign to take an approach that was more sustainable? What evidence was used to create a shift in thinking?
- How was the brief adapted to achieve a brilliant result with more sustainable messaging?

Most importantly, there are the results of the work being submitted. Asking about sustainability opens up a whole range of possibilities, such as:

- What were the results of the carbon reduction stemming from the campaign's effects on consumer behaviour – this could be absolute, relative or in proportion to your company's size or the problem identified, or sales made.

- What insights did you use to inform a more sustainable approach to the brief?

- How do the campaign results show that there has been a more sustainable result from the work, in terms of reduced carbon emissions and, more broadly, a reduced impact on the planet? How is this linked to the objective and to business success?

- Was there a reaction from the customer base and how did that reaction lead to a reduction in carbon emissions?

- Is there any evidence of the work being linked to climate policies or new regulations encouraging a shift to more sustainable practices?

- What learnings did you make during this campaign?

- What were the environmental outcomes?

- What were the commercial outcomes? Will commercial success ensure the continuation of more sustainable outcomes?

- Can you provide a total savings of GHGs as a result of the campaign?

Finally, ask the entrant to reflect on the work they are submitting and its role in helping to build a net-zero economy by promoting a more sustainable product, service and/or behaviour. A good way of doing this could be to ask:

- In your summing up, make the case for why this entry is supporting a business to help achieve its net zero transition plans. Is this a genuine step on the path to net zero? What can others learn and adopt from this?

We hope you can see just how interesting, challenging, and entrepreneurial the possibilities are when it comes to identifying and championing the very best work which is helping to build a net zero economy and a more sustainable way of life on our planet.

Just think, the more we push for this, the more work will be produced that answers these questions, the more we celebrate the right work, the greater the impact we can have on the issue that affects us all – climate change.

Judging the world's best work for sustainability impact

The following is an edit of an interview Matt conducted with Isabelle Quevilly, Meta, a juror of the SDG Lions at Cannes Lions 2023. She is also a Campaign Ad Net Zero judge, helping to shape the awards, and the chair of the sustainability category for the DMA Awards. In 2018, she led The People's Seat campaign to drive climate action for the United Nations UNFCCC at COP24. That campaign reached 1.3 billion people, and Sir David Attenborough delivered The People's message to the world's leaders on behalf of citizens worldwide. The campaign won two Cannes Lions, the WARC Grand Prix, two D&AD Pencils, DMA Best Use of Social Media and many more. She is well qualified to talk about what it takes to win the world's biggest awards for creativity in support of a sustainable future.

Firstly, please could you tell us a little bit about what the SDG Lions is?

Absolutely. The SDG Lions was created in 2018, in partnership with the United Nations. The aim is to recognize and reward work and solutions for systemic change against the UN's 17 sustainable development goals across people, planet, prosperity, peace and partnership for 2030. The main criteria for judging is impact with 40 per cent against the results, then 20 per cent idea, 20 per cent strategy, and 20 per cent execution. It is a very different Lions – with more weight on the impact towards achieving the SDGs.

What were the sorts of things coming through to help recognizing work that genuinely had a positive contribution to the SDGs?

For us, there were three things. The first one was the why, what's the purpose of this work? Is this showing any integrity with what the brand is doing anyway? Is it something genuine? The second was, is this something that can drive systemic change? Is this something new? The third was impact and scalability of the work. Can you see this work duplicated in many markets? Can this campaign make a difference for humanity's biggest problems?

That's quite a high bar, isn't it? Were there clear reasons we can learn from about the work that didn't win?

Yes. The first was if it was a prototype – not yet fully resolved, launched, or scaled. With 40 per cent of the marks linked to results, it is very difficult to sense whether a prototype can really have genuine impact for the SDGs. The second was if the problem was wrong. Sure, it was an important problem and a problem that needed solving, but it wasn't an SDG problem. What we've seen and is a bit disheartening is that it feels like SDG is a box ticked at the last minute when people enter, rather than work designed to progress the SDG – that's a tension that we could see. A lot of the work we awarded was also awarded in other categories.

I'd like to talk now about the Grand Prix winner by Mastercard, a campaign helping Ukrainians to resettle in Poland. When I think about the SDGs I tend to think about climate change, water or conscious consumption, but there's more to the SDGs than that, isn't there, so would you share a little bit more as to why it won and what you think we can learn from and build on?

I can tell you this was a unanimous decision in the room to select this piece of work. It is very aligned to Mastercard's purpose, to connect everyone to priceless possibilities. This is a company in a category that is probably not the most creative traditionally, and not one that would be transformative from a creative standpoint. So, to your question around how can this solve a climate problem? This was about refugees fleeing the war in Ukraine. However, we know fast displacement of population is going to only increase in the coming years. So, climate refugees are only just beginning to really appear, and we must ask, how are brands going to support this? It's super interesting to see the partnership between Mastercard, rental websites, the government and the local city councils, all coming together to pull data points that give refugees settling options. They were very effective recommendations on where to settle, and this shows when you see that 20 per cent of the refugees used this app to settle in Poland (mainly women and children, because the men were mobilized to fight). It's a huge amount of people involved and it's an easy solution to replicate and scale to other refugee crises. That's interestingly one of the criticisms the work has had – why stop at Ukrainian refugees in Poland? There is so much more potential in this idea. What is also super positive in terms of real impact is that it changed perceptions of what refugees bring to the country, and the GDP growth. You see the media saying, the refugees are amazing, they are helping our country. That's brilliant, because that's how we should always consider refugees and immigrants, something great for the country, not something to fear.

What I think is brilliant to hear you articulate is yes, essentially, the idea was dealing with a humanitarian crisis, (i.e., refugees fleeing Ukraine), but the logic is we're entering a period where there will be climate refugees and you are highlighting brands should prepare to support people. How will we deal with climate migration? In a way that's positive, constructive, that doesn't feed a negative narrative?

This is why Mastercard has done something quite impressive. You see a brand taking a position entirely aligned with their business, but also deliver value for society. That's how we need to look at the marketing dollars we're investing – can they work better for society?

More generally, what was the best of the work you saw coming through around climate action?

Specifically on climate action, my favourite piece of work was Prêt À Voter by Solar Impulse in the French market. They connected lawyers and activists to write laws ready to debate and vote for. Lots of people are putting forward policies to drive transformation but this has been very slow. So Solar Impulse wrote up the legislation for increased use of solar energy in France, for example, allowing solar panels on water. They got three laws voted and nine others being discussed. This can be scaled to any market, right? It doesn't need to be driven by political motivations. It doesn't need to take sides. It is effective, it can be debated, it can be acted upon. It's a brilliant idea for legislation.

I loved it. Anything to do with sustainability and climate action, we need to make it easy for people. Essentially what this did was make it easy for politicians to focus on the policy and the vote. And you're right, it is very clearly a scalable kind of mechanic to put into people's hands, you know, at the local level as well as the national level. Anything else catch your eye?

I really love the work that was coming from supply chain issues. It was interesting to see companies like PepsiCo (Lay's) and AbinBev (Corona) looking at their supply chain issues as an opportunity to create new more sustainable processes. For example, Lay's Biochar project. Most farmers in India currently burn the stumps in their fields which goes on to pollute Delhi with smoke and cause real problems. Lay's worked with local universities, local communities and the farmers to create a new chamber to safely burn the leftovers and turn it into biochar. The result is better farming, better soil, and better quality of production.

The role of a big brand and its influence on the supply chain to shift a whole way of doing business, even a bit, to make it more sustainable is so valuable – it feels like something that we'll probably see recognized more and more in awards?

I think we should see more of it. But also, the next step is probably for the marketing team to not be shy of using examples like this in their communications. We should not shy away from talking to consumers about initiatives having an impact.

We've had a comment on the Lay's India example. Yes, it's a creative winner, but isn't it better to turn the stumps on fields into fibre material rather than burn it? There is this constant weighing up when judging work, isn't there – to have room to recognize what's good currently and to continue to push things forward. I think this is a challenge for any judging – accepting what's good as of 2023 versus what we want by 2025 or by 2030. Did you have this sort of tension in the judging process – this is good, but is it good enough?

> Yes. I think it's progress over perfection. What's important is to see big companies trying to change being awarded for it and inspiring the competition to go even beyond. This is all about stimulating innovation, forcing people to have the conversation that creates change and I think that's where we are today. This is also about people; you must convert hundreds of years of heritage of a practice into use of a burning chamber and incinerator that creates the biochar to be used in the soil. That circularity is new, and I think there is always a trade-off to consider when you implement new ways of doing things.

I agree. If we're going to get sustainability embedded into every single award consideration, which ultimately is the end game here, we're going to have to find ways through that sort of tension between 'it's good today, but it's not good enough for the future'. This will be a big factor as we think about the future of awards and the biggest change around sustainability. As an industry we know how to evaluate and present work around commercial metrics, whether that's sales, brand awareness, competitive market share – these are all second nature to advertising professionals. It is not the same for sustainability metrics.

> We all have responsibilities to bring the question up… how can we get a better, more positive impact? We can all raise this when we talk about the brief with clients.

Do you think awards programmes will come under even more pressure if they recognize work that isn't obviously better for the planet, as well? I think it will be hard to defend something as creatively excellent if it can't also evidence it has been better for the planet as a result.

> I completely agree. There is a debate right now about the Effies which have selected three pieces of work as the best of the creative excellence and they're all for companies promoting meat-based food. People were quick to say, 'Is this

really what the world needs today?' We need to remember when we make a selection as a jury, we're sending a message to the world, this is what we want to see more of, this is great. You must ask yourself, is this really the message you want to send?

Embedding 'sustainability' into the heart of all advertising awards

Ascential, the owners of Cannes Lions, made the first step in 2023 by including a question about sustainability in every award entry. Entrants seeking further advice were invited to visit a special section providing guidance on the Ad Net Zero website. The question was voluntary, not mandatory, and any submitted information in the first year was not shared with the jurors. The principal purpose of adding the question in for the first time was to establish a benchmark. It was important to develop an understanding of just how much the advertising industry was considering sustainability in its work.

Steps have been made by other awards organizers. For example, the Data & Marketing Association in the UK included a Sustainability Award for the first time in its hugely popular and successful awards scheme, again modelled on Ad Net Zero. The British Arrows encouraged all award entries to use AdGreen as a means of providing data around the production of the work entered. Sky Media and Channel 4 both introduced the use of AdGreen as mandatory for any submissions to their Zero Footprint Fund and Million Pound Diversity Prize Award, respectively.

In 2023, we are still a way from every advertising and marketing services professional being able to submit the type of data we are aiming for. Most awards organizers are reliant on the volume of entries as a revenue stream. Barriers to entry, like a requirement to submit data that isn't available or accessible for some, will have an unintended consequence. So, a roadmap to make this happen is needed, one where year-by-year, the requirement for sustainability data and evidence is ratcheted up from voluntary for benchmarking purposes, to voluntary in return for additional points, to voluntary with penalties for no information supplied, to entirely mandatory.

Reducing the environmental impact of our industry's events

As we considered the role of awards in helping to drive progress, it became increasingly apparent that many awards were supported by in-person events, with significant carbon footprints of their own.

Not only are we asking our industry to reappraise what we mean by creative excellence, but we are also moving to a world where the *way* we celebrate creative excellence also needs to be reappraised.

This is most obvious in the industry's biggest events such as Cannes Lions, SXSW and the Advertising Week series which travels round the world each year. But there are a multitude of awards ceremonies and industry events run around the world which take place every week of the year, involving thousands and thousands of our professionals. Many of these are run by the biggest organizations in our industry – the agency holding groups, the tech companies, and the national and international trade associations. Advertising is a people business – we work in it because we are interested in people, what makes them tick and how we can connect with them on behalf of the companies and organizations we work for. They are vital for bringing the industry together to strengthen connections and collaborations.

Imagine the impact if best practice in sustainability were applied in all those events; hundreds of thousands of people in our industry would live those sustainable experiences and take away lessons for themselves each time, to apply in their own lives and through the work they make.

As we developed this area further to establish best practice for the advertising industry's awards events, conferences and gatherings, we identified a like-minded partner in the events industry – an organization called isla which had built its own net zero plan for the world of events and experiential campaigns.

For the avoidance of doubt, we are only focused on the B2B events run within our advertising industry here. There could be a book written on the decarbonization of the world's events and experiential industry. Maybe there will be.

Introducing isla

Describing itself as an action-driven network, isla is an independent body founded by events professionals and industry leaders, to help events practitioners confidently and consistently deliver sustainable events. Its focus is on the core areas of sector decarbonization and circularity. It supports knowledge-share with peers in the event industry, offers training to help people develop the skills necessary to act and report, setting targets and tracking progress.

There are two reasons why isla is of particular interest to advertising and marketing professionals involved in industry events. Firstly, it offers a free universal best practice framework for the event industry – proseed – and, secondly, it offers a platform called TRACE which helps to measure and minimize carbon at live, hybrid and digital events.

About proseed

The isla team help you think through the many facets of organizing and running an event. Proseed begins by asking if you are an event organizer, a venue, a caterer, or a production supplier. It then helps you consider factors such as energy usage, food & water, travel and transport, and production, depending on your position in the event's production and the influence you can have over its various elements.

Like all elements of our approach, choice of energy and its usage is critical. The same principles apply for events with those involved in ad production (particularly around set builds), packaging, branding and staff travel. The biggest area of difference is the consideration of the impact of the audience involved in the event and what steps can be taken to reduce that too. A consistent point for consideration is travel and transport options, so truly researching and understanding your audience's desire to be there in person rather than connecting remotely, will inform the way you shape your event in a way that is both sustainable and engaging.

About TRACE

TRACE is a carbon calculator that has been designed for use by all events organizers. The isla team has developed it with all parts of the events ecosystem in mind; in-house teams, events agencies, and beyond the world of B2B advertising and marketing into exhibition organizers and festival owners. It offers measurement capabilities for local and global events and metrics for reporting, which include:

- Emissions from venue energy and temporary power sources
- Impact of event location on travel and accommodation for attendees and crew
- Food and beverage emission impacts for attendees and crew, as well as the waste footprint
- How choice of materials in the event production impact carbon emissions and helps track the lifecycle of these elements
- Production transport footprints from trucking to couriers and overseas freight.

The benefits of using a tool like TRACE are manifest if you're involved in the production of events for advertising and marketing services professionals across our industry. You can plan your event and make estimates of carbon emissions and waste volumes before going on-site; you can understand the implications of different design choices to help make decisions that reduce impact; and you can capture data ready for use in compliance reporting.

Reducing emissions through awards and events: summary

If you are reading this and you are involved in some way with an awards scheme within our industry, think about how you can embed sustainability into the way you are trying to find and celebrate creative excellence. You have tremendous power and influence to shape the work our industry makes. Don't just add one award for sustainability; think about how you can make sustainability a factor in every award and how you can use your awards data to track progress. Help yourself to the template we have published in this chapter. At the same time, in a Sustainable Advertising industry, every event our industry runs will be sensitive to its environmental impact, taking every measure possible to reduce emissions and waste. Review the tools available and consider what is now rapidly becoming best practice when it comes to a sustainable event experience for all.

References

The British Arrows. (2023) *Rules of Entry*. Available at: https://cdn2.assets-servd. host/periodic-openbill/production/files/BA23-RULES-OF-ENTRY-FINAL.pdf (archived at https://perma.cc/RC4Q-BM6Q) (Accessed August 2023)

Campaign Ad Net Zero Awards. (2023). Available at: https://www. campaignadnetzeroawards.com/ (archived at https://perma.cc/RL9S-JBB2)

Cannes Lions. (2023) *Cannes Lions embeds sustainability across the Lions awards in 2023*. Available at: https://www.canneslions.com/news/cannes-lions-embeds-sustainability-across-the-lions-awards-in-2023 (archived at https://perma.cc/ Q65A-35AF)

Channel 4. (2023) *Channel 4's 2023 Diversity in Advertising Award challenges UK advertisers on portrayal of LGBTQIA+ communities*. Available at: https://www. channel4.com/press/news/channel-4s-2023-diversity-advertising-award-challenges-uk-advertisers-portrayal-lgbtqia (archived at https://perma.cc/ Q72Q-YBP8)

isla. (2023) *Here to accelerate the event industry transition to a sustainable future*. Available at: https://weareisla.co.uk/ (archived at https://perma.cc/U7W6-6XTJ)

Johnson, M. (2021) Mediashotz. *DMA Awards' Sustainability gong to reward carbon conscious campaigns*. Available at: https://mediashotz.co.uk/dma-awards-sustainability-gong-to-reward-carbon-conscious-campaigns/ (archived at https://perma.cc/3MNS-UQ7C)

proseed. (2023) *The event industry's first universal best practice framework*. Available at: https://proseed.events/ (archived at https://perma.cc/E6JJ-TR7N)

Sky. (2023) *2023 Winners of £2million Sky Zero Footprint Fund revealed*. Available at: https://www.skygroup.sky/article/2023-winners-of-2million-sky-zero-footprint-fund-revealed- (archived at https://perma.cc/KCV3-AW22) (Accessed August 2023)

TRACE. (2023) *Reduce your event carbon footprint with TRACE by isla*. Available at: https://traceyour.events/ (archived at https://perma.cc/M7VH-6NZA)

Meta. (2023) Interview with Isabelle Quevilly, Meta. Conducted July 11.

09

The big sustainable behaviour change challenge

In this chapter, we will review the legislative and political decisions that are powering the opportunities for advertising and marketing services, and the perspective of politicians. We will then turn our attention to best thinking around behaviour change in support of a sustainable future, what lessons might be applied to increase impact, and also consider how this all adds up to a compelling business case for advertisers.

Political and legislative decisions

Let's begin with the politics, as political decisions will have a huge impact on what is needed from advertising and marketing services, and the sectors they will support. A series of far-reaching and legislative decisions are already shaping how and where advertising will be needed. There will, no doubt, be more after we go to press too.

2022 Inflation Reduction Act

The US Government's Inflation Reduction Act (IRA) in late 2022 has caused the most waves. The Inflation Reduction Act contains $500 billion in new spending and tax breaks that aim to boost clean energy, reduce healthcare costs, and increase tax revenues (McKinsey, 2022). For example, the $11.7 billion committed in the act is described by the US Department of Energy as 'the single largest investment in climate and energy in American history, enabling America to tackle the climate crisis, advancing environmental justice, securing America's position as a world leader in domestic clean energy manufacturing, and putting the United States on a pathway to achieving the Biden Administration's climate goals, including a net-zero economy by 2050' (US Government, 2022).

2023 Green Deal Industrial Plan

In February 2023, the EU responded with its Green Deal Industrial Plan, focusing on four pillars: a predictable and simplified regulatory environment; speeding up access to finance; enhancing skills; and open trade for resilient supply chains.

When launching the plan, Ursula von der Leyen, President of the European Commission, said, 'We have a once in a generation opportunity to show the way with speed, ambition, and a sense of purpose to secure the EU's industrial lead in the fast-growing net-zero technology sector. Europe is determined to lead the clean tech revolution. For our companies and people, it means turning skills into quality jobs and innovation into mass production, thanks to a simpler and faster framework. Better access to finance will allow our key clean tech industries to scale up quickly' (EU, 2023).

The EU estimates that 35–40 per cent of all jobs could be affected by the green transition. This is seismic.

Other programmes

Another significant American policy is the Energy Efficiency and Conservation Block Grant (EECBG) Program, first announced in November 2022 by the Biden/Harris Administration, through the US Department of Energy (DOE). This funding of $550 million dollars has been made available to support communities across the US to develop local programming and deploy clean energy technologies to cut emissions and reduce consumers' energy costs.

Other markets are sure to follow, including China, India, the UK, Australia as well as much of Africa. As demonstrated by US and EU's respective press releases, and the repeated use of 'lead' and 'leader', countries will be participating in an increasingly intense competition to be considered at the forefront of the net zero economy. And wherever there is competition, there will be a need for advertising and marketing services to help businesses promote innovation, market new products and services, and make attractive the new behaviours that will be essential to a more sustainable net zero economy.

Let's consider this for a moment. That's potentially thousands upon thousands of advertising and marketing briefs to help explain and accelerate changes ready to be unlocked from these programmes which are being encouraged with massive financial incentives.

The brief for behaviour change

So, what's the brief for advertising and marketing to truly shift behaviours at scale? In August 2021, the Tony Blair Institute for Global Change published a paper that's worth a closer look. *Planes, Homes and Automobiles: The Role of Behaviour Change in Delivering Net Zero*, written by Brett Meyer and Tim Lord, explores how the pathway to net zero has two common themes. The first theme is that the next phase of transition will be more costly, more visible, and will carry a greater, more obvious impact. This will be seen through the changes that we need to make in how we produce and use energy, how we move around, the buildings we live in, and our environment and countryside. The second theme is that these changes, and therefore the goal of net zero, cannot rely solely on technological solutions. There will be significant behaviour change needed from people (and from a political point of view, voters). This political point is critical for the authors as they believe the changes required will need active support from voters to be enacted by government.

The report argues that citizens should be involved in designing solutions, and to do that they will need to have a better understanding of the changes that will be needed. This approach, if successful, would enable greater political courage, lead to increased deployment of technology to cut costs and help make net zero behaviours a social norm.

The authors of the report highlight three different types of change that will be needed:

- Technology changes: changes to technology and fuel that have no impact on behaviour and require no behaviour change. These might be low-carbon fuels, instead of fossil fuels for industrial production or electricity generation.

- Behaviour changes: changes at both an individual and societal level such as flying less or eating less meat.

- Combination changes: changes which combine technology and behaviour change. For example, the use of electric vehicles versus petrol cars or heat pumps versus gas boilers.

Meyer and Lord argue that these changes have been heavily politicized and require citizens to make significant personal behavioural changes to a degree and of a complexity that has rarely been asked of people in recent decades. The report includes a very clear and helpful table of the six key behavioural changes required for net zero and sets out targets and a timeframe for achieving them, as seen in Figure 9.1.

As the authors say:

> 'It is not necessary for everyone to stop flying – in fact, we need to reduce average kilometres travelled per person by plane by a maximum of around 6 per cent between 2019 and 2035. We do not all need to become vegetarian; on the CCC's pathway, meat and dairy consumption reduces by around 20 per cent in 15 years. We do not need to stop using cars – kilometres travelled per driver need to fall by only around 5 per cent. This is not, of course, to argue that there may not be other reasons to advocate for more significant behaviour change – but it is not required to meet net zero.'

Perhaps there is broad agreement across the political spectrum in many countries (notwithstanding the polarizing views of the political extremes) on what needs to be done, but also on the electoral difficulty around how to do it. This leads to too little change and the loss of the time to act. And the less time there is to act the more radical policy decisions will have to be. While a rational human would act sooner to prevent catastrophe at a lower cost,

FIGURE 9.1 The six key behavioural changes required for net zero, Tony Blair Institute

	Behavioural change	Change, 2019-2035
Homes and consumption	Install low-carbon heating and energy-efficiency measures	~40% of homes on low-carbon heating systems
		All new heating systems are low carbon
		Accelerated installation of energy efficiency
	Reducing waste to landfill through reduced consumption/increased reuse and recycling	Remainig waste per person (after recycling, composting) down 37%
Transport	Increased walking, cycling, public transport in place of car usage	Car km per driver down 4%
	Purchase/use zero-emissions vehicle	~60% car fleet is battery electric
		All new vehicles are battery electric
	Reduce international travel and domestic flights	Plane km per person down 6%
Diet	Reduced meat and dairy consumption	Meat and dairy consumption down by 20%

the average minister might choose to do nothing to upset voters and accept the higher cost, in all senses, of disaster emergency relief when the case would have no opposition. This is why citizens and businesses should act, and frame those changes for ourselves.

While the authors claim that 'we do not all need' to make these sweeping changes, we cannot rely on 100 per cent of the population to be willing or able to make the average changes advised. If those who are prepared to make change only settle for the average required, for instance reducing their kilometres travelled by plane by the stated 6 per cent, the target will never be achieved in total (especially considering the potential for population growth). Instead, those who are able and willing will be making bigger changes in line with what's possible and affordable. For example, taking the train when travelling for holidays is (unfortunately) the expensive option in most cases, and switching to home-cooked food using local produce can be prohibitively costly for some. But if we have the capability to make these changes, it is our responsibility to do so. In other words, everyone should be doing everything they can; not what is required of them.

Our industry can help support the big changes needed in energy consumption and usage, can add appeal to the changes in diet choice and make the case for an aspirational and enjoyable life with different travel decisions.

How to build a net zero society

While at Unilever, Seb worked with David Halpern and the Behaviour Insights Team (BIT). The team was founded in 2010 and has grown from a seven-person unit at the heart of the UK government to a global social purpose company of over 200 professionals across many offices around the world. BIT has incredible knowledge about behaviour change built up through more than 1000 projects to date, including 700 or more randomized controlled trials in dozens of countries. In December 2021, it became wholly owned by innovation charity Nesta. Its mission remains the same: to use evidenced-based insights regarding human behaviour to bring about positive change and help people by developing better systems, policies, products and services.

This is not a book about behavioural economics or 'nudge' theory – there are brilliant books already written on this topic. Understanding how and why people really change what they do, and stick to it, is mission critical. In the next chapter, we will look to identify some of the magic ingredients to foster successful sustainable behaviour change.

How to build a Net Zero society, published by BIT in January 2023, sets out clearly the challenge citizens and politicians face.

> 'Our economy, infrastructure, norms, and media environment are not well designed for those who wish to live sustainably, but without great personal effort or compromise (that is, almost everyone). This may be why some – politicians included – recoil from the idea of widespread "behaviour change", either disavowing what they see as the necessary means (a nanny-state telling people what to do) and/or the ends (an abstemious existence, sacrificing modern conveniences).'

Despite the insufficiency of more sustainable behaviour so far, it's important to overcome the idea that it's impossible to change citizens' behaviours at the scale and speed required.

Some of the most interesting points in the January 2023 paper, *How to build a Net Zero Society*, discuss barriers and ways to overcome them. Consumers want to change, say BIT, stating that 9 in 10 want to make more sustainable choices. But they find it too hard due to information, cost, or convenience barriers. To focus on 'behaviour' is not to imply individuals have the greatest burden of responsibility. An evidence-based and sophisticated understanding of behaviour reveals the interplay between individuals making choices (downstream) and their choice (midstream), which exist as they do due to a system of commercial incentives, regulation and institutional leadership (upstream). There is a critical role for businesses to make green choices easier, more attractive, more socially normative, and timely – the 'midstream' interventions. There is equally a critical role for the Government to make 'upstream' interventions using its regulatory and tax-setting powers to align commercial incentives with greener consumption (thus incentivizing businesses to do their bit).

While there is clearly an important role for informing and encouraging direct individual action, there needs to be greater emphasis on building choice environments which enable greener choices. The biggest impacts of all will come from aligning commercial incentives and regulations with sustainability, in ways which in turn create greener choice environments for consumers and citizens, at scale. That way, we can all consume sustainably by default, and the burden of proactive 'behaviour change' is lifted.

The key role for communications and public engagement is to inform and steer people towards worthwhile steps (given widespread misperceptions of which actions to prioritize). These small 'stepping-stone actions' lead towards the bigger changes that will make the difference overall. The BIT also points out the importance of engaging in two-way dialogue to ensure legitimate interests are heard and that the transition is fair and benefits from widespread public support.

One of the most important points made by the BIT is the utmost importance of communications and the support it provides during moments of change or disruption. Providing tailored communications and relevant support at timely moments makes acting easier for individuals and increases the likelihood of return on investment. We may be more able to make home energy improvements when moving home; more likely to change our travel habits when moving home or job; more likely to adopt sustainable diets when starting university and learning to independently shop and cook, and so on. This approach is also advocated by WRAP (2022) in their citizen behaviour change work for campaigns like *Love Food Hate Waste*. BIT has a word of advice for NGOs too: develop campaigns, content and other communications that make green actions salient, clear, familiar, appealing, normalized and easy to understand and do (rather than just talking about the climate threat).

Matt spent some time with Professor David Halpern, the Chief Executive of the Behavioural Insights Team. He was the first Research Director of the Institute of Government, the Chief Analyst at the Prime Minister's Strategy Unit between 2001 and 2007 and has led the team at BIT since its inception in 2010. Matt asked him what he thought our industry should be doing in support of a more sustainable, net zero society. He explained how advertising in the context of a net zero society was about helping people to make better choices for themselves and suggested there were three areas for people working in our industry to consider.

The first was to think about how we avoid the promotion of detrimental behaviours. David provided the example of an alcohol campaign which might once have made the person appear more attractive if they drink more, and how organizations like The Portman Group have been established to tackle this as a set of standards and expectation within the industry. The group operates a Code of Practice in the Naming, Packaging and Promotion of Alcohol Drinks. His suggestion was that there should be a place within advertising to call out these behaviours and make interventions. Put simply, if we see an ad promoting behaviours that don't seem to support a more sustainable way of life, how does a courageous leader call that out?

The second area was encouraging our industry to focus more and more on the promotion of sustainable brands. His logic was that we want the green brands, the better brands, to win, to gain market share and to succeed. That's our industry's role to help make that happen, and to happen at pace.

The third was around what he termed 'shrouding problems': helping people to understand what is good, what is bad and what is best when it comes to sustainability. He pointed to history and the establishment of Lloyd's Register in the middle of the 18th century, which was established to review the seaworthiness of ships trading between the UK and the Americas and provide a standard for people to make informed decisions against.

This principle can be followed through to today with formal and informal standards like kite marks and TUV, Good Housekeeping or Which? that people can refer to, but this type of comprehensive standard for sustainability is yet to exist. David also warned about the risk of the term 'eco' potentially meaning 'not quite as good' and this was a risk the industry needed to recognize as it helps sustainable businesses succeed. We have a common interest in developing ways of signalling why a product or service is genuinely more sustainable than its competitors. The conclusion of our conversation was that the collective power of advertising and marketing is a tremendous opportunity to make the world a better place.

The challenges for people to adopt new behaviours

The BIT team's Head of Energy and Sustainability, Toby Park, also shared the COM-B model, developed by Professor Susan Richie and colleagues from University City London in 2011. The model explains how people need sufficient **Capability, Opportunity, and Motivation** to adopt a Behaviour (which could be a lifestyle change or a new product, including technology).

Toby discussed how advertising could help to improve capability, opportunity and motivation and he identified several things for us to consider when it comes to the promotion of sustainable behaviours, including:

- How can the advertising help make the behaviour aspirational?
- How can the advertising help normalize the behaviour and allow people to identify with it?
- How can it raise awareness and understanding of the behaviour and provide knowledge about it?

- How can it draw attention to the behaviour and make it front of mind at the right moments?
- How can it help to make the behaviours feel more familiar?
- How can it show that the behaviour is something you can do?
- How can the benefits of the behaviour be highlighted and used for motivation?
- How can the advertising be targeted and tailored according to the audience and their values?
- How can it inform a broader narrative which improves the trust and the credibility of green technology, products and services that support a sustainable future?

All of this is in addition to addressing the challenge of price and convenience/access which are clear barriers for anyone looking to shift from one type of behaviour to another.

We also touched on the design of the advertising, and three key elements to consider:

- The timing, particularly targeting those pivotal moments of change such as a house move, starting a new job, or beginning a family
- The pride in the behaviour, as opposed to trying to guilt people into it
- The need to highlight the solution, not the problem.

For example, BIT's research about the challenge of encouraging adoption of heat pumps has shown that several benefits outperform the environment message, such as the comfort, the always on ambient nature of the temperature, the security of the energy supply and the increase in property value as a benefit of installation. It's clear we don't need to always talk about the environment to bring about more sustainable behaviours. In fact, to drive exponential adoption of more sustainable options, it is sometimes best to avoid it entirely.

Demand side: the business case for action

In May 2022, Meta published its Sustainability Advertising research report produced in collaboration with Accenture. It's a good summary of the growing demand for sustainable products and services. It highlights how consumers are becoming more environmentally conscious, with 65 per cent either very concerned or extremely concerned about the current state of the environment, leading to new purchasing habits (Meta, 2022). Alongside this report, Meta also published the Meta Sustainability Playbook providing tips and guidance on how brands can advertise authentically about their sustainability offerings to people on digital media platforms.

The report suggests that many people believe brands can support them more to live sustainably. To help people find environmentally sustainable products, brands can do more to make people aware that more sustainable offerings exist. The report states that while more and more people are reading information about products' environmental and sustainability credentials, most still do not feel they have enough information about how ethical or sustainable products really are, and this lack of authentic sustainability information is impacting the likelihood of purchase. Unsurprisingly, the authors suggest that social media is a good place to convey this information. Citing the platform's own data, they share that there was 4.2 times more engagement with posts including sustainability hashtags and 7.7 times more interactions with sustainability related posts compared with other content posted by e-commerce brands. Brands can address a real need for people by illustrating how to embed sustainability in their daily lives and educate them on the impact of their purchasing decisions. The brands that communicate authentically about sustainability can gain relevance with an emerging group of customers open to paying more for products that are better for the environment.

Meta presents the example of its work with Asket, a Swedish apparel business, that sells timeless, long-lasting men's clothing. It tested a range of ads during the early phase of a Facebook campaign and found Asket's best performing ad highlighted the company's supply chain traceability and garment production process. This ad was named the 'Ethos of Transparency' ad and, according to Meta's report, went on to generate 50 per cent increase in number of purchases, generating $10 million gross merchandise sales through DTC channels supporting 150 per cent average annual growth from 2015–2020.

The writers also suggest that adopting authentic sustainable advertising can help to achieve stronger financial performance. They concluded that high ESG performance correlated with higher financial performance based on data from Accenture that reviewed the operating margin, growth in operating profit and total shareholder return of a mix of companies against their ESG performance.

Meta's report summarizes four simple but essential components of an effective sustainability communication strategy. The first two are that a brand should set and deliver sustainability commitments; and then communicate their sustainability journey to achieve them by being transparent about operations with externally verified claims. The writers also remind advertisers not to gloss over in-depth understanding of the mindset, wants and needs that put prospective buyers at the heart of campaign strategies. This will help provide them with easy-to-understand and relevant sustainability information and help educate them on the impact of their purchasing decisions.

The business case for demand beyond the niche

As we consider the role of advertising in a sustainable or net zero economy, we need to think about brands' approach to segmentation and pricing. Brands often launch sustainable products at a premium, presumably based on the current low-volume high-cost environment that comes with new products and innovation. However, to drive the sustainable economy at scale, companies will have to plan to make their sustainable products more mainstream, and with that the possibility of more scale to deliver lower unit costs. It will take leadership intent and supply chain planning. What we want to explore is the cost of inaction or self-limiting beliefs and encourage design for mass-market.

To help here, we will reference a report published by Kantar: *Are brands failing their customers on sustainability?* (Kantar, 2023). The report sets out data which shows people believe there is shared responsibility for solving the climate crisis across government (82 per cent), general public (75 per cent), companies (64 per cent), international organizations (59 per cent) and the media (34 per cent).

The findings were critical of what companies are doing so far, with just 14 per cent of people believing that businesses are being ambitious enough, and nearly 2 in 5 people believing that businesses are making the climate crisis worse.

The report challenges business to consider 5 areas:

1 Pricing assumptions

Kantar looked at the products most often bought by sustainably minded consumers in four major European markets and noticed that they sell at a significant premium to category averages. It highlights the problem that sustainability has been positioned as a premium proposition. In Kantar's report, 68 per cent of people said that products that are better for the environment and society are more expensive. This approach will delay the broad-scale uptake of more sustainable products.

2 Think differently about pricing the offer

In the report, Kantar argues that if everything sustainable is priced as a kind of luxury, it will never become mass market. Yet, they are seeing more and more research showing that there is a mass audience for sustainable products and messages.

3 Think differently about costs

Kantar challenges the notion that decarbonizing supply chains is expensive, citing a World Economic Forum study conducted with BCG in 2021 which found that, it is not as expensive as often assumed, adding only 1–4 per cent to the consumer end price for the six sectors examined.

4 Broaden the target market

Kantar splits the sustainability customer base across four groups: 13 per cent are Dismissers, 29 per cent are Actives, while 24 per cent are Believers and 35 per cent are Considerers. Fifty-nine per cent of people fall into the categories of Considerers and Believers. These are people open to sustainability – one is more likely to act on sustainability but lacks belief it makes a difference; the other believes but needs to see others acting too. Kantar suggests this is evidence that evidence and normalization are important. Companies must communicate genuinely sustainable features and provide more accessible price points to address this significant mainstream group of shoppers.

5 Innovate with sustainability as standard

Finally, Kantar says that sustainable innovation means designing with sustainable principles built in from the start, considering the materials and resources right through to the behaviour changes, new business models and routes to market.

In our conversations with the Kantar team for this book, they highlighted the risk for companies if they do not step into the sustainability market fast, and before their competitors. They highlighted the example of one global FMCG company which was lagging on product engagement around sustainability with Actives (29 per cent of their target audience) and in the process missing out on an estimated $1.3 billion in sales annually. That's the risk of not accelerating into sustainability.

For anyone working in advertising and marketing services, you must be ready to make the sustainable business case to go for the bigger market, and not settle for a premium niche. Others will go for scale economics creating competitive commercial jeopardy for brands which don't move fast enough or begin to get the reputation for not being sustainable.

The business case: financial value created by brands' reputations for sustainability

One way of underlining the importance of brand performance in the context of a net zero economy is to place a financial value on its reputation for sustainability. The global trade association, the International Advertising Association, worked with brand valuation consultancy, Brand Finance, to do exactly that with a new study, 'Sustainability Perceptions Index', which it published at Davos in January 2023 (Brand Finance, 2023). In the index, Brand Finance analysed the relative importance of sustainability as a driver of value for brands and revealed major global businesses such as Amazon, Tesla, Apple and Alphabet each have billions of dollars intrinsically linked to careful reputation management of their public commitment to sustainability.

For example, Tesla was seen as one of the most sustainable brands with sustainability worth 26.9 per cent of the EV manufacturer's brand value – more than a quarter of its market worth linked to people's perceptions of the company's commitment to deliver on its sustainability plans. The Sustainability Perceptions Index is based on research of the attitudes of over 100,000 members of the public from over 36 countries about over 4,000 brands. What we see for the first time in this study is the financial value tied to a reputation for acting sustainably, critical to a company's success in a sustainable economy. It highlights just how much financial value the world's biggest brands have riding on their sustainability plans.

The full list in the Brand Finance report covers hundreds of organizations, with the likes of IKEA and Patagonia performing well across a wide range of markets, Lush and The Body Shop scoring highly in the UK, Yves Rocher and tyre brand Michelin standing out in France, and the cosmetics company Natura scoring well in Brazil.

In addition, the Brand Finance research revealed consumers are likely to be reasonably trusting of brands' sustainability related communication, 62 per cent believing brands' sustainability claims. However, nearly 4 in 5 consumers said they had reduced use of a brand after learning it acted in an unsustainable way. The team behind the study used this statistic to reinforce the need to get the communications right about sustainability – to stay quiet about sustainability credentials is a missed opportunity, but to overclaim carries the risk of hundreds of millions of dollars of reputational damage.

The ability to place a financial value on the sustainability factor in a company's reputation with consumers neatly highlights why getting the management of sustainability advertising and marketing is critical as the sustainable net zero economy is built, and the financial risks if you get it wrong.

IAA Global's Managing Director Dagmara Szulce, one of the driving forces behind the study, explained that the Sustainability Perceptions Index aimed to 'harness businesses' profit motive, moving them past the point where they see sustainability as a "hygiene factor", to a point of rapid, concerted action.'

Applying advertising's superpower to the big sustainable behaviour change challenge

Advertising has a superpower. Not in the sense of Captain Marvel, Superman or She-Hulk, but in its ability to normalize and frame choices, and create real change. Matt mentions Uncle Ben's famous line in Spiderman at this point: 'with great power comes great responsibility' (Lee, 1962), to which Seb blurts out that it was Jesus who said that. And Winston Churchill. And some of the leaders of the French Revolution, too. Either way, it's an adage that has significant resonance, a near-universally accepted principle, and lies at the heart of our manifesto for sustainable advertising and marketing.

Never has there been a better moment for responsible leaders in marketing and advertising to mobilize the industry's superpower for good. Our industry has the power to help people become aware and interested in all manner of products, and take up new lifestyle choices and behaviours. Do we currently do that responsibly and, if not, how we can do that with increased responsibility as we tackle the climate emergency? What an opportunity.

We can easily highlight examples of responsible advertising across different parts of our economy and society, but it's difficult to argue that it's ubiquitous, or that it's intrinsic to every piece of advertising we see. Maybe that's never going to be possible, but our manifesto to make advertising and marketing a force for good aims for that greater application of responsibility if we are to achieve the goal of Sustainable Advertising. Our goal to increase exponentially the volume of campaigns supporting a sustainable product, service, or behaviour and to make those campaigns as effective and appealing as possible, delivering changes in behaviour at scale. All to decarbonize the economy, support regenerative nature, and reduce waste for the true benefit of all citizens. To do this, there need to be shifts such as from fossil fuels to renewable energy, from single use and disposable products to longer-lasting biodegradable and repairable ones, or to a higher proportion of plant-based food. Advertising has the proven power to create such a shift in behaviours, moving customers from one type of product or service to another.

To achieve that, there needs to be both a simultaneous shift in advertising (and its media budgets) towards work that promotes better, more sustainable solutions. It also requires an increase in the effectiveness of advertising to change behaviours, raising more campaigns to the level of the best. We call on the courageous leaders to make these behaviour changes: make sure that the work you're involved in is helping achieve that goal. If it isn't, perhaps ask yourself and your colleagues why the work is being made. There is a fundamental shift taking place at the heart of advertising. The best work that our industry is now producing is no longer solely focused on achieving the best sales, but also achieving better results for the planet and its people, and there needs to be a lot more of it. James Murphy, former Advertising Association Chair, and now founder of New Commercial Arts, said it well when the AA's Council met back in summer 2019: 'our industry needs to learn how to sell *better*'.

While it is crucial that addressing the industry's own emissions are executed diligently and thoroughly (not least for credibility and leaving no stone unturned), it is advertising's effect on people's behaviour by selling *better* that will have a far greater impact on global waste, pollution and GHG reduction.

The big sustainable behaviour change challenge: summary

Knowledge is growing about the big behaviour changes that need to happen in countries around the world as governments, investors, corporates and NGOs make informed decisions to support a more sustainable future. This means the challenge for our industry will be to create awareness, desirability and social norming at scale for the key choices around energy, travel, and food, shifting critical sustainable sectors of the economy from niche to mass. With the insights of behavioural science, and the emerging evidence that the business opportunity is out there, are you clear on where our industry can make a real difference? Can you see the commercial benefits ahead for you and your business if you do? Take the information in this chapter and apply it as you consider how you develop and respond to advertising briefs in order to effect the biggest behaviour change possible.

References

2022, Meta, *Sustainability Advertising Playbook*. Available at: https://scontent-man2-1.xx.fbcdn.net/v/t39.8562-6/319179002_824261751995332_953837592008563924_n.pdf/Sustainability_Advertising_Playbook_final_2022.pdf?_nc_cat=111&ccb=1-7&_nc_sid=ad8a9d&_nc_ohc=3oGVlbUxQGUAX_mJulI&_nc_ht=scontent-man2-1.xx&oh=00_AfC28D_nmfUgQ-VJzeMPC1GngUPdnSVCYqN5iVuJVY57oQ&oe=64ED778B (archived at https://perma.cc/E5V9-HYPX)

2022, Meta, *Sustainability Advertising Research Report*. Available at: https://scontent-man2-1.xx.fbcdn.net/v/t39.8562-6/320372781_1472512736492237_7046521443905678675_n.pdf/Sustainability_Research_Report_final_2022.pdf?_nc_cat=111&ccb=1-7&_nc_sid=ad8a9d&_nc_ohc=Jgzav2rvoiMAX9-OlHY&_nc_ht=scontent-man2-1.xx&oh=00_AfCgEvGRZphaZiywqZxU_CWRU6FdZv_DyndV6sYRy3rW4A&oe=64EDF66B (archived at https://perma.cc/6V7J-ACCD)

2023, Interview with Professor David Halpern, CEO, BIT.

Badlam, J, Cox, J, et al (2022) *The Inflation Reduction Act: Here's what's in it.*

Energy.gov. (2022) *Energy Efficiency and Conservation Block Grant Program.* [Online] Available at: https://www.energy.gov/scep/energy-efficiency-and-conservation-block-grant-program (archived at https://perma.cc/MA5K-Q49D)

Energy.gov. (2022) *Inflation Reduction Act of 2022.* [Online] Available at: https://www.energy.gov/lpo/inflation-reduction-act-2022 (archived at https://perma.cc/S4BY-7F2K)

Energy.gov. (2022) *Investing in America*. [Online] Available at: https://www.energy.gov/investing-in-america (archived at https://perma.cc/T29L-S94H)

European Union. (2023) *The Green Deal Industrial Plan: putting Europe's net-zero industry in the lead*. European Commission. February 2023. Available at: https://ec.europa.eu/commission/presscorner/detail/en/ip_23_510 (archived at https://perma.cc/Z6LY-5XWN)

Haigh, B. (2023) *Sustainability Perceptions Index 2023*. Brand Finance & International Advertising Association. [Online] Available at: https://brandirectory.com/reports/sustainability-index-2023 (archived at https://perma.cc/SX6B-FZ2Z)

Kantar. (2023) *Are brands failing their customers on sustainability?* [Online] Available at: https://www.kantar.com/campaigns/are-brands-failing-their-customers-on-sustainability (archived at https://perma.cc/H62U-ZMLG)

Lloyds Register. (2023) *Home*. [Online] Available at: https://www.lr.org/en/ (archived at https://perma.cc/9XT9-FFZS)

Lord, T; Meyer, B. (2021) *Planes, Homes and Automobiles: The Role of Behaviour Change in Delivering Net Zero*. Tony Blair Institute For Global Change. August 2021. [Online] Available at: https://www.institute.global/insights/climate-and-energy/planes-homes-and-automobiles-role-behaviour-change-delivering-net-zero (archived at https://perma.cc/F3GB-SNEV)

McKinsey & Company. (2022) [Online] Available at: https://www.mckinsey.com/industries/public-sector/our-insights/the-inflation-reduction-act-heres-whats-in-it (archived at https://perma.cc/63TE-GCUB)

The Behavioural Insights Team. (2023) *About Us*. [Online] Available at: https://www.bi.team/about-us-2/ (archived at https://perma.cc/H9ZW-8PAR)

The Behavioural Insights Team. (2023) *Home*. [Online] Available at: https://www.bi.team/ (archived at https://perma.cc/3SX3-EDJF)

The Behavioural Insights Team. (2023) *How to build a Net Zero society*. [Online] Available at: https://www.bi.team/publications/how-to-build-a-net-zero-society/ (archived at https://perma.cc/2D79-UH55)

The Decision Lab. (2023) *The COM-B Model for Behaviour Change*. [Online] Available at: https://thedecisionlab.com/reference-guide/organizational-behavior/the-com-b-model-for-behavior-change (archived at https://perma.cc/R2FU-MUCE)

The Portman Group. (2023) *Code of Practice in the Naming, Packaging and Promotion of Alcohol Drinks*. [Online] Available at: https://www.portmangroup.org.uk/codes-of-practice/?_gl=1*srp0gp*_up*MQ..*_ga*MTgzODA5ODIyMS4xNjkyOTUyNDg3*_ga_E75LNN4D72*MTY5Mjk1MjQ4Ni4xLjAuMTY5Mjk1MjQ4Ni4wLjAuMA (archived at https://perma.cc/K8EX-VJBT)

The Portman Group. (2023) *Home*. [Online] Available at: https://www.portmangroup.org.uk/ (archived at https://perma.cc/4ULN-PYED)

10

Sustainable behaviour change: the magic ingredients

What is clear from our review so far is that any big shifts in people's behaviour at scale will need to begin with a forensic understanding of how people make one difficult decision at a time – or don't. In this chapter we first reflect on climate change advertising campaigns before looking at the BIT's models for behaviour change, before identifying some of the magic ingredients from recently published studies that shed light on how and why people actually change their behaviour. Our hope is that understanding what motivates (and doesn't motivate) different people will help us draw out the main constituents of repeatable models for change.

What can we learn from the past 20 years of climate change advertising campaigns?

It's sobering to reflect on just how many advertising campaigns from NGOs and some brands have run over the past 20–30 years, all trying to raise the issue of climate change and the increasingly negative impact of our way of life on this planet we call home. At the Ad Net Zero Global Summit 2022, there was a stimulating presentation by Isa Kurata, of ACT Responsible, and Thomas Kolster a.k.a. Mr Goodvertising which looked at the story of environmental advertising in more detail. ACT stands for Advertising Community Together and is an international non-profit organization, co-founded by Isa. Its goal: to inspire, promote and unite the advertising communication industry to share good practices on social responsibility and sustainable development. Thomas is an internationally recognized marketing and sustainability expert, author of two books – *Goodvertising* and *The*

Hero Trap – and founder and CEO of Goodvertising Agency. He's been one of the frontrunners in shaping the advertising for good movement, which he has dubbed 'Goodvertising'.

At the Summit, Isa and Thomas curated a session in which they took delegates through the history of advertising campaigns to raise awareness of climate change and inspire positive action and behaviour change. It's worth a few moments considering some of the ads the industry has made, many pro-bono, in a bid to help give a megaphone to the big issues we are still grappling with. You can see all the ads on a special playlist from the session.

Isa and Thomas began with United Nations 'Home' by Saatchi and Saatchi Sydney, Australia (2001), an ad that promoted World Environmental Day (WED) which takes place on 5 June every year. It shows the relentless destruction of our environment through the lens of behaviours within a family home, all soundtracked by *What The World Needs Now Is Love*. Watching it back, it's certainly scary, not least the smoking of cigarettes in the living room while children sit and play. As one of the delegates commented at the end of the session, watching it now, doesn't this ad show just how little progress we've made in the more than two decades since it was made?

In the same year, 2001, the car and energy industries joined in with ads to mark WED. Thomas highlighted how this heralded the beginning of greenwashing, branding moments which provided companies with the opportunity to promote the little bit of good they were doing while not being transparent about the wider impact of the company's products or services.

Bund 'Earth' by Y&R Germany Frankfurt am Main is an unforgettable ad with a very simple message from Friends of the Earth: 'Save Our Planet. Save CO_2' which flashes up after we've watched Earth from space light up in a ball of flames and disappear. Scary stuff, again.

There was a Greenpeace ad from 2008 called 'Dreams of Tomorrow' by DDB Paris, France, which features a classroom of children being asked by their teacher, 'What are you going to be when you grow up?' The answers begin with the classic professions but move into the children saying they'd like to study storms, pollution, viruses, another child says they want to be a soldier to help defend their home country from other people, until finally a pupil says they'd like to be an astronaut 'so I can get out of this place'. The theme, the topics, the emotional punch still resonate and are still as relevant when you watch it back now. And again, quite scary.

Isa and Thomas talked about how, over the two decades they were revisiting in the session, brands started to become involved alongside the NGOs.

Examples including MTV Switch 'Walking Over The Sea' by MullenLowe Mexico, using humour to highlight the dangers of rising sea levels to mere mortals who can't walk on water. Their final selection was Patagonia's 'Buy Less, Demand More'; a powerful example of work leading the way in showing how a brand can be successful and sustainable.

But as the session ended, more comments were made by delegates including one who asked whether we might be more effective as an industry in helping to tackle climate change through sector-specific behaviour change campaigns as opposed to the broader dramatization of the existential issue we had seen in many of the ads. The general conclusion was that, while the ads shown have raised awareness of the issues, we remain a long, long way from scale behaviour change to support a more sustainable way of life.

Returning to James Murphy's thought about how to sell *better*, the most effective reasons given to sell those better products may not in fact be environmental or even based on their sustainable credentials. They may be the same reasons that people have always bought their less-sustainable predecessors. While sustainability credentials may sell to some, for others it may require other stories to close the sale. This may be a trap that environmental advertising has fallen into in the past. While many know that most often taking the train has a lower carbon footprint than a plane, would selling a superior passenger experience over the energy system change more behaviours?

But, we mustn't give up, there is hope…

We are now sharing two simple but profound approaches to behaviour change, tested and honed by BIT that all agencies and marketers can use.

The first is the EAST model, developed in 2012 and subtitled *four simple ways to apply behavioural insights*. According to BIT's paper, if you want to encourage a behaviour, make it Easy, Attractive, Social and Timely (EAST). These four clear principles for applying behavioural insights arc bascd on BIT's own work and the wider academic literature. It's quite clear how to apply these to sustainability.

1 Making it easy means making the most sustainable option the default or easiest option; take out all unnecessary actions and steps and make the messages for the most sustainable option simple and clear.

2   Making the more sustainable products and services attractive, using rewards and sanctions to maximum effect also speaks for itself, but is not always observed in the history of environmental advertising.

3   Making it social requires advertising and marketing to show that most people make the desired choice. Be wary of inadvertently reinforcing a problematic behaviour. Use the power of networks. We are embedded in a network of social relationships, and those we encounter shape our actions. Encourage people to make a commitment to others. We often use commitment devices to voluntarily 'lock ourselves' into doing something in advance. The social nature of these commitments is often crucial.

4   Lastly, regarding Make it Timely, prompt people when they are likely to be most receptive. The same offer made at different times can have drastically different levels of success. Behaviour is generally easier to change when habits are already disrupted, such as around major life events. Help people to plan their response to events. There is a substantial gap between intentions and actual behaviour. A proven solution is to prompt people to identify the barriers to action and develop a specific plan to address them.

The Behavioural Insights Team has developed a methodology that draws on experience of developing major strategies for the UK Government, a rich understanding of the behavioural literature, and the rigorous application of tools for testing 'what works'. The EAST framework is at the heart of this methodology, but it cannot be applied in isolation from a good understanding of the nature and context of the problem.

BIT has a method for creating and delivering behaviour change projects, with four stages.

1   Define the outcome

Identify exactly what behaviour is to be influenced. Consider how this can be measured reliably and efficiently. Establish how large a change would make the project worthwhile, and over what period.

2   Understand the context

Visit the situations and people involved in the behaviour and understand the context from their perspective. Use this opportunity to develop new insights and design a sensitive and feasible intervention.

3 Build your intervention

Use the EAST framework to generate your behavioural insights. This is likely to be an iterative process that returns to the two steps above.

4 Test, learn, adapt

Put your intervention into practice so its effects can be reliably measured. Wherever possible, BIT attempts to use randomized controlled trials to evaluate its interventions. These introduce a control group so you can understand what would have happened if you had done nothing. The team's recent experience shows the potential for these ideas, and the methods for applying them, to be incorporated into government actions. For Seb, the part that is often overlooked is the quality of insight creation and testing at step 2. These need to be foundational insights that can be counted on to support all the work that goes into the intervention. No matter how creative or well-crafted the intervention, if based on the wrong insight, effort is wasted.

Testing the effect of different climate narratives in social media content

The Behavioural Insights Team (BIT) worked with Unilever, their agency Edelman, and nine content creators from TikTok and Instagram to test ways for social media content creators to encourage sustainable behaviours around food waste and plastic reduction with specific brands (BIT 2022). The content creators created three types of videos:

- 'Neutral' content (e.g., 'I had an unusual idea for my best friend's birthday')
- 'Climate emergency' content (e.g., 'a major problem with recycling')
- 'Climate optimism' content (e.g., 'thrifty hacks to reduce waste')

The content of the 'climate emergency' and 'climate optimism' videos was informed by BIT guidelines. BIT then tested the relative effectiveness of these videos in a first-of-its-kind large-scale rigorous online trial. It recruited a sample of 6,013 social media users from the UK, US and Canada, and randomly assigned them to watch one of the three types of content. BIT then measured their immediate responses to the content, and their reported food-waste and plastic-use behaviours 2–3 weeks later.

Results, published in March 2023, validated the influence of social media in shaping sustainable lifestyles. Eighty-three per cent of participants said social media is a good place for advice on how to live sustainably, ranking it as one of the more trusted sources for this information. Experts, activists, family and friends are trusted more, but social media trump the government, politicians or other media (newspapers or TV). Social media also has the biggest influence on behaviour change, according to participants. Content from Instagram or TikTok is the most inspiring, on a par with TV documentaries.

The type of content that people in the study said they valued the most is content that is instructive, easy to follow and giving concrete advice – most in line with the 'climate optimism' guidance frame that the BIT prepared for content creators. Here are the two sets of guidance that were used.

Climate emergency frame

1. Highlight problem behaviour

Shine the light on individual behaviours that are problematic when it comes to food waste.

2. Sound the alarm about future consequences

Focus on loss. Talk about the local consequences and costs if we don't change our collective behaviour.

3. Emphasize key data and statistics

Use simple facts, figures and helpful analogies to illustrate the size of the problem and the need for action.

Warning: Point at the problem but avoid fear-based appeals or placing blame and guilt.

Climate optimism frame

1. Show the solution is easy and normal to do

Model helpful behaviours to show what to do and how to do it, and to demonstrate that it's commonplace. Focus on behaviours that are relatable and relevant for many (e.g., cooking from leftovers), rather than niche and too specific (e.g., pickling watermelon rind).

2. Show how it benefits YOU

Focus on personal, non-eco benefits, not on sacrifice. On how good it feels for you, not how much good it does for the world.

3. Make it surprising

Make the content memorable in a surprising way. Use humour, curiosity, surprise or… your pets.

So, what should we conclude from the study? Here are the recommendations for businesses looking to support the promotion of sustainable products, services and behaviours:

- Firstly, temper expectations. Where significant real-world barriers to behaviour change exist, social media communication alone should not be relied upon to significantly change behaviours. However, companies like Unilever have a unique opportunity to offer practical solutions with its products, alongside sustainability messaging.

- When using social media, there is value in both climate emergency and climate optimism content. Each seem to trigger different psychological mechanisms, and both therefore drive motivations and intent, likely in complementary ways. BIT suggest that climate emergency framing should be used when targeting easy behaviours for already knowledgeable audiences, while climate optimism framing may resonate more for harder behaviours, less familiar to the target audience.

- Attitudes towards the branded content were generally positive and, as such, there is no evidence to suggest branding will ring as inauthentic or risk reputational damage, provided the content itself is suitable.

These findings indicate that businesses with well-positioned brands can use their marketing in effective ways to support behaviour change while promoting a product or service to a customer. However, the framing narratives around climate change need to be carefully crafted, depending on the degree of behavioural change required, and communication alone will not be sufficient for very stretching behaviour change.

One of the communication challenges for sustainable products and services to manage is the very wide differences in what citizens already know and think about the climate emergency or inter-related issues around nature, pollution and waste. What is increasingly affecting people around the world is personal experience of the effects of more extreme climate events.

Understanding the growth in personal experience of climate change

In 2023, Meta Foresight published *Culture Rising*, a trend report pulling out some 20 trends. They analysed 4 million global conversation trends on its platforms, Facebook and Instagram, and surveyed 21,000 people in seven countries. Researchers found that anxiety about climate change is rising, as is the desire for practical action, and the problems causing anxiety are increasingly personal: from a jump in heating bills to difficulties obtaining drinkable water (Meta 2023). Seventy-three per cent of the users surveyed in those seven countries report climate change is important to them personally with many having had experiences of a natural disaster or abnormal weather in the past year. This covers extreme temperatures (40 per cent) frequent/more severe storms (27 per cent), flooding (22 per cent), drought (19 per cent) and forest fires (14 per cent). Forty-three per cent of respondents say these environmental events disrupt their lives, reporting effects on mental health (46 per cent) and physical health (22 per cent). This was most apparent in emerging markets covered by the research, such as Brazil and Vietnam. The fast-growing topics of conversation on social media picked up in the study can be grouped around three key themes: water (and scarcity), more sustainable lifestyles, cities and villages (including bicycles and biodegradability of waste) and energy (included vehicles and smart meters).

According to the Meta Foresight team, many people have been stuck, unable to act, despite having high levels of awareness about environmental issues. They report indications that this could now be changing. For instance, 74 per cent of consumers across the seven countries say finding renewable/sustainable energy sources is important to them, highlighting the opportunity to accelerate change in addressing this demand. The report highlights that millennials are more aware of the impact of climate change on their personal lives, and more aware of their own environmental impact (nearly 50 per cent wish they had less impact).

Meta Foresight concludes that people are looking for brands to provide products that are budget and planet friendly, want information on which behaviour shifts make the biggest difference, and demand evidence of companies' own environmental impact reduction. This research shows that there is a huge behaviour change gap to be exploited when it comes to sustainable products – companies with sustainable offerings need more effective ways of communicating to the right people.

Sustainability messaging and the importance of personal benefits

From a global study covering seven countries, we now zoom in on the US. The NYU Stern Center for Sustainable Business (CSB) published new research in June 2023, in partnership with Edelman. It sought to highlight which environmental sustainability claims are most motivating to people and, crucially, why.

The study – *'Effective Sustainability Communications: A Best Practice Guide for Brands & Marketers'* – was conducted in partnership with R&D, innovation, sustainability and marketing teams for nine leading global brands. The brands included Mars, The North Face, Unilever and HP, Inc. The supporting brands spanned apparel, food and beverage, technology, household items and personal care, with the researchers investigating the views of 2,700 consumers. These were its findings:

- People care most about themselves and their family, so the strongest performing claims connected the sustainability benefits to the impact on individual lives, families and experiences.

- People react strongly to claims regarding animal health, sustainable sourcing, local sourcing, and children and future generations. Audiences also care about claims regarding support for local farmers. Leading with 'local farmers' improved the performance of claims which connected to non-industrial approaches to agriculture.

- People are notably less interested in the scientific reasons behind a brand's sustainability unless tied to a self-centred reason to care or related to the outcome of specific action(s). For example, 'reduced air pollution' alone versus 'reduced air pollution for cleaner air to breathe'.

- People respond universally to products made without harmful ingredients to human health in all product categories. Resonant claims include 'grown without harmful ingredients' or 'made without chemicals harmful to humans/the environment'.

- Apart from 100 per cent recycled packaging claims, other sustainable packaging claims do not resonate with people without that extra reason to personally care, such as 'micro plastic-free packaging for human and ocean health'.

- Category claims (e.g., 'tastes great') are paramount and non-negotiable. People look for benefits that are intrinsically linked to the category.

The research showed a wide range of people are attracted to simple, jargon-free sustainability messages that connect directly to them, their family and the world around them. Within the top performing claims, which followed the best practices detailed above, the researchers found no demonstrable demographic or psychographic differences nor political polarization. Effective sustainability messages had a powerful amplifier effect for brands that use them correctly and in a way that highlights the personal benefit (NYU Stern CSB, 2023).

Matt spoke with Jaclyn Murphy, Managing Director, Purpose & Impact, at Edelman, who was working on this project, for some views on the wider implications.

What surprised you most about the research findings?

For each brand, when we looked at the top performing sustainability claims (which linked sustainability to category benefits and connected with consumers on a human level), there were virtually no demographic differences – including gender, education levels, income levels, generations and political affiliation. In contrast to current narratives around the divisiveness of topics like ESG and 'woke capitalism', we found that top performing sustainability messages resonate across demographics, for all 9 of the brands we tested – helping to dispel common myths about which consumers care about sustainability. In the US the narrative is that sustainability matters to a coastal, liberal, wealthy or Gen Z consumer. When you frame it right, that's just not true – it matters to everyone.

Overall, the top performing messages are personal and linked to the consumer's world: my health (better for me, e.g., harmful ingredients removed), my family, my wealth (provides a good value, more durable), my community (e.g., working with local farmers). We saw that by focusing on 'local farmers', you can dramatically increase the appeal of a regenerative agriculture message. This can humanize a topic that can otherwise feel unfamiliar or esoteric.

How are you are applying these research findings to your work with clients?

One key thing we're landing with clients is the idea of the 'amplifier effect'. We found that a top performing category claim will net you roughly 44 per cent of your addressable audience. And category claims remain paramount – people need to know your product is going to work. If you couple that with a top performing sustainability claim, it will increase the appeal of your message between 24–33 percentage points, which is significant. This proves when you communicate sustainability the right way it has significant, mainstream reach and appeal.

How confident are your clients when making credible sustainability claims?

Overall, clients are not confident on this topic. Companies are concerned about the ESG backlash – hopefully this research points a way forward by demonstrating that when you focus on personal benefits, sustainability messages can be universally appealing. Greenwashing is a real concern, one that must be addressed by 'doing what you say and saying what you do' and communicating with context, along with aligning with local standards.

Companies have told us they don't know how to communicate sustainability benefits. NYU, our partner in research, does incredible work tracking the growth of sustainable market share with Circana in a study called the NYU Sustainable Market Share which shows that sustainable products are growing twice as fast as conventional but are still at only 18 per cent of the market in the US. Our lead researcher Randi Kronthal Sacco, senior scholar at NYU Stern, often gets asked, how do we get that number from 18 per cent to 50 per cent or higher? We need more mainstream brands to adopt sustainability in their core business and to communicate it at scale. Being accurate and transparent in communications is critical to advancing the sustainable agenda. Fundamentally, your goal needs to be to inform, engage, inspire – your goal can't be to make consumers think that you're better than you actually are.

On trust, when I think of the brands most loved for sustainability; they are the most transparent about not only where they have gotten it right, but where they fall short or continue to struggle. People understand this work is hard. So, brands would do well to embrace humility and honesty in how they communicate their sustainability journey. Celebrate how far you've come and be honest about how far you have to go.

Are you anticipating a growth in sustainability-driven campaigns as the impact of climate change becomes more real and apparent to people?

Massively. Consumers, employees, markets are demanding this. Companies need to listen and to invest meaningfully in the kinds of innovations and solutions that are going to help make their businesses and products more relevant and more resilient in the future.

The problem is right now so much of the conversation is coming from a place of fear (understandably), but we need to go beyond doom and gloom – showing how sustainable products/services can benefit people's health, their wealth, their family, their community as well as the climate. Show how changes that are better for the climate can be better for people too. Innovation, behaviour change theory and marketing have a big part to play in all that.

Media Bounty's 'Beyond The Climate Bubble'

Media Bounty is a UK agency with the ambition of being the leading independent ethical creative and media agency by 2026. In March 2023, they published a report called Beyond the Climate Bubble, which coined the term 'Persuadables'. This built upon an original research project – 'Britain Talks Climate' – by Climate Outreach (2020) which presented seven audience segments.

In summary, 14 per cent of people in the UK are already very engaged in climate issues, while 17 per cent are not and won't be convinced otherwise. In the middle are five segments, representing 69 per cent of the UK population, open to change. They understand climate change is happening and, when asked, tend to agree that taking action for the environment will benefit them in the long term. However, they're not yet engaged, and they aren't talking about it. Price, familiarity with the brand, and reliability take priority over environmental or social impact in their decision making. They represent a large, untapped market for sustainable products and services.

Media Bounty strategists Florencia Lujani and Harriet Kingaby researched cultural attitudes and perspectives on climate change issues among 'Persuadables'. The researchers teamed up with Bricolage, a cultural insights agency, to run the project. The 'Persuadables' included Urban 'Somewheres' (a reference to David Goodhart's *The Road to Somewhere)* from Newcastle, rural (mostly white) dwellers in Yorkshire from a variety of backgrounds and ages, and British Black and Asian communities in Birmingham.

The first thing to note is that 'Persuadables' are often already under economic pressure. These groups are feeling heavy pressures on their quality of life. The cost-of-living crisis is front of mind, with many concerned about making ends meet. They're also seeing cuts to local services: the NHS is struggling, public transport services are reduced, and many local businesses are having to close their doors for good. They are looking for stability, but recent years have not given them that. They also feel excluded from the climate conversation; conversations around climate are seen as 'too London-centric', 'too leftist' and 'too white'. As such, the research shows 'anything and everything green' is just not for them. However, while they struggle to engage with the topic of climate on a global scale, it matters when the researchers touched on the issues closer to home.

10 Tips to appeal to 'Persuadables'

These nuggets drawn from the research are an essential checklist for engaging a wider customer base so critical to scale the sustainable economy beyond the 14 per cent of ethically minded sustainable shoppers.

1 Connect to local issues

'Persuadables' are connected to their local communities, which translates to purchasing behaviours. They connect better to products with tangible local benefits than nebulous, global ones. How does your product or service connect with the places where they live?

2 Normalize new choices

People's choices are influenced by social norms and deep-rooted beliefs. How can you challenge misconceptions about sustainability and make what you're offering feel like it seamlessly fits into their everyday lives?

3 Ditch the green tax

'Green' products tend to be more expensive, creating a gap between intentions and actual behaviours. Where can you help customers by reducing costs across the value chain to deliver savings?

4 Lead with a strong, personal benefit

'Persuadables' are more likely to make purchasing decisions based on personal benefit – product familiarity, reliability, cost, convenience or enjoyment – than abstract sustainability benefits. How can you lead with these personal benefits to broaden appeal?

5 Find your trusted messengers

'Persuadables' are more likely to be influenced by people similar to themselves and are unlikely to listen to 'green' campaigners, especially protesters. A US campaign to encourage vaccination during the pandemic enlisted highly decorated US army veterans to encourage people to get the jab by tapping into the values of freedom, strength, and duty. Who are the equivalent of the US army veterans to help you reach new customers?

6 Crack the cultural code

During the research project, if asked about sustainable products, 'Persuadables' tended to answer that 'they're not for me'. This is about reflecting families, neighbourhoods, accents and ways of living. What are the important cultural nuances which will help create interest and relevance for your audience?

7 Sell to men too

A theme which surfaced among some respondents was that buying green didn't fit their concept of masculinity. Can you remove any gender cues or conversely incorporate some traditionally masculine signals in your marketing?

8 Buy media where your audience trust it

'Persuadables', like many audiences, have fragmented media habits, but broadcast channels remained as important as ever, especially in the cost-of-living crisis. Social media was the least trusted channel in the research for these groups. How are you varying media channels for trustiness to different audiences?

9 Funny or die

The research highlighted once again that humour can play an important role in reframing an issue or creating strong emotional associations. What might you do to help your customer laugh (or simply smile) when they encounter your product or service?

10 Match hope with a concrete plan

'Persuadables' are too cynical for hope and loathe buzzwords. When talking to them, balance emotional connection with hard evidence that change is happening, and especially that people like them are making those changes too.

It's almost a chapter in itself how humour is so often prevalent in ads challenging the status quo. The team at Media Bounty highlighted the Will Ferrell GM ad – No Way Norway, which first aired in the Super Bowl in 2021 for a US audience. Here in the UK, two challenger brands are seeking to disrupt the toilet paper sector, and both are using humour on a significantly lower budget. *Who gives a crap?* started with its name and carries a cheeky message on every pack. *Serious Tissues*, winners of the 2022 Sky

Zero Footprint Fund, employed animation and talking trees to make the pitch amusingly to potential customers. Humour very effectively bridges the gap between a new brand and potential customers and is effective at communicating serious topics without appearing preachy or prescriptive.

Creating social and environmental change: right time, right place

Behaviour Change is a not-for-profit social enterprise, founded in 2009. It is an organization which helps to create social and environmental change, through big ideas grounded in behavioural science. Since January 2022, it has become an integral part of climate action charity WRAP where Seb is Chair.

Matt spent some time talking to Founder David Hall and Head of Strategy Kate Brennan-Rhodes. They were very clear that they 'don't do advertising' but they do deliver campaigns and interventions which have the objective of changing people's behaviours. This echoes the BIT recommendation not to rely on communication alone where change is most challenging for citizens. It's interesting to consider their approach as we look at all the different opportunities to help build a more sustainable future.

The Behaviour Change team start with the fundamental realities: simple knowledge of a behaviour is not sufficient to make it happen, nor even an intention to adopt the behaviour, not even with a positive predisposition to a brand. It takes much more to fundamentally shift people's behaviours and the team outlined three key factors:

- **Ease** – someone is far more likely to do something if it's easier.
- **Pressure** – people don't like to be in the minority and are more likely to do something if it is a social norm. People can also be put under pressure in other ways, such as incentives, penalties, commitments and feedback.
- **Right time, right place** – the moments and locations are critical for when you make an intervention into someone's life and bring about a change.

How they go about achieving this can be seen in the campaigns in which they have been involved, including their work preventing sewer blockages, originally for Northumbrian Water, in a campaign called Bin The Wipe. The campaign to give free bins to customers who didn't already have one in their bathroom was hugely successful, an intervention which has stopped millions more wipes being flushed down the toilet. This attention to right time, right place, and aligning all the influences to come together at the same moment is informing much of their future work.

Start with the most accessible actions and earn trust

In May 2022, Google worked with research partner Ipsos to understand what sustainability means to people in the UK. It reviewed Google Search data across 16 product categories, conducted in-depth interviews, focus groups, and conducted a quantitative survey of more than 1,700 UK adults. The results presented three insights to help advertising and marketing professionals consider how to drive greater engagement and uptake of sustainable products and services.

1 People care deeply, but are drawn towards the most accessible actions

The quantitative analysis showed 78 per cent of UK adults agree climate change was as big a concern as the cost-of-living crisis, with 80 per cent of people feeling responsible for looking after the environment for families and future generations. However, the research also highlighted people prioritize more accessible actions, like recycling (85 per cent) or using low energy lightbulbs (72 per cent) versus more difficult or costly options such as not driving or using a car (27 per cent) or driving an electric or hybrid car (12 per cent).

Google suggests this means sustainability messaging alone is not enough to shape purchase decisions. It has to be combined with other attributes such as quality and price, something we're seeing in other research too. There is a gap between intention and action – businesses must help people choose the more sustainable option. Google cites the example of Ikea as a company which nudges customers towards more sustainable behaviour throughout the processing of buying something from its range, offering tips to extend the product lifecycle and online filters for environmentally friendly options.

2 Striking differences in the perception of sustainability across product categories

In Google's study, 64 per cent of people agreed sustainability was an important influence for purchasing physical products such as groceries or clothing against just 47 per cent for buying a service like broadband, insurance or banking. The study's authors reason this may be because people find it harder to connect sustainability to less tangible purchases.

It suggests there is a strategic decision to be made by companies in the service – invest in educating customers about sustainability options now or pause sustainability marketing, with the risk of being left behind by players in the longer term. Conversely, it recommends tangible products such as food, fashion or cars can benefit from proactive positioning and, by doing so, secure competitive advantage in the near term. It cites the example of Oda, a Norwegian online supermarket, which saw a drop in the number of carbon-intensive products sold after adding estimated carbon footprints to shop receipts.

3 Trust needs to be earned

As part of the research, an Ipsos segmentation divided respondents into different groups based on their attitudes towards sustainability. Only 16 per cent of respondents considered themselves as highly engaged, stating they 'want to do as much as they can' and believe they 'can always do more'. The study's authors recommend that businesses need to be open to sharing product sustainability credentials, as well their processes, and their own net zero progress.

The study says it is possible for mass-market brands to engage people who aren't already actively making sustainable choices, and this can be done most effectively through clear, simple, and relatable communication with any green claims backed by strong oversight and quantifiable data.

The study concludes that many people are yet to commit to more challenging lifestyle changes that can have a bigger positive impact. The authors urge businesses to do their part in make sustainable solutions accessible to everyone.

Helping consumers understand sustainable jargon

Mail Metro Media, the company selling advertising for the *Daily Mail*, *Mail on Sunday*, *MailOnline*, *Metro* and *i* published a research report in April 2023 called *Greenwash: Exploring Consumer Understanding of Sustainable Jargon*. Using its Matters panel of over two thousand, a sample of readers shared their understanding of sustainability terms, their frequency of exposure and their trust of claims made by brands. The key findings were:

- All demographics, from young to old, consider the issue of climate change is important to them personally, and almost all understand it is caused by human activity.
- The word 'sustainability' alone is very powerful and elicits lots of positive sentiment and connected themes, such as recycling, green and reuse.
- Plastic pollution was the top environmental issue for most.
- Older people believed brands should minimize packaging, waste and improve recyclability of products.
- There was a general view that the responsibility is with 'big business' to drive change.
- People said they are willing to make simple changes to help the environment, like buying food from the UK or walking, cycling, and using public transport, with older people more likely to be currently making sustainable choices in everyday life (examples given include cutting energy usage and re-using shopping bags).
- There was the view that brands need to do more, and more products are required to make 'sustainability' easier for consumers. Only one in four of the respondents believed there are enough products and services available currently to support a more sustainable lifestyle.
- Beyond food and drink, few respondents are spending money on sustainable products in other categories, despite placing importance on there being sustainable options available.
- 'Net zero', 'zero emissions' and 'carbon neutral' are the top climate jargon phrases readers see in advertising. 'BCorp certified' is less seen overall but is significantly more recalled by younger audiences.
- Readers are much more likely to think these terms are important when they are shown an explanation of what they mean.
- Only 41 per cent of readers have a good or partial understanding of what net zero means and feel they could comfortably explain it to others, while just 42 per cent of readers could explain what BCorp certified meant.

It's notable that there is a lot of focus on recycling packaging, food miles and transport but a lot less about home energy, holidays, or electric cars. Matt asked Ryan Uhl, Chief Brand Strategy Officer, Mail Metro Media, to explain why they commissioned this research.

> After attending the Ad Net Zero summit last year, I was encouraged to see the research on climate jargon from the ASA. We commissioned this piece to better understand our readers views of these terms. What is clear is that people are not using this language in day-to-day conversations with friends and family and so there is a big divide in understanding of what they truly mean. I hope that brands think about the words and terms they are using on their advertising and test it out on real people to check that they are understood and are believable.

What should advertisers and their agency partners have most front of mind when looking to drive sales of a sustainable product or service with your readers? What's the biggest mistake they could make?

> Readers in the main love to know that something is more sustainable; it makes them feel better when they make a purchase, but they care about quality and value. I would encourage brands to talk in simple language, not over claim and remember that sustainability is just one aspect of a purchase decision. The worst thing we can all do is talk in jargon that people don't understand. The campaigns that work best are when sustainability is woven in as a facet of the narrative. Brands which launch products but also aim to encourage behaviour change of the whole category will make more impact with readers.

Testing power of including sustainable messaging in TV ads

In April 2023, Sky Media released new research with Savanta to look at the effectiveness of advertising campaigns promoting sustainability benefits. Research covered 52 campaigns, across seven categories, surveying a UK-representative audience of 5,300 people, supported by qualitative interviews and groups.

The research compared campaigns with sustainable messages against others without, and demonstrated sustainability messaging helps to influence the brand choice for three in five of Sky's customers. The research showed the sustainability ads in the test evoked stronger emotions, which led to better ad engagement and persuasion. The sustainability ads even outperformed the *best* non-sustainability ads for engagement and persuasion. This was true across all categories of advertising, but there were some sectors such as finance and energy, which had more work to do convince people.

Sky's research also analysed its library of effectiveness studies, comparing 600 campaigns across 7 categories. The research showed 15 per cent higher positive brand perception for sustainability ads vs non-sustainability ads, 5 per cent greater engagement and persuasion and up to 12 per cent increase in recall.

So, why was this happening? The Sky report identified four key factors to consider when it came to the creative execution of the ads:

- **Credibility** – Show what you've done already or why you are to be believed. Back up the claims with actions. Be ready to acknowledge the behaviour of the past and show you are a partner in the fight against climate change.
- **Clarity of message** – What sustainability action is being undertaken? Vagueness tends to be heavily associated with greenwashing. Avoid any ambiguity.
- **Correct tone** – Who is delivering the information and how? An impassioned voice of authority/influence is liked if coming from a credible source; telling people what to do with no obvious expertise is counterproductive. Make the tone positive, confident and achievable.
- **Creative execution** – Is the ad truly sustainable in everything it is saying and showing? Make it human by involving people in the ad, especially children, and documentary-style ads can help with engagement. Talking about sustainability brings all aspects of execution under closer scrutiny: factors such as location choice can undermine green credentials.

The greenprint – themes to consider for your sustainability advertising

As we approached final deadline, we were given a preview of a study called *The Greenprint* – a collaboration between System1 and ITV, which draws on insight from behavioural scientist Richard Shotton (The Choice Factory, 2018; The Illusion of Choice, 2023). System1, using their methodology based on emotional engagement, looked at how people responded to different types of environmental messages within a bank of ads identified together with the team at ITV. The following is a summary of *The Greenprint* key themes, outlined by Chiara Manco, Creative & Media Partnerships Director, System1. They neatly bring together some of the different areas we have been discussing during this chapter.

1 Hope over fear

If you make people feel guilty, they put their head in the sand: it's what behavioural science calls 'the ostrich effect'. So, while you may feel like communications around the environment should reflect the seriousness of the climate crisis, think about how you could educate or raise awareness of issues while ensuring the lasting feeling is one of hope and optimism.

An incredibly effective way to spark hope is humour. At System1 we found it to engage audiences even more strongly during times of hardship, like the Covid pandemic and subsequent recessions. If you can land a serious point in a way that makes people laugh, it will pay major dividends.

2 Stories over stats

We know from decades of ad testing that storytelling is extremely effective in engaging audiences emotionally. As humans, we are wired to better respond to concrete, human cues, not abstractions. However, as the climate crisis is global in scale, messages around it tend to often be very abstract. Focusing on real people or recognizable characters adds warmth and personality to ads while making the topic of the environment less anonymous and green behaviours feel more achievable.

3 It might be about climate, but it doesn't need to say climate

In our research, we found that the best way to make an appealing environmental ad is to make an appealing ad first and foremost – with strong characters, dialogue, a dynamic storyline – then weave in the environmental message. You also don't necessarily have to mention climate change to drive environmentally responsible behaviour. The behavioural principle of 'appeal vs duty' tells us that if you can align an issue with what the audience naturally cares about, they will gravitate towards it because they find it appealing, not because they feel it's their duty to do so. This avoids moral licensing: when people feel so pleased about having done something positive that they engage in less 'good' actions they might otherwise avoid.

4 Solution not sacrifice

Given the magnitude of the climate crisis, people can feel like making a
difference will require huge lifestyle changes, but we know small changes
can make an impact. Here is where one of the key tenets of behaviour
change – make the change as easy as possible – can be extremely valuable.
Take plant-based food: people worry the products won't taste as good as
their meat or dairy counterparts, which triggers the well-known behavioural
principle of loss aversion. As people feel more strongly about avoiding losses
(in this case taste) than about making gains, the most successful brands in this
space concentrate more on reassuring people there is no loss of taste than on
promoting the environmental benefits of switching.

5 Use the right messenger

Who delivers the message has a powerful influence on consumer behaviour.
Partnerships can be especially useful in this context as they build relevance
and trust: delivering an unfamiliar message through a familiar entity achieves
a level of 'optimal newness' which makes change easier. Children can also be
effective messengers, often acting as adults' conscience, urging them to think
about the impact of their actions for future generations. While choosing the
right messenger is important, so is ensuring they deliver the message in an
emotionally engaging way: communication between characters, for example, is
more effective than a monologue to camera.

6 Triggers for change

Cultural context is key to driving change: social challenges like Veganuary or
official events like COP can heighten the relevance of environmental issues and
act as powerful triggers brands can leverage to their advantage. We also know
people are more likely to change their behaviour in fresh-start moments: from
the start of a new year to a lifestyle change, these are moments where behaviour
change messages can land more strongly.

These six themes usefully bring many of the learnings in this chapter together.
What's clear to us is how much overlap there is between these studies.
Despite each piece of research having slightly different goals, System1's findings echo so much of this chapter: BIT's conclusion to avoid the placement
of blame and focus on positivity; NYU's finding that people care about real
people (especially those close to them); the consistent finding that humour
helps deliver messages effectively; and much more. These are all principles
that advertisers and marketers can take into their work on sustainability.

Sustainable behaviour change: the magic ingredients: summary

In this chapter, we have selected and summarized research studies about people's attitudes to sustainability, building on the framework of behavioural science. We reviewed work with insights into the attitudes of people fabled to be hard to reach with sustainability messages. We learnt that living more sustainably appeals to over three-quarters of the population if brands are prepared to close the gap with personal relevance, specificity, transparency and humour. There is a time and place for the 'climate emergency' messages, but when it comes to sustainable behaviour change choices in everyday life make it personal, connect the choice back to the familiar and the local, make messages practical and clear, remove jargon, line up relevant influencers in the right media as well as advertising, and bring it all together along the whole customer journey to shrink the change.

But what is also clear is that for many people around the world the changes being made are most often still the easier ones. We all have our work cut out to engage with citizens and customers on the bigger changes and less obvious sectors.

References

2023, Interview with Jaclyn Murphy, Managing Director, Purpose & Impact, at Edelman.

2023, Interview with Ryan Uhl, Chief Brand Strategy Officer, Mail Metro Media.

2023, System 1 & ITV, Sustainable Research preview – August 2023

2023, The Greenprint, ITV / System1 / Richard Shotton. Previewed August 2023.

Act Responsible. (2023) *Great Ads for Good*. [Online] Available at: https://act-responsible.org/great-ads-for-good/ (archived at https://perma.cc/R625-WEGT)

Act Responsible. (2023) *Home*. [Online] Available at: https://act-responsible.org/ (archived at https://perma.cc/GVV9-CZSW)

Ad Age. (2021) *General Motors "No Way, Norway"*. [Online] Available at: https://adage.com/video/general-motors-no-way-norway (archived at https://perma.cc/6UN6-9NFX) [Accessed August 2023]

Ad Net Zero. (2022) *22 Summit Playlist, ACT Responsible*. [Online] Available at: https://act.adforum.com/creative-work/playlist/24536 (archived at https://perma.cc/H5VU-HG5G)

Ad Net Zero. (2022) ACT Responsible + Mr Goodvertising. [Online] Available at: https://adnetzero.com/news/act-responsible-mr-goodvertising/ (archived at https://perma.cc/95NS-ENGE)

Ad Net Zero. (2022) *Global Summit 2022*. [Online] Available at: https://adnetzero. com/the-ad-net-zero-global-summit/ (archived at https://perma.cc/3JVM-2PGC)

Behaviour Change. (2023) *Home*. [Online] Available at: https://behaviourchange. org.uk/ (archived at https://perma.cc/M243-WKXS)

Behaviour Change. (2023) *Northumbrian Water Group: Bin The Wipe*. [Online] Available at: https://behaviourchange.org.uk/case-studies/bin-the-wipe (archived at https://perma.cc/7PY5-JYGX) [Accessed August 2023]

Breatnach, G; Cracknell, L. (2023) *Sustainable behaviours: How U.K. marketers can make a difference*. Think With Google. May 2023. [Online] Available at: https://www.thinkwithgoogle.com/intl/en-gb/future-of-marketing/management-and-culture/sustainable-business-consumer-behaviour/ (archived at https:// perma.cc/Z6CF-A5GP)

Bricolage. (2023) *Home*. [Online] Available at: https://www.bricolage.ie/ (archived at https://perma.cc/2MX2-48VU)

Bund "Earth" by Y&R Germany Frankfurt am Main. Available at: https://act. adforum.com/creative-work/playlist/24536/ad-net-zero-22-summit-playlist/ play#50191 (archived at https://perma.cc/X88U-9RXN)

Climate Outreach. (2020) *Britain Talks Climate*. [Online] Available at: https:// climateoutreach.org/reports/britain-talks-climate/ (archived at https://perma. cc/7HKK-WT2J) [Accessed August 2023]

Doerrer, B. (2023) *Unilever study shows creators influence sustainable choices*. Campaign. [Online] Available at: https://www.campaignlive.co.uk/article/ unilever-study-shows-creators-influence-sustainable-choices/1815933 (archived at https://perma.cc/3MV7-7HST)

Esteban, A. (2007) Ad Net Zero 22 Summit Playlist: MTV's Walking Over the Sea by MullenLowe Mexico. [Online] Available at: https://act.adforum.com/ creative-work/playlist/24536/ad-net-zero-22-summit-playlist/play#6699830 (archived at https://perma.cc/7LV9-E5SU)

Kalchev, A; Thirache, S. (2008). Ad Net Zero 22 Summit Playlist: Greenpeace's Dreams of Tomorrow by DDB Paris. [Online] Available at: https://act.adforum. com/creative-work/playlist/24536/ad-net-zero-22-summit-playlist/ play#12653969 (archived at https://perma.cc/9EHR-KS2P)

Kellerman, Y. (2001) *Ad Net Zero 22 Summit Playlist: United Nation's Home by Saatchi & Saatchi*. [Online] Available at: https://act.adforum.com/creative-work/ playlist/24536/ad-net-zero-22-summit-playlist/play#19443 (archived at https:// perma.cc/VYA8-VUF5)

Kolster, T. (2012) *Goodvertising: Creative Advertising That Cares*. 1st edition. Thames & Hudson. London.

Kolster, T. (2020) *The Hero Trap: How to Win in a Post-Purpose Market by Putting People in Charge*. 1st Edition. Routledge. Abingdon-on-Thames.

Mail Metro Media. (2023) *Mail Metro Media unveils 'Greenwash' research.*
[Online] Available at: https://www.mailmetromedia.co.uk/news/mail-metro-
media-unveils-greenwash-research/ (archived at https://perma.cc/X9CB-DULC)

Media Bounty. (2023) *Beyond The Climate Bubble.* [Online] Available at: https://
mediabounty.com/beyond-the-climate-bubble/ (archived at https://perma.cc/
8NE8-DFGZ)

Media Bounty. (2023) *Home.* [Online] Available at: https://mediabounty.com

Meta. (2022) *Culture Rising 2023 Trends Report.* Meta Foresight. February 2023.
[Online] Available at: https://www.facebook.com/business/news/insights/
culture-rising-2023-trends-report (archived at https://perma.cc/BW3P-FKBA)

NYU Stern CSB & Edelman. (2023) *Effective Sustainability Communications:
A Best Practice Guide for Brands & Marketers.* [Online] Available at: https://
www.stern.nyu.edu/experience-stern/about/departments-centers-initiatives/
centers-of-research/center-sustainable-business/news-events/news-insights/
new-research-csb-and-edelman-identifies-most-effective-sustainability-messages-
across-wide-ranging (archived at https://perma.cc/25WB-35H5)

Patagonia. (2020) *Ad Net Zero 22 Summit Playlist: Patagonia's Buy Less, Demand
More.* [Online] Available at: https://act.adforum.com/creative-work/playlist/24536/
ad-net-zero-22-summit-playlist/play#34629844 (archived at https://perma.cc/
VXP2-BJM3)

Sky Media. (2022) *Serious Tissues Announced as £1m Grand Prix Winner of the
2022 Sky Zero Footprint Fund.* [Online] Available at: https://www.skymedia.
co.uk/news/serious-tissues-announced-as-1m-grand-prix-winner-of-the-2022-
sky-zero-footprint-fund/ (archived at https://perma.cc/G53F-STDG)

Sky Media. (2023) *Sky research reveals the 'green halo' of sustainability advertising: 3 in 5 say sustainability messaging in advertising influences their brand
choice.* [Online] Available at: https://www.skymedia.co.uk/news/sky-research-
reveals-the-green-halo-of-sustainability-advertising-3-in-5-say-sustainability-
messaging-in-advertising-influences-their-brand-choice/ (archived at https://
perma.cc/2T22-S7GK)

The Behavioural Insights Team. (2014) *Four Simple Ways to Apply EAST
Framework to Behavioural Insights.* [Online] Available at: https://www.bi.team/
publications/east-four-simple-ways-to-apply-behavioural-insights/ (archived at
https://perma.cc/KTP2-THEF)

The Decision Lab. (2023) *EAST Framework.* [Online] Available at: https://
thedecisionlab.com/reference-guide/management/east-framework (archived at
https://perma.cc/94AB-5GW7)

Who Gives a Crap. (2023) *Home.* [Online] Available at: https://uk.whogivesacrap.
org/ (archived at https://perma.cc/KKS4-QQYA)

11

What 'good' looks like now, and in the future

As we discovered in Chapter 8 on awards, determining commercial and sustainability success is highly complex. For commercial brands, their ability to do good is predicated on continuing commercial success. Growth campaigns for a start-up/disruptor which has 'sustainability' baked into its business model from the outset is evidently good (and investors are looking for business potential rather than actual margin at the early stages). But for established players, 'good' is about constructive steps towards net zero along a pathway, while continuing to deliver margins and cash, influencing thousands or millions of 'better choices'. We believe it is right to encourage progress made by businesses with good intent, and not let perfection be the prohibitor of progress and the cause of 'greenhushing', where companies fear any public discussion of progress. Research among the public supports this approach as long as it's transparent about how much more there is to do and avoids greenwashing.

In this section, we're going to unpack what good can look like with a range of recent examples that have won awards already: a brand (Hellmann's), a media owner (Sky Zero Footprint Fund), and an NGO (WRAP). We're also going to explore an initiative helping to push the expectations of 'good' further into a sustainable future (#ChangeTheBrief), and consider the implications for the way an advertising sales team might operate 'sustainably' (ITV). But first we'll start with the 'best of the best' work winning Cannes Lions, through the lens of sustainability and positive impact on the planet.

Learning from the world's best creative work

The International Festival of Creativity, Cannes Lions, is widely regarded as the global benchmark for creative excellence and the festival has been recognizing the world's best creative work every year since 1954. Its goal is to celebrate and showcase creativity from around the world to the world's largest and most influential advertisers and marketers. The festival's catalogue of Lions winners across seven decades comprehensively demonstrates how the most creative companies consistently grow faster, are more profitable and can shift culture. We've seen some Lions-winning work that accelerates more sustainable brands and offerings but imagine if the creativity of every campaign awarded were another step towards a net zero economy.

Matt has been part of the Cannes Lions UK Representative team at the Advertising Association for several years. The association took the role on in late 2018, establishing a collaboration with industry partners and the UK government to adopting a 'Team GB' model for UK creativity and the association has been successfully running trade missions to the festival each year (including virtual missions during lockdown periods). It also runs the UK Young Lions event each year and hosts events back in the UK to share learnings from the winners. Matt first grasped the scale of the Lions community when he attended the two-day gathering of reps from around the world and connected with colleagues from across Europe, Asia, North and South America. Everyone shares the same goal – to bring the very best creativity from their country to the festival, to compete (and collaborate) on the world stage, before taking learnings home to their own creative communities to help the biggest creative solutions be analysed, understood and built on. Standing on the shoulders of giants, year after year.

Simon Cook, CEO, Lions, gave us his perspective and aspiration for Lions into the future.

> We know that creativity has the power to drive change because we have seen evidence, through our Lions-winning work, that creativity can shift consumer behaviour, redesign supply chains, or reimagine the way products are manufactured, or services are delivered. We've seen it in shortlisted and Lions-winning work for many years. And we're increasingly seeing work that inspires consumers to choose more sustainable brands or engage in more sustainable practices. This shift in behaviour is driving real progress and business growth – and it is all underpinned by creativity.

The volume of sustainability-focused work increased during the pandemic from 4 per cent of all shortlisted and Lion-winning work in 2019 to 8.5 per cent in 2023. This rise suggests that the pandemic gave the global creative community greater impetus to take action against climate change and other sustainable initiatives. Across most of the last 10 years, work that is related to sustainability has enjoyed a higher success rate in the Lions than the average for all work. When we look at the sustainability-related entries in 2023, 10.9 per cent of them were subsequently shortlisted, ahead of the Cannes Lions 2023 Festival average of 10.3 per cent – though 2.9 per cent went on to win a Lion, dipping slightly below the Cannes Lions 2023 Festival average of 3.2 per cent for the first time since 2017.

More broadly across the Festival, we saw entries linked to sustainability across all 30 of the Lions in 2023, with the Sustainable Development Goals (SDG) Lions accounting for 12 per cent of these entries. The SDG Lions celebrate creative problem-solving, solutions or other initiatives that harness creativity and seek to have a positive impact on the world. Work needs to demonstrate how it contributed to or advanced the 2030 Agenda for Sustainable Development across people, planet, prosperity, peace and partnerships. Our SDG Jury was looking to recognize work that supported environmental and ethical ambitions but also delivered long-term business impact. It wanted to ensure that these initiatives could deliver growth so that they could maintain and sustain that positive change.

Lion-winning work is helping brands and agencies understand how to make a difference to the industries they serve and drive business growth – while at the same time driving progress for people and planet.

It's good to hear Simon's passion for promoting the power of creativity to address sustainability challenges and we really hope the number of entries supporting behaviour change in some of the most necessary sectors will help that 8.5 per cent of Lions-winning work double and double again over the next few years.

Matt had the opportunity to tour the exhibit of winning work at Cannes Lions 2023 and captured examples from across the winners, shortlisted work and entrants which might have relevant learning or inspiration for sustainable advertising.

1 Leading by example

A German media agency offering carbon-neutral OOH (out of home) campaigns wanted to convince more agencies and clients to book environmentally friendly OOH campaigns. It recycled old posters to create new sustainability reports. Each copy is unique, gets delivered by a bike courier, and readers can only borrow the sustainability report – it must be returned. Just 50 copies were made and then promoted to target customers via the agency's homepage, a short film on YouTube, Social Media Postings & Stories Banners, DOOH (digital out of home) – and PR. The campaign generated a 110 per cent increase in sales of carbon-neutral OOH campaigns and saved 50 kg of wood through the upcycling production. This was entered into multiple awards.

2 Making climate change consequences visible to everyone

Denmark's largest public broadcaster, launched 'Our Earth, Our Responsibility' in Spring 2022, complete with TV programmes focusing on innovative solutions that can lead to a more sustainable future. But to raise awareness of the implications they made a simple change to a Danish design icon – The Copenhagen Bench – elevating it by 85 centimetres to match the UN Climate Report's estimate for the rise of sea-level by the year 2100. Fifteen elevated benches made from upcycled metal and recycled wood were placed at central locations in the largest cities of Denmark, initially with no messaging or branding.

Then 20 famous ambassadors posted photos sitting on the bench through their social channels, again without a clear ownership to spark further debate, before the broadcaster took ownership through national PR and an integrated campaign consisting of outdoor, print, TV, and digital advertising. The campaign made 1 out of 3 Danes talk about climate change, with more than 50 per cent of Danes recognizing the organization as the Danish media brand with the biggest focus on climate change. Eight out of ten Danes agreed that 'all have a responsibility in changing course for a more sustainable future'. It won a Bronze Lion in the Special Build category in Outdoor.

3 Sparking conversation about the future of food and sustainability

A winner from Singapore was inspired by the classic game of 'truth or dare' to engage with Gen Z about the future challenge of a severe shortage of sustainable protein sources facing a global population of 10 billion by 2050. The food brand challenged TikTok creators and global followers to taste, cook and share recipes using insects – one of the most sustainable protein sources available. The campaign was executed in February 2023 and went on to develop 188 pieces of content. The campaign's talents, a partnership with 70 TikTok creators, with a cumulative following of over 40 million across eight countries, were invited to a dinner party to try sustainable and planet-friendly dishes like Grasshopper Tacos or Mealworm Loaded Nachos. The results secured over 100 million views and 1.45 million engagements and helped to get people talking about food choices. It was shortlisted for Corporate Purpose and Social Responsibility in Media.

4 Turning your advertising assets into renewable energy sources for your supply chain

A multi-national brewer created a campaign called 'Beer Power' to solve a problem facing bar owners in Brazil due to rising energy prices. It mapped the billboards it used that were most exposed to the sun, adapted them to generate energy and then plugged these 'Solar Billboards' into the bar's electric system. The company's social networks promoted this to all other bars that could receive the same energy for free. At the time of entry, 26M KwH had been channelled to bars, powering 1,843 bars, saving R$17 million (£2.8 million) on bills with a further 5,417 bars on the waiting list. It was shortlisted in categories including Outdoor, Food & Drink and Special Build.

5 Using pollution to create cleaner air with a positive social return

A nasal health brand runs a worldwide 'Actions to Breathe Cleaner' campaign to mitigate the impact air pollution has on children. Pollution Pencils kicked off in July 2022 in Bengaluru – India's asthma capital where the company partnered with an award-winning clean air start-up to identify three low-income schools in the industrial areas of Hegganahalli, Peenya, and Mallasandra where self-cleaning, sustainable and energy-efficient air purifiers were installed. Two billion cubic feet of air was cleaned, and particulate residue was collected. This residue was then combined with graphite to produce 10,000 child-safe Pollution Pencils at a local pencil factory and distributed to students and used to raise funds. Over 1,500 children are breathing cleaner air in Bengaluru, over 6,800 children in Delhi schools will benefit once the second batch of air purifiers are installed, and there is a long-term commitment by the brand to keep this programme running for years to come. It was shortlisted in categories including Healthcare and Corporate Purpose and Social Responsibility.

The following three case studies are detailed examples of how and where we can start to see and understand what 'good' looks like, and the type of work we'd like to see everywhere.

CASE STUDY
Brand case study: Hellmann's

Aim

In the UK, 1 in 6 bags of groceries and 1 in 8 prepared meals are binned every year (Millward Brown, 2021). Because it emits methane, food waste in landfill is responsible for 25 million tonnes of greenhouse gasses, the equivalent of 10 million cars. Meanwhile, unused food costs UK households a collective £19 billion per year (WRAP – Food Surplus and waste in the UK, 2020). Sounds like one of Seb's speeches: is he recycling the same one at WRAP from when he was at Unilever?

These insights were the inspiration for Hellmann's to drive positive change in people's approach to food waste – creating a nation of food lovers that say 'Yes' to taste and 'No' to waste. Hellmann's approached Mindshare, their global media agency network, part of GroupM/WPP, with an interesting brief, challenging them to approach things differently, with a #ChangetheBrief mindset (coming up in a few pages) to drive behavioural change.

Action

To inspire people to be more resourceful with food and waste less, Mindshare joined forces with Channel 4 and BBC Studios' Science Unit to create *Cook Clever, Waste Less* hosted by one of Britain's best loved cooks, Prue Leith, and social media food and health expert Dr Rupy Aujla (aka The Doctor's Kitchen). The unique branded four-part series was designed to raise awareness of the scale of food waste in the UK, as well as the small steps and food rescue behaviours households can take to turn their leftovers into delicious meals. The campaign was the first sustainability-focused Branded Entertainment show in the UK and was created from scratch by Mindshare's Invention team – from developing the concept to getting it commissioned.

The decision to build a campaign around Branded Entertainment was based on the insight that broadcast programmes have produced real behaviour change before. Famously, 88 per cent of 'Blue Planet 2' viewers changed their plastic usage habits (Waitrose Food and Drink Report, 2019). Hellmann's recognized TV as the best way to influence behaviour change and make a positive environmental impact while utilizing one of the brand's selling points: transforming leftovers into enticing meals.

The programme was broadcast in four 30-minute episodes aired in peak time on C4 and All4. To accompany the programme, an advert was made featuring Dr Rupy which set out Hellmann's commitment to food waste, as well as sponsoring the show, along with bespoke brand idents for airing on C4.

To further extend the campaign's reach, digital assets were produced, including trailers and snappy recipe videos, which were circulated online throughout the campaign. A downloadable recipe book was created, giving people a resource to implement the change they had been inspired to make.

Result

Cook Clever, Waste Less drew in 3.4 million viewers – over the 3 million viewers target that was initially set – and the first episode was the top-performing show of the day on Channel 4.

According to research by Channel 4 Research, 32 per cent of those who watched the show said they would start using leftovers to make meals. That would be a whopping 3.1 million kg of food saved from landfill and 5.9 million kg of CO_2 emissions if everyone acted as they claimed.

The commercial and brand results were equally impressive, demonstrating that true sustainability advertising can be more than financially viable. The campaign drove a 15 per cent uplift in the number of people who agreed that 'Hellmann's helps use food that would otherwise go to waste' and eight out of ten viewers said they would choose Hellmann's next time they bought mayonnaise. Traffic to Hellmann's website increased by 500 per cent and over 40,000 recipe books were downloaded.

The ingenuity and creativity, as well as the genuine value that this campaign offers to its audience, make it a shining example of what good looks like. Follow up research on the conversion of intent to action on food waste would make it even more outstanding, to inform future executions from the brand around the world.

CASE STUDY
Media owner case study: Sky Zero Footprint Fund

Aim

Time for a confession from Matt. He loves this initiative by Sky and believes it brilliantly shows what ad breaks of the future might look like. What caught Matt's eye was when Sky launched a series of special carbon net zero ad breaks timed to run during COP26 which took place in Glasgow, Scotland. The ad break was 'presented by Sky Zero' and it featured all five winners of the first year's fund, in an ad break that ran for two weeks across Sky Nature and Sky News. Sky was a Principal Partner and Media Partner of COP26, and this was a first for British TV – all ads produced were carbon net zero with every ad promoting a more sustainable way of life to the Sky viewers. An inspiring vision of the future, sustainable advertising in action today.

Action

Sky has been working on its own sustainability for more than 17 years and was the first media company to go carbon neutral back in 2006. It has won multiple awards for its Sky Ocean Rescue work. Through its sustainability strategy, Sky Zero, it has set a net zero carbon target of 2030, across its film and TV programming but also the technology which enables Sky services in people's living rooms, the fleet of engineer vehicles and how it encourages its customer base to live more sustainably too.

Sky's main revenue source comes from subscription revenues, but it has a large and respected advertising sales operation too, Sky Media, which represents a wide range of channels, not just Sky channels, including Paramount (Channel 5), Warner Bros. Discovery, A+E Networks, AMC Networks, National Geographic and more. Through these channels it has a reach of over 93 per cent of the UK population (Sky Media, 2023).

Sky launched the Sky Zero Footprint Fund in March 2021, originally a £2 million campaign to inspire change and help fast-track sustainable initiatives. It set out as a competition to find five winners which would feature in ads on Sky TV, with the most impactful and creative idea securing £1 million in advertising support and each of the winning businesses guaranteed at least £250,000 of airtime.

The competition launched with a fantastic line-up of judges from across the industry and set out clear standards from the outset, including the requirement that all the winning ads had to be produced in line with the standards set by AdGreen (covered in the earlier chapter on sustainable ad production). Winners of the prize come from a range of sectors, from a challenger period product to sustainable toilet paper and established brands like Royal Mail.

Result

Many of the winning brands can show sales uplifts or distribution in more stores that they wouldn't have had without winning the Sky Zero Footprint funding. For example, Here We Flo's win helped them open up conversations with new retailers, and since winning the fund, the brand extended its distribution in Superdrug.

During the TV campaign, the business saw an average sales uplift of 18 per cent and highest-ever website engagement with site visits +1,000 per cent year on year (Sky Media, 2023).

In that Sky Zero ad break Matt also saw a glimpse of an attainable future for our industry, helping people make sustainable choices rather than encourage unsustainable ones. How can we accelerate that change across all ad inventory to the point where every ad is made sustainably and is in support of a sustainable way of living? What if every media owner could have its own version of the Sky Zero Footprint Fund – a way of accelerating the growth of the sustainable businesses that are emerging in all parts of our economy? Imagine if the sales teams of media owners and platforms around the world could be incentivized to put more and more focus on turning this vision into reality.

Meanwhile, the Sky Zero Footprint Fund goes from strength to strength, winning multiple awards including British Media Award's 2022 Best Sustainability Initiative, Campaign's Ad Net Zero's 2022 Media Award, and the 2023 Media Leader Sustainability Excellence Award. In 2023, the initiative is expanding further with the introduction of an additional fund for local businesses and initiatives. This is called the 'Local Heroes' Fund and Sky is using its AdSmart technology to help connect regional businesses to their local community and enabling the public to take part in voting for their winner.

Sarah Jones, Director of Planning at Sky Media summed it up when she said, 'It's clear that there isn't a silver (or even a green) bullet but since the launch of the fund, we're learning more about what kind of sustainable communication cuts through, and what doesn't. If TV has the power to change behaviour, why don't we use TV to get people to buy more sustainable products and establish more sustainable habits?'

CASE STUDY
NGO case study: WRAP

Aim

WRAP (The Waste Resources and Action Programme) is an NGO dedicated to tackling the emissions that cause climate change and promoting a regenerative circular economy working with governments and industry in food and drink, textiles, packaging and recycling.

WRAP runs a campaign for Food Waste Action Week each year to directly address the huge food waste problem with the public – 6.5 million tonnes wasted every year in the UK alone. In order to create the biggest impact with the more modest resources available (compared with commercial brands) the team decided not to aim the campaign at the demographic of the fastest increasing wasters (households 35–44 years old) but instead aim for those most likely to make a change, people who attach high importance to nature and the environment with high 'biospheric values'.

Action

The campaign was launched through video, out-of-home and digital channels. To support the campaign, WRAP used the tagline 'Wasting food feeds climate change' to be used as consistent messaging running throughout the campaign. This simple message was used to solidify the link between wasting food and climate change; something that is frequently underestimated as a contributing factor.

Out of 165 kg of real food waste (equivalent to the average UK household's annual waste), the WRAP team created a ten-foot planet with the intention of creating a visual shock to represent the scale of the problem within each household.

Result

With an initial goal of driving action from 50 per cent of people exposed to the campaign, the result of 55 per cent taking action and 4.4 million people changing their behaviour was a huge success. Of people who saw the campaign, the number of people who drew a clear link between wasted food and climate change jumped significantly, from a pre-campaign level of 37 per cent to 49 per cent in 2022.

The widespread dissemination of the campaign was demonstrated by the fact that one in three people saw or heard something about food waste during the week: equivalent to 17.7 million UK adults. While WRAP doesn't have the budget or scale to produce something on the level of the Hellmann's campaign, the clarity of purpose with the WRAP campaign produced a powerful message that was successfully delivered to a huge and largely receptive audience. The campaign won a DMA Gold award for Sustainability in 2022.

The #ChangeTheBrief Alliance

A key part of the original Ad Net Zero action plan was an initiative called #ChangeTheBrief. Matt spent time with one of its founders, Rob McFaul, who shared his experiences over the last few years with him.

#ChangeTheBrief was an idea originally introduced by Marco Rimini – global chief development officer at Mindshare and (in Rob's own words) industry legend, recently retired. Marco was taking part in the Purpose Disruptors' first Climate Crisis summit which took place in July 2019, and came about as a response to the question: 'What does collective action look like in response to the climate crisis?' Follow-up workshops facilitated by the Purpose Disruptors with summit attendees developed a range of ideas emerging from the summit including #ChangeTheBrief.

Mindshare, where Rob worked, launched #ChangeTheBrief in November 2019 on Mindshare Day (a regular event in the industry's annual calendar encouraging partners to share ideas with Mindshare staff and clients). Mindshare invited the industry to adopt the #ChangeTheBrief concept and asked the Purpose Disruptors to build out #ChangeTheBrief into an alliance, recognizing the entire industry needed to work collectively on the 'bigger than self' problem that is the climate crisis.

Here is the letter that Marco wrote as an initiative to others to join the Alliance:

> When the challenge is so big, we need to help each other to help ourselves. That is why we want you to join the #ChangeTheBrief Alliance.
>
> The #ChangetheBrief Alliance is a thought and action platform that seeks to reduce depictions of unsustainable attitudes, lifestyles and behaviours in commercial communication and increase depictions of attitudes, lifestyles and behaviours that will lead to a net zero emissions society.
>
> The Alliance is seeking a broad collective of agencies, bound together by the singular desire to help solve the climate crisis through the use of their collective communication skills, enabled by the investment their clients make in advertising.
>
> As the climate crisis is a 'bigger than self' problem, the Alliance represents a rare opportunity for the industry to act as one. To work in solidarity, not in competition, to meaningfully tackle climate change. You will enter the Alliance with an open and collaborative attitude, with a desire to change the future, to stimulate and share ideas that can change the world and to work together for a better future.
>
> By signing up to the #ChangeTheBrief Alliance you will be committing to help solve the climate crisis by using your skills as communication agencies (whether Design, PR, Experience, Media, Creative or any other). You will be committing to help effect behaviour change at scale through responding to client briefs in a way that encourage the attitudes, lifestyles and behaviours which are consistent with a transition to a carbon-free world.

The Purpose Disruptors has agreed to act as our spine. More than anyone they've galvanized the industry to respond to the climate crisis and have collected the best network of experts to help us help each other and energize our wider Alliance.

As members of the Alliance, you will have access to what will become the world's most extensive pool of case studies and research on sustainable attitudes, lifestyles, and behaviours. This will enable your agency to knowledgably respond to client briefs and deepen your sustainability credentials. Additional services will be designed and delivered based on Alliance member needs e.g., training courses.

The #changethebrief Alliance is modelled on the successful 'Unstereotype Alliance' that seeks to eradicate harmful gender-based stereotypes. In the UK, activity by the 'Unstereotype Alliance' has resulted in a change in the ASA ruling on the depiction of negative gender stereotyping in advertising.

Below we set out the practicalities of what it means to join the Alliance. I hope you agree with the aim and can sign up and contribute whatever you can afford for the next 18 months.

Please be generous with your people, time, and money. It is really important.

Together we can #ChangeTheBrief.

Marco Rimini

Global Chief Development Officer

Rob takes up the story:

#ChangeTheBrief Alliance is an initiative grounded in action so that we not only understand that every campaign is an opportunity to normalize the behaviours, the products, the services, and the attitudes we all know we will need to adopt to achieve sustainable living, but that we also have access to the knowledge, skills and ideas to put this into practice.

We developed a learning programme and content platform to support the industry in upskilling in response to the climate transition. Our ambition is that the Alliance will generate a new skill set so we are future fit for a net zero world.

What I believe to be unique about the Alliance is that members share with each other their learnings and experiences of embedding #ChangeTheBrief in their organizations, as well as help shape future content and learning experiences.

This is great example of the industry transcending its deeply competitive nature so that it can accelerate our creativity and strategic firepower to meaningfully address the climate crisis.

What exactly do you mean when you say let's change the brief?

It's an invitation for everyone involved who touches, influences and responds to the brief to change it so that the work it inspires brings forward a thriving, sustainable future. Because the work starts with brief. It's the foundation of every campaign and every piece of marketing activity. The role of the brief is to clarify the task ahead so what we create great and effective work. And if we understand the responsibility of marketing and advertising in restoring and preserving the health of society and the environment, we know we must rethink what great and effective work looks like.

So, how do you go about challenging a brief?

If you are a marketing director, this is can be about challenging your teams to include objectives for encouraging sustainable behaviours in the target audience.

If you are agency-side, there is an opportunity to positively challenge the brief by suggesting a response that also promotes a sustainable behaviour.

But in all cases change starts with a conversation. To generate effective work, we have to connect with and empathize with our target audiences. The same principle applies to our colleagues and work partners. A vital phase in changing the brief is to consider what conversation will connect your team and stakeholders.

You could be the kindling and be the one who starts the conversation that your colleagues didn't know they wanted to have. A simple way is to add just one additional response to the brief. This extra response only needs to be a kernel of an idea that serves as a way to ignite the conversation on the opportunity and responsibility to promote sustainable lifestyles.

Or you can be the one who stokes the fire in cases where the brand is well advanced in its setting of climate and sustainability targets. Here you have an opportunity to show that through advertising and marketing's brainprint, you can help meet those targets, and that it all starts with the brief.

Ultimately your role is to demonstrate the vital part that marketing and advertising can play in accelerating brands' transition to future-fit business models. You can lay the groundwork for this by encouraging briefs and responses to change the image and change the behaviour.

Can you give examples of how the brief might be changed to create a more sustainable campaign as an outcome?

Firstly, think about how you can change the image or language of the work to normalize a net-zero world. We can choose and direct creative to show a positive sustainable world that doesn't always have to be central message to the campaign. In our briefs and responses, we can choose and direct creative imagery that normalizes sustainable behaviours and a net-zero world. A great example of this is the EDF/Havas London 'busy doing nothing' campaign. A campaign designed to promote a new energy tariff backed by 100 per cent renewable energy for EV charging. The ad showed vehicles in everyday UK neighbourhoods charging overnight just like we charge our phones, and so normalizing an approach to running an EV.

Secondly, change the outcome/impact/behaviour: Align a brand, product or content and product positioning with a relevant behaviour change from one of the following six lifestyle areas: how we eat, how we buy, how we travel, how we use less, how we waste less and how we connect with nature. A good example here is the inaugural winner of Ad Net Zero Awards for Campaign of the year; Hellmann's and Mindshare with their 'cook clever, waste less' campaign. An ongoing campaign and purpose for Hellmann's to help reduce food waste and as a consequence the methane emissions from the 1 in 6 food shopping bags that get thrown away every week.

Finally, and the bigger ambition for the industry, change the business: Accelerate a brand's transition to a future-fit business model. How will your brand and category need to transition to be commercially successful when it operates within planetary and societal boundaries? What is your business model for a net-zero world? In nearly every case, you will need your customers and target audience to be using your produce or engaging in your service in entirely different ways. The key question to ask is what's the role of marketing, media and creative and advertising in making that mainstream and desirable? An example here is IKEA and their ambition to be a circular and climate positive business by 2030. They are working on all products to be re-used, refurbished and remanufactured. There's a role for customers then to return products back into their system. A simple design and communications idea was the creation of disassembly instructions for their products, so customers can return them to the store of reuse and refurbishment and resale.

Everyone in your agency and team needs the confidence, knowledge, and inspiration to encourage sustainable living well and effectively.

#ChangeTheBrief Alliance, supported by the major advertising groups and convened by Purpose Disruptors, is an accessible resource for agency-side and client-side teams to learn how to promote sustainability across a range of categories.

A 'sustainable' ad sales team at ITV

At the sharp end of a sustainable advertising eco-system, ad sales teams incentivized through revenue targets to help fund the business they work for, are faced with the question of what to do about climate change and sustainability. For decades, the most successful media businesses, a vital part of the advertising eco-system connecting highly valued audiences with advertisers, have been rewarded and recognized for hitting sales targets. Thousands and thousands of jobs depend on this funding, particularly journalists, presenters, and content creators, all of whom have an important role in presenting well-researched and high-quality information and entertainment through programming and editorial.

So, how do you manage the transition to net zero within this commercial context? That is the question that leaders at the UK's biggest commercial media owner, ITV, are asking and looking to answer as part of their own business plans for future success in a net zero economy. They are preparing for a world where carbon disclosure requirements for reporting, as well as investors making financial decisions about the company, are asking how much advertising revenue is aligned with the Paris Agreement and 1.5 degrees. There's also the self-regulation code that is increasingly focused on monitoring 'green' claims in advertising and potential pressure from consumers and regulators in the future, which might make it harder for companies in some sectors to advertise. How much of that revenue might be at risk, and how much might new sector revenue streams be worth in the future? When and how can the businesses with the best chance of success in a net zero economy become advertisers? Are there disruptive shifts coming in the economy to accelerate the net zero transition, or government interventions that the business should plan for? And the faster an ad sales portfolio is made up of business with products and services in line with a net zero economy, the quicker advertising can help to make that economy a successful one.

During conversations with ITV's Kate Waters, Director of Client Planning and Strategy and Jeremy Mathieu, Head of Sustainability, for the research of this book, we explored how they are working to prepare the sales team for a net zero future: and the following are our reflections on the themes they are wrestling with.

Firstly, it's important to recognize this isn't easy and there isn't a perfect answer. The first step for the sales team leaders is to train their sales colleagues about sustainability and climate change, to turn any understanding into genuine knowledge that they can relate to at an individual level and then apply that with scale to the work they do. All to secure more and more advertising revenue in line with that 1.5 degree future.

To that end, the ITV team has created a year-long programme of training for the entire commercial team covering climate science, the role advertising can play in driving climate action, green claims, greenwashing and carbon calculators. Attendance is mandatory and linked to the ESG element of every individual's performance bonus. In addition, specialist training is being provided for teams involved in ad production and for the commercial sustainability squad, who are the climate action champions within the commercial team.

The second is to work out how to add sustainability metrics to the advertising revenue sheet. This will be important for the sales team to have visibility of how much revenue might be at risk, and how much revenue could be unlocked from the fast-growth areas of a net zero economy. Exploring this question is increasingly required as part of disclosure reporting from organizations such as the Taskforce for Climate-Related Financial Disclosure and CDP. So, an objective, transparent and fair methodology will be required (ideally developed in collaboration with other broadcasters) to help the business to categorize its advertising customers in the context of net zero opportunity and risk.

The third area of focus is for the sales team to consider how to encourage advertisers to bring more sustainable products, services and behaviours to their commercial breaks, sponsorship packages and media partnerships. We've seen earlier in this book just how influential a media owner like ITV can be in supporting positive behaviour change through the right brand advertising activity. So, how does it responsibly create propositions for advertisers that encourage investment behind the more sustainable products and services within an advertisers' portfolio?

Remember the motto, 'make the better brands bigger, and the bigger brands better'? Certainly, there is no desire to leave any advertiser behind, but there is a commercial imperative for growing sales revenue based on a combination of those two goals.

Imagine what would be possible if ITV's commercial team is able to drive revenues in a way that significantly future proofs ITV's revenue and carbon footprint, using the full gamut of advertising products including airtime value, sponsorship, and partnership with ITV brands across its linear channels and on-demand services. How would you best deploy all these opportunities to grow revenue and manage the transition to a net zero advertising portfolio?

The fourth area for the ITV team is to think about what interventions and nudges they can build into their own sales process that can help support a more sustainable advertising industry. An example being considered is the expectation that an advertiser buying one of its premium sponsorship packages should run the production through AdGreen as a standard part of the process. Considering the advertiser's customer journey through a sustainability lens can help to normalize these types of behaviours.

Within the PSB legal remit, shaped by regulators and shareholders as well as viewers, there is a viable destination for ITV's sales team, and many others across the industry, to transition to a trading model and sales process with sustainability baked in.

What 'good' looks like now, and in the future: summary

In this chapter we have seen examples of what good is beginning to look like across the whole length of the industry from advertisers, both businesses and NGOs, to agencies and media owners. Glimpses of what can and is being done already to make Sustainable Advertising a reality. What's apparent is just how much commitment, how much thought, reflection and granularity is required to truly move a business to a more sustainable footing.

For some, the progress we've recorded here will simply not be enough nor is it happening at a fast enough pace. That said, we need room to discuss what good looks like now, to help identify what will soon become standard and to foster a competitive desire to be even better. Ultimately, as we reflect on the examples of good in this chapter, the question is how fast can we see these things happening everywhere?

Good sustainable advertising means looking into the future, identifying a major relevant sustainability challenge, and showing leadership on how you can help address it. Not only that, it also means successfully aligning the sustainability results with your own commercial or organizational success.

References

2023, Interview with ITV's Kate Waters, Director of Client Planning and Strategy and Jeremy Mathieu, Head of Sustainability.

2023, Interview with Rob McFaul, Purpose Disruptor.

Ad Net Zero. (2022) *Ad Net Zero Global Summit 2022, Day 1: Action 5: Harness Advertising's Power to Support Consumer Behaviour Change.* [Online] Available at: https://adnetzero.com/the-ad-net-zero-global-summit/ (archived at https://perma.cc/SR9P-7PPQ)

Advertising Association. (2023) *Cannes Lions UK Representative.* [Online] Available at: https://adassoc.org.uk/our-work-category/cannes-lions/ (archived at https://perma.cc/GE3N-H32U)

Cannes Lions. (2023) *Home.* [Online] Available at: https://www.canneslions.com/ (archived at https://perma.cc/FAS6-QTA8)

#ChangeTheBrief. (2023) *Home. [Online]* Available at: https://www.changethebrief.org/ (archived at https://perma.cc/9WTV-EPMV)

Lions: The Work. (2023), *Home.* [Online] Available at: https://www.lovethework.com/en-GB/ (archived at https://perma.cc/K5FK-EHLN)

Montoute, J; Wren, N. (2021) *Cook Clever, Waste Less with Prue and Rupy.* Channel 4. May 2021. Available at: https://www.channel4.com/programmes/cook-clever-waste-less-with-prue-and-rupy (archived at https://perma.cc/ZJB4-889K)

Sky Media. (2021) *British TV's first Net Zero Carbon Ad Break.* [Online] Available at: https://www.skymedia.co.uk/news/sky-media-launches-net-zero-carbon-ad-break-featuring-footprint-fund-winners/ (archived at https://perma.cc/CQ5X-2FFM)

Sky Media. (2021) *Sky Zero Footprint Fund launch.* [Online] Available at: https://www.skymedia.co.uk/news/sky-launches-the-sky-zero-footprint-fund/ (archived at https://perma.cc/N4EM-M2J8)

Sky Zero. (2023) *Our Story.* [Online] Available at: https://www.skyzero.sky/our-story (archived at https://perma.cc/U9NJ-2AWD)

WRAP. (2023) *Food Waste Action Week.* [Online] Available at: https://wrap.org.uk/taking-action/citizen-behaviour-change/love-food-hate-waste/key-campaigns/food-waste-action-week (archived at https://perma.cc/9C45-VS4L)

WRAP. (2023) *Home.* [Online] Available at: https://wrap.org.uk/ (archived at https://perma.cc/N7M3-BR6R)

12

Sector review: Energy, travel and tourism

In the next two chapters we will look at advertising's opportunity to effect behaviour change at scale. Changing behaviours on a societal level will be critical for the industry to land significant decarbonization. Governments will define the rules of transition and industry players will lead and execute the change, but they won't get there without us taking action as responsible citizens. The question for each of these sectors is how advertising can help shift our collective appreciation of more sustainable products or services, and how quickly. The sectors have their own challenges, but they all have one in common: motivating people to make significant changes to their behaviour to achieve a successful transition. This will require matching new product and service availability to the adoption rate generated by advertising and marketing, or the other way around.

The sectors we have chosen – energy, travel, tourism, food, fashion and finance – are where the biggest and most significant changes are needed. Between them they account for most greenhouse gas emissions (Ritchie & Roser, 2020). Although every sector has its own sustainability challenge and opportunity, we can't get to them all into one volume, but we hope this chapter and the next will sketch out the opportunities ahead for marketing and advertising and the role you can take to accelerate a more sustainable future in some of the most challenging sectors.

Energy companies, advertising, and the net zero transition

It's impossible to write this book without first considering the energy sector and the role advertising for energy companies needs to play. The transition from fossil fuels to renewable energy is the single biggest opportunity to disrupt the current climate change trajectory. Ultimately, the brief here for advertising is to do everything it can to help shift citizens and business customers to renewable energy sources as quickly as possible. To support the behaviour changes required to make that possible, such as the adoption of heat pumps, installation of insulation, acceptance of wind farms onshore, normalization of solar panels and adoption of electric and hydrogen powered vehicles. Advertising should promote innovations, drive competition, and help accelerate the renewable energy market as rapidly as it can. That sounds straightforward, doesn't it? We're not going to go into the history of the type of work that has been done by agencies (across advertising, public relations and lobbying) for oil and gas clients in the past. This book is about what needs to be done now, envisaging how the advertising industry can best help the transition to a sustainable future. We write at a pivotal point in this transition, where the debate rages over which fossil fuel companies, if any, should be represented by businesses in the advertising industry and where their advertising should appear in the media.

The Shell media business (by no means a small account) came up for pitch in the summer of 2023 while we were writing this book, and protestors have been standing outside the offices of the large agency groups in central London making their voices heard. The protests don't stop there – we've heard of staff of agency groups that work for fossil clients being targeted with personal ads on LinkedIn, stunts in the receptions of companies and more and more voices calling for all work on fossil clients to be stopped. The main reason given most often is that advertising gives companies a social licence to operate (SLO), and that this, in the campaigners' view, lends implicit support for activities that needs to stop. The parallel most often cited is tobacco advertising. Activists speak passionately about decades of greenwashing, and reference companies and campaigns in the USA to back up their point of view.

In the UK, oil and gas company advertising spend is, for the large majority, from two companies, BP, and Shell and their 2022 advertising spend can be broken down as follows (Credos, 2023):

TABLE 12.1 Shell & BP

BP	Total	%
Sustainable products	4843810	25.8
Fuels and lubricants	1,036,519	5.5
Brand building	9,801,760	52.1
Other (apps, utilities etc.)	3,120,096	16.6

(continued)

TABLE 12.1 (Continued)

Shell	Total	%
Sustainable products	183859	4.1
Fuels and lubricants	363075	8.2
Brand building	3,049,845	68.7
Other (apps, utilities etc.)	840,185	18.9

When you see the figures and the split like in Table 12.1, you can see very little spend promoting petrol at the pumps to car drivers, but that won't make any difference to whether a car owner (when their car is low on fuel) heads to a petrol station. Most of the spend is on sustainable products, brand building and other (apps, utilities, etc). This is why the argument about social licence to operate is so front and centre. One argument would be that companies are using the advertising to promote their products and plans to transition to net zero. The other is that they are using it to present a version of their company entirely at odds with the reality. If you compare the share of ad spend with the reality of the share of sustainable products in the businesses, or even the share of capital investment for future business, perhaps the closest measure to intent, the advertising is far off the reality. It is perfectly legitimate to ask why and to also scrutinize what this advertising is saying and how. It's all about intent and, as we will see, that is somewhat intangible, linked to trust, and can be heavily influenced by political events.

In June 2023, three adverts for Shell that publicized its climate-friendly products were banned (Sky News, 2023). The Advertising Standards Authority (ASA) ruled the ads created the impression that 'a significant proportion of Shell's business comprised lower-carbon energy products' and misleadingly 'omitted' information that oil and gas made up the 'vast majority' of its operations. The three adverts showcased the renewable power that Shell provides and its clean energy services, including electric vehicle charging. For example, Shell UK's TV ad said 1.4 million UK households used 100 per cent renewable electricity it had supplied and that the company was working on a wind project to power six million homes and planned 50,000 electric car chargers nationwide by 2025.

The following is a line from the captioning of the ad on its YouTube channel: 'From electric vehicle charging to renewable electricity for your home, Shell is giving customers more low-carbon choices and helping drive the UK's energy transition. The UK is ready for cleaner energy.'

Shell UK's rationale for the ads was that it wanted to raise awareness about its range of energy products that were better for the environment than fossil fuels and increase demand. For context, in 2022, Shell spent 17 per cent (£3.5 billion) of its total capital expenditure (£20 billion) on 'low-carbon energy solutions', which include renewable wind and solar power as well as things like electric vehicle charging, biofuels, carbon credits and hydrogen filling stations.

In response, the ASA said this: 'We understood that large-scale oil and gas investment and extraction comprised the vast majority of the company's business model in 2022 and would continue to do so in the near future. We therefore considered that, because (the ads) gave the overall impression that a significant proportion of Shell's business comprised lower-carbon energy products, further information about the proportion of Shell's overall business model that comprised lower-carbon energy products was material information that should have been included. Because the ads did not include such information, we concluded that they omitted material information and were likely to mislead.' It ruled that the ads must not appear again.

After the ruling, Shell responded: 'No energy transition can be successful if people are not aware of the alternatives available to them. That is what our adverts set out to show, and that is why we're concerned by this short-sighted decision.'

Meanwhile, BP is under pressure for a 'Backing Britain' campaign that it ran during May–July 2022 to promote its investments in low carbon energy solutions for the UK market. The campaign ran on social media as a carousel ad with four different parts, three on the types of investments it is delivering, and the fourth was a caveat, which read as follows: 'Today, most of the energy we produce is oil and gas. But as we transition towards net zero that will change. This decade we plan to increase to 50% our capital expenditure on our transition businesses globally and reduce oil and gas production by around 40%.'

There have been public challenges to the accuracy of this statement, but in it there is acknowledgement of the context of what the business is doing overall, and a statement of intent in the public domain. However, in August 2022 Channel 4 News pointed out that data from BP showed that the company had invested only 2.5 per cent of 2021 profits (£300 million) in H1 2022 into renewables and low-carbon projects combined (noting that it wasn't possible to break out renewables from this) versus 31 per cent in oil and gas (£3.8 billion). Furthermore, by February 2023 the 40 per cent commitment was pared back to 25 per cent (Financial Times, 2023) despite profits from fossil fuels more than doubling in the context of global supply shortages. The explanation given to the FT by the CEO was that 'governments and societies around the world are asking companies like ours to invest in today's energy system.'

So, what's the way forward? There are options. The solution may be a mix.

- A Government ban on all ads by the fossil fuel companies. A ban won't impact petrol or diesel purchasing, but some people would argue this would stop oil and gas, and the companies selling them, being socially acceptable. Others argue the world needs these companies to make the transition work. Whether they are transparent or not, their investment in advertising new products can help people understand the newer low-carbon energy options that are emerging. But if there is not a substantial portfolio change, without drag and delay, this would be greenwashing. There is a tension here between banning a whole sector and banning individual companies that are not doing enough.

- Include a full disclosure element in every ad. This might be possible through self-regulation with mandatory information – for example, the percentage spend of investments in low-carbon energy vs fossil, and the validation of their transition plans to science-based targets on an annual basis. SBTi introduced a policy in March 2022 to pause target commitments and validations for fossil fuel companies while guidance development work continues (Science Based Targets, 2023). The advertising industry can't set this 'standard', which leaves government regulators like Ofcom to set and enforce such a standard, if the self-regulatory system cannot. But is there evidence for the effectiveness of such statements on advertising?

- Agencies clarify and publish policies for carbon-intensive industries in line with the transition to net zero. Many agencies work in some way for fossil companies at the time of writing. There is a growing group of independent agencies under the collective banner of the Clean Creatives who commit to not working for fossil companies and that includes an individual pledge which can be made by creative professionals. Both WPP and IPG have published specific policies relating to representing clients in the energy sector, which has the benefit of being evidence-driven, company by company. Another angle being explored is the full disclosure of fee income to ascertain how much is earned from fossil companies.

- Media owners and tech companies could set their own boundaries around what they will and won't run. For Public Service Broadcasters this might require clarification from Ofcom on what could comply with the 2003 Act that tasks the regulator to ensure 'a broadcaster must not unduly discriminate between advertisers that seek to have advertising included in its licensed service'. The ASA code states in the section on Compliance: 'the fact that a marketing communication complies with the Code does not guarantee that every publisher will accept it. Media owners can refuse space to marketing communications that break the Code and are not obliged to publish every marketing communication offered to them'. *The Guardian* has enforced its own ban on fossil company advertising (in place since February 2020), and to the positive, one of the Sky Zero Footprint Fund beneficiaries in 2021 was renewable energy company Ovo.

In the UK, the Labour Party (2023) announced plans to create a publicly owned renewable energy company (Great British Energy) that would enter the energy market to take advantage of the lower supply costs for renewables (an exciting prospect if it happens). Which advertising agency wouldn't want to work on a brief for that new company?

The Global Energy Alliance for People and Planet (GEAPP) is an alliance of philanthropy, local entrepreneurs, governments and technology, policy and financing partners to develop the renewable energy sector. Its mission is to support developing countries' shift to a clean energy, pro-growth model that ensures universal energy access, bring power to one billion people, and create 150 million jobs. Matt met Kate Willis, GEAPP's Chief Communications Officer, during Cannes Lions 2023 who explained how the initiative wanted to create a green energy industry revolution, focused on emerging markets with a fund to incentivize investment in businesses across solar, hydro and wind to build the commercial market and in the process take coal off the list. Another exciting prospect to keep an eye on.

It's also worth bearing in mind the role that brands outside the energy sector can have in influencing the uptake of renewable energy. We will discuss electric vehicles later in the chapter as one of the catalyst purchases to renewable electricity. Budweiser was a winner of a Campaign Ad Net Zero award in 2022. Through The Budweiser Energy Collective, the company helped its supply chain of bars and restaurants to switch to renewable energy by acting as the bulk buyer on their behalf. A big company which is interdependent for commercial and sustainable success with thousands of SMEs using its scale for the benefit of all stakeholders. That approach shouldn't be limited to just one company in the drinks sector; it is scalable.

Meanwhile, the energy company E.ON launched a new campaign in summer 2023, 'It's Time To Act', led by a TV advert featuring people performing the lyrics of 'Time' by The Rolling Stones as apocalyptic scenes of environmental destruction caused by climate change take place around them. The events happen with them seemingly unaware until the final scene, when a character notices the burning forests and a voice-over calls on the viewer to act today, not one day, but now, pointing to E.ON's solutions to help people shift to renewable energy. The company's website shares more on this shift through sustainable homes, businesses, and cities, highlighting that 100 per cent renewable electricity is provided to all customers at no extra cost, and presenting a range of sustainable solutions including solar panels, smart meters, EV chargers and air source heat pumps.

The advert isn't for the faint-hearted. It goes against the advice of 'positive climate framing', more along the lines of the big NGO crisis ads we've seen for decades. At the same time, though, it is bold and new for a commercial energy company to take this line.

There's a second film on the website about the making of the ad. It describes how the team made every effort to reduce the climate impact in creating the ad, by keeping the amount of travel and number of crew as small as possible, minimizing set waste and using second-hand wardrobe. E.ON partnered with a provider of high-quality carbon removals to remove the residual emissions that it could not eradicate operationally. E.ON and their advertising partners changing the way they work and changing the work they make.

In conclusion, events are moving quickly. If you want to do the right thing, adopt the goal described at the outset: take on briefs to shift citizens and business customers to renewable energy sources fast. Normalize the behaviour changes required to make that possible, through brilliant advertising that is honest, truthful, transparent and is always in line with the aims of the Paris agreement. The faster our industry helps to replace oil and gas, the better, and this should be in mind approaching every brief.

IPG POLICY

IPG and its affiliates announced in September 2022 that it will proactively review the climate impacts of prospective clients that operate in the oil, energy and utility sectors before accepting new work. It has developed a set of questions that it expects prospective clients to affirm before any new contracts are signed, including:

- Have these potential clients set specific emission reduction goals that are aligned with 1.5°C ambition to achieve net-zero GHG emissions by 2050 or sooner with no greater than 10 per cent off-setting?
- Are these companies publishing clear climate reporting, including scope, baseline, timeline, and the tracking of Scopes 1,2 and 3 emissions?
- Are their goals in line with the goals IPG has made in our own ecosystem, and reported on publicly?
- Have these companies ceased any controversial forms of oil and gas production?

Additionally, IPG states it does not support or engage in marketing or communications aimed at influencing public policy that seeks to extend the life of fossil fuels. It has reported that it has already declined new business briefs because of the new approach. It acknowledges a small number of IPG agencies create marketing for carbon-intensive clients, including oil, gas and utility companies and that historic work does not meet current standards, but all future work will be line with IPG's own sustainability values. It has also committed to reviewing the approach on a bi-annual basis.

Travel behaviour change

One of the most important areas of behaviour change is in the way people travel, for work and for leisure. This means switching the use of petrol cars and planes to taking public transport, replacing cars journeys with bicycles or electric scooters as well as electric vehicles, and flying less.

The transition is huge and the time to do it is short. Matt is reminded of an image Rob McFaul, co-founder of the Purpose Disruptors, presented at an event with magazine publisher, Hearst. He showed a street in New York heaving with horses and carriages alongside a picture of the same street just over a decade later, now lined with cars. This seismic transition has been done before. We need to do it again.

Let's start the way many journeys start these days. Let's look at the best way to make our journey, using all the nuances and preferences we can now set in the map and travel apps made freely available by advertising.

Google is one of the largest companies in the advertising eco-system, funded by advertisers through their spend on Google Search and YouTube. This ad spend has helped Google invest in services free at the point of use to people worldwide. As part of its sustainability commitment which we referenced earlier in this book, Google has used its Maps product to help people make more eco-friendly travel decisions in the US, Canada, Europe and Egypt.

The product feature launched in late 2021 uses a routing model to let drivers see and choose the most fuel-efficient route to their destination. It uses insights from the US Department of Energy's National Renewable Energy Laboratory and data from the European Environment Agency. As of the end of 2022, fuel-efficient routing is estimated to have helped prevent more than 1.2 million metric tons of carbon emissions since launch – equivalent to taking approximately 250,000 fuel-based cars off the road for a year (Google, 2023).

Google provides other options to help people make more eco-friendly travel decisions. For anyone looking to make a trip, Google Maps offers multiple navigation options, whether that is the most fuel-efficient (therefore lower carbon emissions) or options to take public transport, cycle or walk. There's also the ability to map a route for an EV vehicle via EV charging stations, including details on port types, charging speeds and, where possible, live data on availability.

The routes suggested for cycling include a more detailed breakdown showing whether there might be heavy car traffic or steep hills that can be avoided. It also offers data on bike and scooter shares in more than 400 cities around the world.

For journeys on foot, live directions and visuals of the location you're walking in make sure you're in the right place – especially useful for emerging from an underground station. The level of sophistication for planning bus, train, underground or ferry journeys, includes times, transfers and optimizing for preferred modes of transport.

A healthy competitor to Google Maps, Citymapper, founded in 2011, focuses on an increasing list of big cities, with accurate real-time data from multiple sources and sustainable travel information for its users to be able to make decisions on route as the situation changes.

How can advertising help inspire and normalize more sustainable journeys? Updating or replacing the tropes of travel – for example, the freedom of an open road or the luxury of private jets. New ideals for travel and transport experience need to be celebrated.

Google has opened the fuel-efficient options in its Google Maps Platform to third-party developers. How can services like Google Maps be enhanced and supported by businesses promoting sustainable travel and transport? If you're thinking about advertising and marketing work in this space, providing people with the right inspirational information to make better choices about their trips could be a good area to focus in on.

Advertising aviation

Of all the sectors, the aviation industry faces one of the biggest challenges to decarbonize within the timeframe it has been set. The UK government's Department for Transport published its Jet Zero strategy paper in summer 2022, setting out how it plans to deliver net zero aviation by 2050. It aims to rapidly decarbonize the industry while retaining all the benefits that the industry brings of connectivity, jobs, and economic benefits.

It is also heavily challenged by other voices on how feasible this is, whether it will be possible and the reliance on yet-to-be realized new technologies. The Royal Society, for example, has raised concerns about the viability of alternative fuels which the industry proposes to use (2023). As *The Guardian* pointed out, 'the UK would have to devote half its farmland or more than double its total renewable electricity supply to make enough aviation fuel to meet its ambitions for "jet zero", or net zero flying.'

But this isn't going to put the industry off. Virgin Atlantic has announced plans for the first net zero transatlantic flight, planning to use Sustainable Aviation Fuel (SAF). This is made mainly from waste oils and fats (like used cooking oil) and works with no modification needed in the Rolls-Royce Trent 1000 engines of one of its flagship Boeing 787 jets. These 'moments' will be a critical part of the industry's marketing and no doubt they will be challenged.

Advertising for the aviation industry is under intense scrutiny as calls intensify for people to fly less. There are high profile examples of ads being publicly shamed for breaking the self-regulatory codes.

A campaign by Lufthansa is one such example. In March 2023, an ad was banned by the ASA for giving a 'misleading' impression of the environmental impact of flying. The ad included the text 'LUFTHANSA GROUP. CONNECTING THE WORLD. PROTECTING ITS FUTURE. #MakeChangeFly'. The ASA ruled the claim in the ad was not clear and it had not been adequately substantiated. The ad also caused a stir among advertising commentators for the image of the front of a plane in flight, with its undercarriage replaced by earth from space.

This was quickly followed by another ASA ruling against an airline, this time for Etihad Airways, again for 'misleading' consumers over the environmental impact of flying. The ASA ruled, 'while we noted steps were being taken by Etihad to reduce the environmental impact of its service, we understood that there were currently no initiatives or commercially viable technologies in operation within the aviation industry which would adequately substantiate an absolute green claim such as "sustainable aviation" as we considered consumers would interpret it in this context. We concluded, therefore, that the claim exaggerated the impact that flying with Etihad would have on the environment and the ads breached the Code.'

These rulings from the ASA in the UK are very clearly setting boundaries on absolute green claims from airlines for this market. Companies in carbon-intense industries will not be permitted to make green claims for steps being taken if they do make a significant impact on the total carbon footprint of the product or service. Airlines are going to come under pressure all around the world.

France have moved fastest, bringing in a ban on short-range domestic flights of up to 2.5 hours, in favour of people taking more sustainable travel options. Travel guides like Lonely Planet were the first to cover the news and encourage travellers to get on board the 'excellent and wide-ranging rail network' instead. The ban may be more symbolic to begin with, as the exception clauses allow it to be whittled down to three routes for now, but it does signal that the French government believes curbing or changing people's behaviours around flights is essential for driving down emissions.

Advertising for French train companies stepped up in a bid to make the most of the regulatory intervention. A campaign from OUIGO, a low-cost train service provider offering conventional and high-speed trains to customers in France, launched in early 2023, highlights how taking the train is an easy way to do something more sustainable. Called 'Going Green Without Even Trying', it presents a series of scenarios in which small things can have a more positive environmental impact – sharing a shower, unplugging the kids' games consoles, getting off a scooter – and equating those to making a trip on a train. The company business model is based on the insight we came across already from the behaviour insights section of this book: taking the train is most likely to be a choice based on low prices, rather than a conscious effort to reduce emissions. Longer journey times versus planes will also need to be countered by higher convenience and amenity. However, for French trains there is also a 96 per cent reduction of emissions when compared to travelling by petrol car and, as for flights, well you might find you can't do that anyway.

All this begs the question, how will advertising for public transport options develop over the coming years? It's safe to say that the push to include sustainable travel options in your trips, whether for work or for leisure, is going to become more important, more visible and more central to the way we respond to climate change. Advertising is going to be asked to help normalize those behaviours in countries around the world.

Car advertising

The transition to electric vehicles (EVs) is one of the most obvious areas of behaviour change being supported by advertising. It is certainly the one where we can see the clearest shift in ad spend.

That analysis of what is happening to car ad spend in the UK was a result of Matt's experience in front of the House of Lords Environment Committee who asked for tangible evidence for cases where advertising was effective in promoting more sustainable products and services to help build a net zero economy. Thinkbox and Credos ad spend data shows how the share promoting hybrids and Evs had moved from 7 per cent to 73 per cent in just four years (Figure 12.1). And while share of sales lags share of spend, those numbers are moving too.

This means that advertising is portraying and normalizing ownership of EVs and hybrids for different market segments ahead of reality, creating desire and aspiration to own a vehicle that is more sustainable than the one many people own right now. It seems that the car companies are now reinventing their model line-up for significant change from now on in line with UK Government phase out dates for Internal Combustion Engines in 2030 and hybrids in 2035. This medium-range clarity from Government is a good example of how legislation can bring certainty to industries to plan how to succeed.

Many of the big car companies are grabbing the opportunity, using high-profile advertising campaigns and major advertising moments including the Super Bowl in the US to raise awareness of their EVs. As mentioned in Chapter 10, one of the best examples was the General Motors 'No Way Norway' ad featuring Will Ferrell which ran during the 2021 Super Bowl, which used humour to bring the slow pace of EV adoption in the US to the

FIGURE 12.1 UK ad spend on Hybrid / Ev / Alt. cars, Credos/Thinkbox (2022)

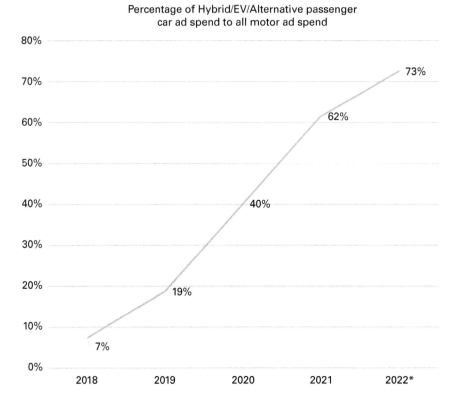

attention of the American public. Just look at how Audi and Ford Norge responded to get a sense of the impact it made.

In conversations for this book, what became clear was how the advertising of EVs and hybrids is now moving from early adopter (aspiration) to mainstream (normalization). Advertising is not just helping to create a new sector and a new behaviour but will need to help deal with all the questions and challenges that this behaviour shift will raise, to help bring a world of EV ownership to life.

And there are small (but significant) nudges taking place all around us – many of which can be accelerated and amplified. For example, a fascinating partnership has developed between GM and Netflix, which shows just how powerful an impact popular culture can have on shaping how people see a product – in this case, EVs. Many people talk about marketing's 'brain print' but there is a greater influence than the one shaped purely by marketing – the one built through all elements of popular culture.

GM launched its 'Everybody In' campaign in 2021, to help accelerate the adoption, forming a partnership with Netflix which at its heart is good old-fashioned product placement. They agreed to add a minimum of one electric car to every Netflix show (where it makes sense). Netflix has form on impacting upon popular culture: 'Stranger Things' helped Kate Bush return to the top of the charts again with 'Running Up That Hill', and chess set sales rose 87 per cent following the launch of The Queen's Gambit (Netflix, 2023).

Does it work? It's hard to know what the incremental impact was, however, searches for GM vehicles increased 50 per cent on Cars.com, and edmunds.com saw increases across the board for GM vehicles, including 160 per cent increase for Cadillac Lyriq, 6,970 per cent increase for Chevy Silverado EV, and 1,374 per cent increase for GMC Hummer EV. Forbes named it the Most Effective Ad in its 2023 awards, and it won a Silver Lion for Corporate Purpose and Social Responsibility in Film (Lions, 2023).

Meanwhile, EDF's 'Busy Driving Nothing' campaign by Havas takes another approach to normalizing a new behaviour when it comes to EV ownership. This ad shows a series of EVs being quietly charged at night while their owners are asleep, normalizing the action of charging your car before you go to bed, adding it to the list of other things you plug in like your mobile.

Volvo noted that today's backseat drivers will be tomorrow's drivers, so designed a campaign titled, 'Celebrity School Run' in which comedian Ellie Taylor drove kids to and from school in a new Volvo EV. Ellie was tasked with answering questions covering all things sustainability, as well as anything and everything else on her passengers' minds. The footage was split up into multiple channels, with the branded social film debuting as a 30 second spot on Celebrity Gogglebox and then being launched on Channel 4's YouTube, Instagram and Facebook accounts. Shorter, targeted campaigns supplemented the main content. Awareness of the XC40 Recharge improved by 8 per cent because of the campaign, while the brand's rating for sustainability also improved by 7 per cent (Channel 4, 2023). Real success will come from the changing of attitudes towards electric vehicles and the resulting sales shift.

A final example of advertising solving the challenge of making EV ownership a normal, enjoyable, and hassle-free experience is how Renault won the Creative Strategy Lions Grand Prix in June 2023 for its campaign 'Renault – Plug Inn', by Publicis Conseil, Paris. It developed an app that shows drivers of electric vehicles a network of private chargers in France, connecting EV drivers looking to explore rural France with café owners relying on travelling tourists for income. The Cannes Lions jury recognized that Renault was open to other brands also being involved and demonstrated category leadership through its efforts to advance the electric vehicle category.

Advertising sustainable tourism

As we write this section, familiar tourist destinations in Europe are in the news, reporting the impact of climate volatility and fires at or near resort locations. There is no doubt that what travel companies choose to advertise will be influenced by the impact of climate change over the coming years and these companies have a tremendously influential role in addressing how and where people choose to holiday. An opportunity to really make a difference. New destinations with more temperate weather will no doubt come into fashion and spread the load of holiday travel more evenly, opening the possibility for alternative modes of transport to be design in too.

Let's consider the powerful role of an industry media title, one that is funded by commercial ad spend from the sector it serves. Every sector has at least one title like this – Seb is an avid reader of *The Grocer*, and relates how the publication put a powerful spotlight on food waste a few years ago. How trade publications embrace the issue of sustainability and a transition to net zero could be central to a sector's pace of change.

In the case of the travel industry, it's the Travel Trade Gazette (TTG), which was established in 1953 as a weekly newspaper for the travel industry with the goal of connecting travel suppliers – the hoteliers, the cruise ship companies, the flight operators – with travel sellers – the travel agent community.

That role remains the same today, but four years ago the company articulated a new purpose and mission – to promote smarter, better, fairer travel and help the industry it sits at the heart of to be kinder to the environment and to the people who work in it. A crucial part of this is helping travel (and the many thousands of holidays sold every year) to be sustainable, to influence travel suppliers to make their offerings more sustainable and to equally influence travel sellers to promote more sustainable holiday choices.

Matt's conversation with the CEO and owner of TTG Media, Daniel Pearce (also former editor of TTG), was fascinating as he explained what we've seen elsewhere in this book, that most people just want a cheap holiday and they are not, in the main, likely to opt-in to offsetting their flights. Their expectation is that the travel industry itself will solve the problems of sustainability. Holidaymakers expect travel sellers to clearly signpost and help them make choices that are more sustainable without an extra premium.

TTG has approached the transition by making itself an organization which is proactive about sustainability, publishing its own climate action plan and committing to the Glasgow Declaration for Climate Action in Tourism, supporting the global mission to cut tourism emissions in half by 2030 with the rest reduced to zero by 2050 at the very latest (TTG Media, 2023).

Through its Climate Action Plan, TTG commits to its own measurement, tracking emissions from 'Business Operations' and from 'Events', making these publicly available on its site. Once emissions have been measured, the natural next step is taking action to reduce those emissions through actions including moving to a monthly frequency from weekly print magazine with a reduced print circulation and adopting paper wrappers to replace biodegradable polywrap. It has taken a similar approach to its events, reducing carbon-intensive menus further and introducing more vegan options, and incentivizing event delegates to use public transport.

TTG recognizes its own footprint is relatively small, but it can influence the travel industry community into acting on climate change through its own progress with carbon reduction and initiatives such as TTG's Sustainable Travel Heroes and TTG's Fairer Travel Week, which includes a full-day conference on Sustainable Travel.

TTG is helping to showcase and set the standard for sustainable travel and a net zero economy, supported by ad spend from commercial partners looking to promote their businesses to current and prospective customers. Every sector has at least one TTG, a dynamic B2B publisher at its heart leading the way on the changes we need to see, the catalysts of the transition taking place within the business supply chain. Their role as champions of, and critical friends to, the business communities they service is crucial.

Securing a sustainable future for travel and tourism

EdenLab is a business, made up of sustainability, innovation and marketing consultants, that describes itself as a sustainable innovation company and venture studio. Its mission is to help client companies build their net zero future through a technology-enabled and data-driven approach. It has an approach which it describes as 'The 3D framework':

- Diagnose the green growth opportunity
- Design green growth revenue programmes
- Deliver transition at scale

Its founder and CEO is Leo Rayman, former CEO and CSO of creative agency Grey London, who has spent 25 years advising global clients on marketing, branding, innovation, culture-change and sustainability. He is also an adviser to Carbon13, the venture builder for the climate emergency and he holds a distinction from the Cambridge University Institute of Sustainability Leadership. While researching this book and the challenges facing the travel and tourism sector, we had the opportunity to speak with Leo about the work that the sector needs to do.

Can you describe the challenge faced by businesses currently operating in the travel and tourism sector?

Two words: stranded assets. Many operators own planes and ships and old hotels. The question facing all companies in this sector is how do you supply a joyful travel experience without the emissions?

What are the steps a company in this sector needs to consider to achieve a sustainable footing?

1 Accept that travel needs to change
2 Rebuild the offering to incorporate lower carbon alternatives (e.g., trains)
3 Measure the baseline and set stretching targets
4 Be honest about the challenge of achieving it

Whose responsibility is it to make this happen: the business, the government through regulatory intervention or the customer? Or a combination of all three?

It's such a big systemic challenge that we're all going to have to pay for the transition one way or another. While we wait for government to step-up, it's incumbent on progressive leaders to inspire and enable their customers to make better, more sustainable, choices.

What is the role of advertising and communications to help customers take holidays that are enjoyable and sustainable?

Inspire, inform, and innovate. Let's reframe what a great holiday is. It certainly doesn't involve spewing out lots of carbon dioxide. Make choice available, explain in relatable terms what the impact of those choices are. Ensure that the business is taking an integrated approach, i.e., pricing, product offering, services, ancillaries – all in aid of decarbonization.

How could data be used to make holiday choices more sustainable?

Data is the lifeblood because how else might you uncover more sustainable holiday choices? Unfortunately, the travel sector lags on high quality sustainability data, for example, hotels are self-reporting using a wide variety of accreditation systems. It's my contention that within 3–5 years data standardization and universally applied standards will help resolve this problem.

What is the risk to a travel company that lags competitors on sustainability and securing a net zero future?

They will face fines and regulations on one hand and an inability to finance their transition away from stranded assets on the other. High-emitting plane operators will have to lower prices to attract customers – particularly the young – while regulators will fine them.

What does 'good' look like for a travel company's customer experience through a sustainability lens?

1 Focused on the holiday experience first, not the sustainability.
2 Easy to understand and inspiring more sustainable travel propositions.
3 Easy to use tools to help navigate and understand the impact of the travel choices people make.
4 Rewards and incentives for making more sustainable choices.
5 Transparency and open-source customer feedback on how to make trips more sustainable.

Are there examples for others to learn from?

Intrepid Travel. TUI's climate pledge. Travalyst's cross-industry data consortium.

CASE STUDY
The Palau Pledge

This campaign won the Grand Prix in the 2019 Care Awards particularly because it appears to be easily scalable and involves all stakeholders involved in travel and tourism to Palau. The idea is simple: the world's first 'eco-pledge' to be stamped in the passport of every visitor to the island. The advertiser was the Palau Legacy Project, and the campaign was developed by Australian agency, Host Havas.

For context, Palau is an island in the Pacific archipelago and high-volume tourism represents a threat to its future. At the same time, tourism, which began to scale massively in the 1980s, and the income it brings is important to the island's future. The Palauans are looking to protect their children's future by modelling a responsible way to enjoy the island. The Palau Pledge was a powerful way to shape this for everyone involved. It started with children from Palau who helped to draft what they would like visitors to consider when they arrive. That pledge to act in an ecologically and culturally responsible way on the island, for the sake of Palau's children and future generations of Palauans, became a visa stamp in every passport. Each visitor was asked to read and sign the pledge on arrival at Passport Control. Visitors are also encouraged to support Palau Pledge certified businesses. Palau describes itself as the first nation on earth to change its immigration laws for the cause of environmental protection.

The campaign has generated over 800,000 pledges from visitors to date and comes with a simple guide of do's and don'ts to help people uphold it during their stay (Palau Pledge, 2023). It is an idea that goes beyond advertising and has become an integral part of the communications between the Palauans and their visitors.

What struck Matt in conversations with leaders in the travel sector is how travel customers are, to borrow a phrase from another book, 'prisoners of geography'. Where someone holidays *from* matters, and transport solutions will need to transition to support travellers from all countries. This will trigger some fundamental rethinking about the holiday business model, as highlighted by Leo at EdenLab, addressing the risks, but also the opportunities that the traditional holiday companies face: new challenges for advertisers and new briefs for their agencies. Big behaviour changes for the industry, and for travelling customers. Tourism advertising, with sustainability at its heart, can help reframe what a great holiday looks like.

Energy, travel and tourism: summary

Energy, travel and tourism: the big carbon-intense sectors where major behaviour change on a worldwide scale is required of the industries and citizens alike, away from activities rooted in fossil fuel usage. The level of debate surrounding these hot-button topics is representative of the scale of the task ahead and is actually a positive for the industry. We need fierce debate from all corners – brands, regulators, activists, and industry professionals – to make progress. We don't claim to have the solutions, but we do hope that we have provided some contexts and case studies for you to consider how you might respond, and how you will contribute to this conversation. Whether in marketing or advertising, what part can you play to deliver behaviour change campaigns at scale, to help change the brief, and make the more sustainable options desirable, aspirational and accessible?

Coming up next are three equally critical sectors: food, fashion and finance.

References

2023, Interview with Daniel Pearce, CEO, and owner of TTG Media.

4Sales. (2021) *Volvo powers all-electric future with Channel 4 branded content.* Available at: https://www.4sales.com/latest/2021-07/press-releases/volvo-powers-all-electric-future-channel-4-branded-content (archived at https://perma.cc/63FE-QVW7)

ASA CAP. (2023) *01 Compliance.* [Online] Available at: https://www.asa.org.uk/type/non_broadcast/code_section/01.html (archived at https://perma.cc/D6JC-D77D)

ASA CAP. (2023) *ASA Ruling on Deutsche Lufthansa AG t/a Lufthansa.* [Online] Available at: https://www.asa.org.uk/rulings/deutsche-lufthansa-ag-a22-1169419-deutsche-lufthansa-ag.html (archived at https://perma.cc/PAN9-KPZL)

ASA CAP. (2023) *ASA Ruling on Etihad Airways.* [Online] Available at: https://www.asa.org.uk/rulings/etihad-airways-a22-1174208-etihad-airways.html (archived at https://perma.cc/5U59-LEGG)

ASA CAP. (2023) *ASA Ruling on Shell UK Ltd t/a Shell.* [Online] Available at: https://www.asa.org.uk/rulings/shell-uk-ltd-g22-1170842-shell-uk-ltd.html (archived at https://perma.cc/BL9J-DMXU)

Bootlis, P. (2018) *Care Awards 2019: Palau Legacy Project - "World-first eco-pledge stamped in all visitor's passports".* Available at: https://act.adforum.com/award-organization/6651769/showcase/2019/ad/34591189 (archived at https://perma.cc/HM6M-HJFM)

Creative Salon. (2021) *Havas London's Campaign For EDF Showcases Its Zero Emissions Capability.* Creative Salon. August 2021. Available at: https://creative.salon/articles/work/havas-edf-electric-vehicle (archived at https://perma.cc/F97F-U9V8)

E.ON. (2023) *It's time to take climate action.* [Online] Available at: https://www.eonenergy.com/climate-change/take-climate-action.html (archived at https://perma.cc/FR97-883L)

Eden Lab. (2023) *Home.* Available at: https://www.edenlab.co/ (archived at https://perma.cc/Z5UW-C8BV) [Accessed August 2023]

Financial Times. (2023) *BP slows oil and gas retreat after record $28bn profit.* [Online] Available at: https://www.ft.com/content/419f137c-3a83-4c9c-9957-34b6609bcdf7 (archived at https://perma.cc/3EFY-KJGK)

Gauthier, M. (2021) *Audi And Ford Norge Respond To GM's "No Way, Norway" Super Bowl Ad With Videos Of Their Own.* Carscoops.com. February 2021. Available at: https://www.carscoops.com/2021/02/audi-and-ford-norge-respond-to-gms-no-way-norway-super-bowl-ad-with-videos-of-their-own/ (archived at https://perma.cc/RKZ3-ACLX) [Accessed August 2023]

Global Energy Alliance for People and Planet. (2023) *Home.* [Online] Available at: https://www.energyalliance.org/ (archived at https://perma.cc/7Z69-Z9JF)

Google Sustainability. (2023) *Empowering Individuals: Google Maps.* [Online] Available at: https://sustainability.google/empowering-individuals/#google-maps (archived at https://perma.cc/H5NR-FERG)

GOV.UK. (2021) *Consulting on ending the sale of new petrol, diesel and hybrid cars and vans.* Department of Transport & Office for Zero Emission Vehicles. July 2021. Available at: https://www.gov.uk/government/consultations/consulting-on-ending-the-sale-of-new-petrol-diesel-and-hybrid-cars-and-vans (archived at https://perma.cc/6HZQ-DN3F)

GOV.UK. (2022) *Jet Zero strategy: delivering net zero aviation by 2050.* Department For Transport. July 2022. [Online] Available at: https://www.gov.uk/government/publications/jet-zero-strategy-delivering-net-zero-aviation-by-2050 (archived at https://perma.cc/CLF7-KASZ)

Labour. (2023) *Labour's plan for GB Energy.* [Online] Available at: https://labour.org.uk/issue/clean-energy-by-2030/ (archived at https://perma.cc/VSK7-86R8)

Lewton, T. (2022) *Revealed: BP's 'greenwashing' social media ads as anger over fuel costs rose.* The Guardian. August 2022. [Online] Available at: https://www.theguardian.com/business/2022/aug/06/bp-social-media-influence-ads-labour-windfall-tax (archived at https://perma.cc/UU29-RDH6)

Ofcom. (2018) *Code on the prevention of undue discrimination between broadcast advertisers.* [Online] Available at: https://www.ofcom.org.uk/tv-radio-and-on-demand/broadcast-codes/code-on-the-prevention-of-undue-discrimination-between-broadcast-advertisers#1 (archived at https://perma.cc/VHZ2-MHNE)

Ormesher, E. (2023) *ASA bans Lufthansa ad over misleading environmental claims.* The Drum. March 2023. Available at: https://www.thedrum.com/news/2023/03/01/asa-bans-lufthansa-ad-over-misleading-environmental-claims (archived at https://perma.cc/82EE-MA8C)

Palau Pledge. (2023) *Home. [Online]* Available at https://palaupledge.com/ (archived at https://perma.cc/VG7E-QT3G)

Paris, R. (2023) *Going Green Without Even Trying – OUIGO.* YouTube. March 2023. [Online] Available at: https://www.youtube.com/watch?v=wB5lYy6FhRg (archived at https://perma.cc/6VSK-LY87)

Ritchie H; Roser M. (2020) *CO₂ and Greenhouse Gas Emissions*. University of Oxford. [Online] Available at: https://ourworldindata.org/emissions-by-sector (archived at https://perma.cc/DGT7-85RS)

Roach, S. (2022) *Energy companies investing just 5% of profits in renewables*. Channel 4 News. August 2022. [Online] Available at: https://www.channel4. com/news/energy-companies-investing-just-5-of-profits-in-renewables (archived at https://perma.cc/M66L-CTMT)

Science Based Targets. (2023) *Oil and Gas*. [Online] Available at: https:// sciencebasedtargets.org/sectors/oil-and-gas (archived at https://perma.cc/C7HL-FN48)

Seabrook, V. (2023) *Misleading' Shell adverts about low-carbon products banned*. Sky News. June 2023. [Online] Available at: https://news.sky.com/story/ misleading-shell-adverts-about-low-carbon-products-banned-12897524 (archived at https://perma.cc/762W-H7CJ)

Staff. (2022) *The Energy Collective by Revolt London for Budweiser*. Campaign. [Online] Available at https://www.campaignlive.co.uk/article/campaign-ad-net-zero-winners-2022-drink/1804960 (archived at https://perma.cc/WGX7-9UJJ)

The Royal Society. (2023) *Net zero aviation fuels: resource requirements and environmental impacts*. [Online] Available at: https://royalsociety.org/topics-policy/projects/low-carbon-energy-programme/net-zero-aviation-fuels/ (archived at https://perma.cc/2ECZ-CV6K)

Topham, G. (2023) *Scientists pour cold water on UK aviation's net zero ambitions*. The Guardian. February 2023. [Online] Available at: https://www.theguardian. com/business/2023/feb/28/scientists-uk-aviation-net-zero-ambitions-half-farmland-double-renewable-electricity (archived at https://perma.cc/ 7RY2-ZMKL)

TTG Media. (2023) *TTG Media's Vision*. [Online] Available at: https://www. ttgmedia.com/ourvision (archived at https://perma.cc/5CQC-EBQE)

Virgin Atlantic. (2023) *World first 100% SAF transatlantic flight taxis closer to takeoff*. [Online] Available at: https://corporate.virginatlantic.com/gb/en/media/ press-releases/world-first-SAF-transatlantic-flight-taxis-closer-to-takeoff.html (archived at https://perma.cc/Z9UY-98NU)

Walton, J. (2023) *France has banned some short flights - what does this mean for travelers?* Lonely Planet. May 2023. [Online] Available at: https://www. lonelyplanet.com/news/france-short-haul-flight-ban-2023 (archived at https:// perma.cc/7WTD-MEKS)

13

Sector review:
Food, fashion and finance

In this chapter we're going to consider three sectors where a sustainable advertising industry can make a major contribution to supporting positive behaviour changes. We start with the role advertising can play in reducing emissions from food consumption and waste reduction, then address fashion with a staggering 56 per cent of textiles ending up in landfill (WRAP/ The Times, 2023), before finishing with the role finance brands can play in helping people spend their money in more sustainable ways.

Food

One of the key sectors to building a sustainable future is food and drink. WRAP (2021) data confirms that food production and consumption are responsible for around 30 per cent of global carbon emissions. By creating space for agriculture, they also contribute to between 60 per cent – 80 per cent of biodiversity loss through the destruction of natural habitats (WRAP, 2023). As we'll show in this section, many companies are already harnessing advertising to change underlying behaviours at scale, but much more needs to be done.

There are several actions we can all take to improve the sustainability of our food choices. Before weighing up the pros and cons of specific dietary choices, every person must make sure they are not wasting huge amounts of food: we featured example of work by Hellmann's and WRAP earlier.

We know that people need to eat less meat that is farmed in carbon-intensive ways (including that which is contributing to deforestation).

The emergence of better farming techniques and meat alternative products present two opportunities for advertising and marketing professionals.

There are many social norms including macho masculine tropes to be challenged and unpicked when it comes to meat consumption, typified by the modern-day BBQ and recipes like the beer can chicken. And the opposite: anyone for quiche? Plant-based alternatives to meat, egg and diary are a highly contested, high innovation-rate market with new brands fighting for awareness, market share and funding.

According to the Good Food Institute, the category raised $2.1 billion in 2020 – the most capital raised in any single year in the industry's history and more than three times the $667 million raised in 2019. A record $5 billion was invested in alternative proteins in 2021. The global plant-based meat market size was estimated by Grand View Research at $5.06 billion in 2021 with estimates the market will be four times as big by 2030, reaching a value of $24.8 billion.

As of 2021, plant-based meat's share of total meat was only 2.7 per cent of retail packaged meat dollar sales, or 1.4 per cent of the total meat category (including random weight meat) (Grand View Research, 2023). Paradoxically, while growth rates are flattening in 2023 for the first time, there's still a lot of scope for growth if new behaviours can replace the old ones and attitudes change to the old tropes: a job for marketing and advertising.

Analysis of UK adspend data by UK advertising think tank Credos identified a tipping point in 2022 as plant-based alternative products commanded more than a 50 per cent share of the media spent on advertising. The shift from traditional meat products to plant-based alternatives may be a gradual one, but advertising is already playing an essential role in supporting behaviour changes that will need to continue.

Quorn is a well-known plant-based meat-alternative product. According to Statista, brand awareness of Quorn is at 82 per cent in the UK. Seventy per cent of meat substitutes users in the UK use Quorn. In May 2022, about 46 per cent of UK meat substitute users had heard about Quorn in the media, on social media, or in advertising over the past four weeks (Statista, 2023). London-based agency, adam&eveDDB created a campaign for Quorn to challenge social norms in different ways and, by doing so, shift people's behaviours towards more sustainable options.

The first ad is for the launch of a new range of delicatessen-style meats. As the woman in the ad, Lisa, tucks into a delicious-looking sandwich, a voice is urging her to enjoy the treat and to absolutely, never, ever, consider the alternative. As the camera pulls out, we see the voice is coming from a puppet of a pig, and as the word 'alternative' is mentioned, startled-looking puppets of a chicken and a cow pop up on the other side of Lisa, asking what that 'alternative' might be. The comic ad promotes the taste of the product, while reminding the viewer of the reality behind the alternative to this 'alternative'. It's a powerful nudge and reminder of humour's ability to engage with uncomfortable or difficult topics, as we saw in Chapter 10. The second advert shows night-time street scenes typical after closing time at the pubs. People, hungry after a night out, hitting the fast-food outlets. Revellers tuck into their kebabs, burgers and wraps, but the chicken products being served are all Quorn, filling all the same needs as the originals. It will be interesting to see how many vendors add 'alternatives' to their menus in the years to come. Both ads are simple examples of ways to promote sustainable alternatives.

Before we go further into considering the work of advertising to support the growth of this sector and achieve the goal of mass behaviour change, let's have a quick look at some behavioural science specific to this sector that might help. Governments and supermarkets are extremely reluctant to tell people what to eat. Nobody is a fan of being preached to or coerced into behaviour, so the way that advertisers and brands pitch their products is so important.

Studies have found that neutral labelling is in fact more effective at selling vegetarian dishes to omnivores than the use of explicit labelling. The theory is that this removes the risk of reactance and allows for moral licensing – a person's perception that they may pursue whichever option they desire, without consequence or judgement. Understanding how to position better options without diminishing choice, as a totally free choice, is the psychological insight for success.

For example, the Journal of Environmental Psychology published "*A vegetarian curry stew*" *or just a* "*curry stew*"? – *The effect of neutral labeling of vegetarian dishes on food choice among meat-reducers and non-reducers* – which included five useful findings:

1 Neutral labelling versus explicit vegetarian labelling increases vegetarian food choice

2 Neutral labelling outperforms explicit labels in both meat-reducers and non-reducers

3 Explicit labels may act as exclusion criteria, create reactance or moral licensing

4 Neutral labelling is particularly powerful among ethically concerned meat-reducers

5 Neutral labels nudge non-reducers with low meat-eater identity to vegetarian dishes

Most people who eat meat won't be sold by the plant-based element; they are convinced by other product benefits such as improved taste, better price, or perhaps improved health because of consumption.

In practical terms, though, the topic of neutral labelling is becoming increasingly tricky for the companies who provide these alternatives. As of early 2023, Italy, France and South Africa have all brought in bans on products which do not differentiate themselves clearly enough from meat-based products. Finding the line between following labelling regulation and avoiding explicit plant-based labelling will be a real challenge for the marketing teams of these brands going forwards.

The challenge becomes even more intriguing when considering the prospect of promoting lab-grown meats. Or is that cultured meat? The current consensus seems to be 'cultivated meat', but expect a new iteration to emerge soon as innovation thrives.

What a creative challenge! To take something that is a country's favourite meat, develop a new way of producing it (sustainably) without animal involvement, and then convince millions and millions of customers to eat it every day. That's what UPSIDE Foods is looking to do in the US, starting with chicken. Its spokesperson even talks about more possibilities than just great tasting nuggets, adding in health benefits that could even be personalized to their own dietary needs. An Australian company, Vow has resurrected the flesh of the long-extinct woolly mammoth, and has pitched the idea of mammoth meatballs, unveiling the dish at a Science Museum in the Netherlands. The company is promising to invent new meats in the battle to change behaviours and encourage people to move away from consuming meat produced through industrialized farming techniques. Fancy a cheeky NanDodos, anyone?

Helping customers make better, more sustainable choices – Tesco

Food production and consumption are responsible for around 30 per cent of global carbon emissions (WRAP, 2021). The UN's Sustainable

Development Goal 12.3 is to halve food waste by 2030. To achieve this in the UK, further reductions in food waste of 1.8 Mt are needed, 1.3 Mt from homes and over half a million tonnes from across the supply chain (WRAP, 2021). Tesco is the UK's biggest supermarket by market share. Matt spent some time with the Tesco team during the process of writing this book to understand what they are doing to support a more sustainable way of life on our planet, whether the customer might be directly aware of this or not.

The company's core purpose, *serving our customers, communities and planet a little better every day,* is very holistic, and under the leadership of Dave Lewis and now Ken Murphy, inspired not only operational improvement but also customer propositions and campaigns to help customers to make better choices for health and sustainability. Like many shoppers, a large majority of Tesco customers are not going to do something if it is hard or too expensive. Instead, it needs to be easy and that means better choices that are simple, tasty and affordable.

Tesco's Better Baskets proposition launched in May 2022 when the company updated its position on customer health and the environment. The role of the Better Baskets campaign was, and remains, to help a customer find something better… better for them, better for their pocket and better for the planet. Consider the mindset of a Tesco customer for a moment – no one walks in store actively thinking 'today I really want to buy some things which are bad for me and are going to do some more damage to the planet'. They're thinking 'will the kids like it?' and 'can I afford it?'.

As they developed the *Better Baskets* proposition, Tesco uncovered that the two largest barriers to health, according to customers, is the want to treat themselves (35 per cent of customers surveyed) and that customers consider healthy food to be too expensive (33 per cent). Further barriers included the lack of inspiration on what to cook (22 per cent) and so the goal of the Better Baskets campaign became clear: to make healthier choices easy, affordable, and inspirational.

During Matt's conversations with the Tesco team, they talked about the role of communications and their marketing and advertising activities to help join the dots between what David Attenborough is saying on customers' TV screens about the planet and what they put in their shopping basket. It's about education and demystification, but also being conscious of the so-what factor for customers. That message about 'soil improvement' – it's probably not something the general Tesco customer cares about, but it is a critical message when it comes to talking with partners within the industry about positive steps forward in sustainability.

Ultimately, the Tesco team know that the Better Baskets proposition must be better for a customer's pocket, particularly in times where there is pressure on the cost of living. So, that recommendation in a recipe to use a blend of meat and vegetables in tonight's recipe is cheaper, yes, but it is also a good thing from a health point of view and contributes another small gain in the crucial reduction of the UK's meat consumption. The goal for the company's communication with its customer base is always to empower the individual, never to preach about what is best for them.

In May 2022, Tesco introduced Better Baskets into stores with a campaign that aimed to tackle the barriers that customers come up against when looking to fill their basket with better choices every time they shop. The campaign spotlighted products with the Better Baskets logo, including:

- Foods that are high in fibre
- Plant-based options
- Low- and no-alcohol drinks
- Snacks and treats under 100 calories
- Products that have reusable, reduced and recyclable packaging

To support the campaign, chef Jamie Oliver worked with Tesco and WWF (World Wildlife Fund) to create new veg-packed recipes, to inspire customers. The *Better Baskets* campaign was supported by TV, print and outdoor advertising, along with social media and online. Tesco is working closely with its partners, WWF, and WRAP (Waste & Resources Action Programme), to halve the environmental impact of the average UK shopping basket and has improved packaging for more than 1,500 different products and removed 1.6 billion pieces of unnecessary plastic, including multipacks, additional lids, films, and bags since 2019.

Sustainability, though, is a new area for the marketing team and is adding a new dimension to the consideration around language used in campaigns. The marketing team is being asked to adapt and consider new ways of substantiating why this is 'better' along with new types of evidence to explain and back that claim. This strive to talk consistently about 'better' in the context of sustainability is present across all areas of Tesco's communication – its paid, owner and earned media channels.

The initial approach of short term 'spikes' of communication about Better Baskets, accompanied by trade events in store only drove short term uplift in sales of healthier and more sustainable products (+9 per cent uplift of Better Baskets product versus previous period). The team also discovered that pulling 'better' products out of their parent categories and into high-visibility promotional space ('the power aisle') made it harder for customers to understand what they were *better* than. As such, showcasing a product with 'reduced packaging' didn't make sense if you can't compare it with the original version - the context of the rest of the aisle was required to help customers understand better choices.

The team ran into difficulties with the Better Baskets campaign in June 2022 when its advertising of the Plant Chef Burger as 'better for the planet' was the subject of a successful complaint to the ASA, with all the public attention that type of decision causes. The month before the campaign appeared, the CMA published its Green Claims Code with new guidance around product specificity. Despite the careful consideration Tesco had taken collaborating with both internal Sustainability and Legal teams, and external sustainability partner WWF, the ASA ruled that the ad must not air again.

While not wilfully misleading, the ruling put a new focus on how a company like Tesco ties a broad message like 'better for the planet' into a specific product. This shines a light on the inevitable tension between getting to the so-what quickly for customers and the specificity being required by regulators to ensure accuracy, which will almost certainly introduce more technical language to shoppers over time.

The team has used the experience to develop its knowledge and understanding of how to qualify such a statement when comparing products with the aim of stating that the one in the spotlight is the one that is more sustainable. It shouldn't be underestimated just how difficult a thing this is to do, particularly as supply chains for products are constantly evolving. But it is a message that is central to the *Better Baskets* campaign.

The Tesco team turned its lost ASA challenge on its Plant Chef Burger ad into a rigorous approach for how it now substantiates any 'better for the planet' claims. It runs a full Life Cycle Analysis on any product featuring this claim, meaning the company can confidently explain why the product is better than a comparison product. All this information is made available online so that customers can verify this themselves if they want to. Tesco is now directing customers towards naturally plant based products that are proven to be better for the planet – its latest Plant Chef Frozen Veg Burger performs better than frozen Tesco beef burgers on all sustainability metrics (88 per cent less global warming impact, 56 per cent less water use and 90 per cent less land use). It's good for people too as it's low in saturated fat (with no reds on the pack's traffic lights, and a healthy Nutrient Profiling Model score).

Looking forward, the Tesco team is now delivering a sustained communications approach whereby the brand becomes intertwined with customers' lives through the Better Baskets campaign – such that it is consistently showing up with helpful, timely and relevant nudges to support them making better choices. This is no longer about those campaign spikes that might run for a 6–8 week period (perhaps a more traditional way of thinking about an advertising campaign), but to consistently be a positive and supportive presence whenever customers make decisions about what they buy. This approach is achieved through surfacing products that are currently in-store or online that will help customers make easy choices, things that they might not know about. Tesco has an array of marketing options to choose from across its own channels, whether that is to use its website, its smart screens in-store, a tannoy to make an announcement, or a feature in the Tesco magazine. In essence, the team has moved to what it described as a 'surround sound of helpful nudges'. An example of this might be Tesco choosing to highlight its new range of own-brand snacks that are healthy and offers value-savings on Clubcard Prices, or a feature in the magazine titled '3 ways to use cauliflower'. Or, it might be via the company's collaboration with Jamie Oliver where he helps inspire families to try healthy, inexpensive products like chickpeas by weaving them into a recipe that is perfect for a busy family. Or when he helps families use under-valued store cupboard products, like a can of black beans, in a drive to use up other commonly wasted food in the fridge. The latter is a particularly effective strand for the Better Baskets campaign to leverage as there is a clear cost-saving benefit in 'using up' food with a net result of reducing food waste (a major source of GHG emissions).

This all-year-round engagement has shown promising signs of more lasting behavioural change and uplift in healthy product sales. For example, in-store Better Baskets zones have been shown to increase sales – a 12 per cent uplift in volume of the healthy products within these zones versus the rest of the range. These zones are permanently dressed bays in aisles that group together and promote healthier options, for example, wholemeal bread which is high fibre. The zones are being rolled out gradually and will be in 97 per cent of stores in some form. The online Better Baskets zone page, featuring information about what Better Baskets is, and buy list which feature better products, with 80 per cent of customers who visit the page adding something to their basket. Meanwhile Better Baskets emails connect with millions of customers and the Tesco Instagram channel provides recipe inspiration and videos.

The core principles of *Better Baskets* are clear: make it affordable, make it easy and make it simple and inspiring. The Tesco team has strict criteria for any products that feature – an in-house nutritionist approves any health claims working alongside fellow stakeholders in healthy sustainable diets, as well as the sustainability team.

Recent rises in cost-of-living have had a significant impact on how the campaign is delivered. The team has acknowledged customers are now less likely to try new food, as there is risk it will go to waste – customers are filling up with cheap carbs while cutting down on meat and veg. Value linked to health and sustainability is even more important and the team has stepped up its 'too good to waste' messaging with Jamie Oliver where the focus is on using up commonly wasted items to reduce food waste and save customers money.

To conclude, a supermarket like Tesco has a hugely influential and complex role in shaping more sustainable decisions around food and drink that are made by millions of people every single day. Matt was struck by just how much responsibility sits with the marketing team of a brand like this – to be the front line in the contact with customers and to help them to be healthy, to be able to afford the food and drink they need and to do this in a way which supports the planetary system. The Tesco team were at great pains to say that we should never think their customers do not care about climate change or the planet, but that pressures like cost-of-living or eating more healthily mean a brand like Tesco must help them do all of this in an easy, accessible, and affordable manner. All the time allowing the customer to be in control of their own decisions, and to do this in a way which consistently remains in line with what is expected from the advertising industry's own self-regulatory system and from any regulations that the government of the day might choose to introduce.

On that final point, Matt couldn't help noting an absence of government messaging to positively support the work of companies like Tesco to help people understand why and how to live more sustainably. We touched on the positive role of communications from government to citizens earlier on in the book, when we referenced the public health campaign around Covid. Matt reflected afterwards, while considering everything the Tesco team deals with daily to help the UK deal with a cost-of-living crisis at the same as the global issue of climate change, surely, it is not just the role of brands to help people eat and drink in a way that supports a sustainable future?

Advertising and the fashion industry

Some of the most famous, world-renowned fashion imagery is from advertising, created by brands seeking to sell their products to customers around the world. Think Kate Moss in Calvin Kleins or Supreme, Nick Kamen in Levis, the 90s work of Gap including its 'Who Wore Khakis' campaign, Tommy Hilfiger's 'family' – the list goes on. An entire media sector, helmed by the mighty Vogue, has built up around it. But as you consider these campaigns, what emerges in more recent times is how quickly and fully fashion has embraced social media marketing. Campaigns like DKNY's State of Mind, Prada's partnership with Charli D'Amelio on TikTok for Milan Fashion Week, all capitalizing on, and harnessing, a dynamic shift in the advertising marketplace. The advent of social media, the birth and growth of fashion influencers and the connection which has been made possible via technology have all supported growth in ecommerce. It has become possible to see, select and buy any 'look' night or day, and add it to your wardrobe, often at a greatly reduced cost than the original high-end items on show and all too easy to return if a size isn't right.

The Fast Fashion Global Market Report 2023 states the fast fashion industry was worth $106.4 billion in 2022 and will grow to an estimated $256.7 billion by 2032. It defines fast fashion as the design, development and marketing of apparel designs that places an emphasis on giving consumers access to fashion trends fast and affordably. Fast fashion meaning garments that move quickly from the catwalk to the stores to meet the new trends and it cites the major players in the fast fashion market as Zara (Inditex), H&M Group, Fast Retailing (Uniqlo), Gap, Forever 21, Mango, Esprit, Primark, New Look and River Island; all household names and big advertisers in the fashion category. The reasons for growth, according to the report are linked to rising disposable incomes in developing countries, growth in apparel export volumes, changing consumer preferences, increasing social media penetration, and increasing youth population. In the UK alone, the fast fashion market was worth $4.1 billion in 2022 and is expected to grow to $5.5 billion in 2027 after recovering from a 25 per cent drop in 2020 for the pandemic. These products are generally currently made of polyester, acrylic and/or nylon. WRAP, in its work around textiles, estimates that £140m worth of clothing is sent to UK landfill each year.

Shein, the Chinese brand, is probably the 'trophy' example of a fast fashion business that has grown through the power of social media marketing.

It is worth $100 billion in 2022, up from $5 billion in 2019 (The Times, 2023). Shein stocks hundreds of thousands of individual items, releases thousands of new styles daily and products, with an average price of just a few pounds, are shipped to more than 150 countries worldwide. Let's consider for a moment how it used TikTok to build its business. Influencers were paid to share their haul of clothes in different styles, sizes, colours, asking people if they should return the clothes. The campaign's hashtag #sheinhaulover has had more than 9.1 billion views on TikTok, while #shein itself has had 53.5 billion. A shop feature, introduced in 2021, helps convert views into sales. TikTok isn't alone in offering this functionality. The quick and easy user experience is successful for fast fashion companies, offering free returns, size-match tools and constantly updated new 'personal' styles, just a click or two away. All this is often linked via affiliate marketing with a share in profit going to the influencer or media channel that has helped generate the sale. Much of the commercial media space with links to fashion and apparel is dependent to some extent on the income it generates in this way. Houston, we have a problem.

Matt had first-hand experience of just how complicated this all is to unpick when he presented to the sales team at a major commercial media owner at their annual sales gathering in late 2022. He had 20 minutes to share the thinking behind Ad Net Zero and encourage the sales team to put a greater consideration on sustainability in their day-to-day work and targets. Lots of interesting questions and lots of nice feedback. But before him was a presentation about the media owner's investment into (and early success with) its digital sales operation, offering new, high-impact ecommerce solutions to advertising partners, facilitating sales, and evidencing the power of the media brands to influence those sales. And he was followed by a leader from a big agency group sharing results of new audience research, evidencing the global consumers' desire for easy shopping online. There was one short film embedded in the presentation, in which an influencer made a nod to 'sustainability' by excitedly saying, 'If you show us that this amazing bag is sustainable, we won't buy just one, we'll buy them all!' And, of course, if that's helped by the sales team through an affiliate partnership, then that's more money back into the business for content, journalists, tech and sales team hires and bonuses. He left the event deflated, thinking there's a big hungry, never-satisfied monster sitting right in the middle of this sweet spot of consumers, influencers and ecommerce. It will keep feeding and feeding the fast fashion habit unless something gives.

The rise of low-cost, easy-to-access, easy-to-discard fashion items of all kinds has created an enormous issue, some call it over-consumption, but in truth it's over production, making more than people need to the point where it ends up in landfill. Cheap because many of the costs are driven into externalities outside the P&L of the companies in the industry, like the cost of disposal, the cost of pollution and greenhouse gas emissions and the social cost of underpaid workers.

The industry must rapidly reduce the environmental and social damage it causes through the production process and subsequent waste. Advertising is locked in here, as we've seen at the beginning of this section, advertising helps (alongside other creative industries including film, tv and music) to create the aspiration for an always-moving, always developing abundance of fashion styles. Fashion, as portrayed by advertising, allows us to express who we are and where we 'belong', but the rate at which people can buy, change and throw away clothes is simply unsustainable and something which must be addressed.

This is all pointing to the urgent need for complete system renewal within the fashion industry. There are some emerging better practices, with more sustainable business models, that must be supported, normalized and, indeed, made aspirational through the support of advertising.

The Sustainable Fashion Communication Playbook

Matt spoke with Rachel Arthur, advocacy lead at the United Nations Environment Programme. Rachel has worked with the UN on The Fashion Industry Charter for Climate Action, guided by its mission to drive the fashion industry to net-zero Greenhouse Gas emissions no later than 2050 in line with keeping global warming below 1.5 degrees.

Rachel has been behind the development of the 'Sustainable Fashion Playbook' for the UN which links to the charter and was launched at the Global Fashion Summit in June 2023. It has been designed to help fashion communicators – marketers, brand managers, imagemakers, media, influencers and beyond – and it lays down some fundamental challenges and changes to the way fashion is promoted and advertised.

It very clearly sets out the need to redirect fashion communication towards sustainable and circular solutions, and explains how to communicate environmental claims, summed up in eight principles for communication change as follows:

Lead with science: Ensure relevant information is clearly and transparently shared, providing an evidence-base that is verifiable and comparable while adhering to relevant regulatory policies.

- Principle 1: Commit to evidence-based and transparent communication efforts.
- Principle 2: Ensure information is shared in a clear and accessible manner.

Change behaviours and practices: show how consumers can enjoy fashion while living within the limitations of the planet and respecting human rights and dignity. Encourage lower impact options and circular solutions that normalize more sustainable behaviours.

- Principle 3: Eradicate all messages encouraging overconsumption.
- Principle 4: Champion positive changes and demonstrate accessible circular solutions to help individuals live more sustainable lifestyles.

Reimagine values: actively seek to separate the belief that consumption and ownership lead to happiness and success. Paint a picture of how positive new values can look when considering wellbeing, equity, and community.

- Principle 5: Spotlight new role models and notions of aspiration or success
- Principle 6: Focus on inclusive marketing and storytelling that celebrates the positive ecological, cultural, and social values of fashion.

Drive advocacy: use your platform and influence to empower consumers in their role as citizens. Educate internally and externally on the level of change required, supporting dialogue with policymakers on a just transition towards a sustainable and circular global value chain.

- Principle 7: Motivate and mobilize the public to advocate for broader change.
- Principle 8: Support dialogue with leadership and policymakers to enable wider industry sustainability.

A powerful set of principles to reinvent fashion communication, in which people employed in communicating about fashion are asked to:

- counter misinformation and greenwashing

- reduce messages perpetuating overconsumption
- redirect aspiration to more sustainable lifestyles
- empower consumers in their role as citizens to demand greater action from businesses and policymakers.

The playbook attempts to define overconsumption, acknowledging that there is no signed-off definition as it stands today.

More work is needed for a clear, agreed definition, but it can tentatively be proposed that overconsumption is a) beyond the physical and core social needs of an individual, b) primarily driven by peripheral social needs (e.g., personal image and identity), and c) inconsistent with all other people on earth having the same level of consumption while ensuring planetary sustainability (UNEP, 2023). Fair fashion consumption will differ by market, with some people needing to consume less, while those who still need to meet basic needs consume in a way that is different from contemporary materialism (UNEP, 2016).

Coming back to the reframing of over-consumption as over-production and over-selling:

The Playbook does not however suggest the onus for change is on individual action – it recognizes the role consumers can play but does not imply they are solely or mainly responsible and able to fix the fashion sector's issues. As with UNEP's Textile Value Chain Roadmap report, the Playbook places its emphasis on how organizations (public and private) with power and influence can change systems, create incentives, and shift expectations to support consumers in adapting their behaviour and values towards more sustainable patterns.

This 'overconsumption' challenge isn't unique to the fast fashion sector, but it is perhaps most obvious as we consider how and where massive behaviour change is needed. The playbook contains a series of questions which fashion communicators are posed as they develop their campaigns:

- Do communication materials demonstrate product longevity over disposable or one-off buys?
- Are sales promotions and media buys thoughtful and considered, rather than promoting overconsumption?
- Does the communication activity inspire and encourage consumers to engage in more sustainable lifestyles at large?

- Is the 'why' of sustainable products or services clearly stated and explained? Do the benefits inspire and motivate behaviour change?
- Are all products fairly priced in relation to their environmental and social costs?

There is a major transformation about to take place at the heart of the fashion industry – the question is how quickly this can happen and how rapidly fashion advertising can adopt these new practices. Can fashion brands (including the big fast fashion companies) and the many campaigns they deliver every year help build a world where all fashion is sustainable?

Redefining 'fashionable'

There are all sorts of challenges emerging around the words and phrases that companies will increasingly use to encourage people to buy their more sustainable fashion products: precise and evidenced use of 'organic', 'carbon neutral', 'circular', 'regenerative', 'zero waste' will be critical.

Examples of advertising campaigns that are helping normalize more sustainable behaviours are emerging. Let's look at the growth in advertising of second-hand or 'pre-loved' clothing.

Oxfam's 'Second-Hand September' is a campaign to encourage people to buy only second-hand items for 30 days in the month of September. It has been running since 2019 to inspire people to shop in a more sustainable way. Some 26,413 people pledged to say yes to less in September 2022, the first few thousands committing to consume less, look out for people and planet, raising money and awareness to fight climate change and end poverty (Oxfam, 2023).

In April 2023, pre-loved fashion platform Vinted announced it would be working with Channel 4 on the broadcaster's biggest cross-platform branded partnership to date. Vinted returned as sponsors of Channel 4's hit soap series, *Hollyoaks*, with newly created idents. In addition, a star of that show, Jorgie Porter, presented a new short-form digital series, *Second Hand Style-Up*, with stylist Emma Winder surprising people looking for a make-over by taking the profits of clothing sales on Vinted to purchase second-hand outfits. The show brought to life how selling what you don't wear can help you purchase items you can wear, and when that's second-hand, it's a win-win for wallet and the environment. The show featured on Channel 4's YouTube shows and across the company's Facebook, Instagram and TikTok accounts.

CASE STUDY
ITV, Love Island and eBay

Aim

Love Island and eBay were both brands struggling to find their place in their respective industries following periods of reduced consumer awareness and ratings – Love Island was still a show with enviable cultural clout, but by the time we emerged from lockdown in the summer of 2021, viewing figures were some way off their 2019 pre-pandemic high. Meanwhile eBay, while well-known as a general marketplace, was not broadly appreciated as a treasure trove of unique fashion. The aim, then, was to reignite the country's love and awareness of eBay and Love Island by reframing desirable fashion; putting a spotlight on pre-loved clothing and bringing it more firmly into the mainstream for every fashion-conscious consumer.

Action

ITV launched a collaboration between Love Island and eBay in their bid to revitalize both brands, bringing the concept of a 'pre-loved fashion partner' into the show. Knowing the power of Love Island to set fashion trends and shape audience behaviour – a bespoke dress made for a contestant in 2019 sold over 1600 units within 10 minutes of airing – the ITV team knew that there was potential to make real change while smashing their business objectives.

The ITV and eBay team enlisted a professional stylist to work with the Love Island contestants to put together bespoke pre-loved wardrobes, turning the Love Island cast into an ongoing advert for eBay, as well as showing off the power of recycled fashion through a shared wardrobe that encouraged the islanders to re-wear each other's outfits throughout the series. The collaboration then went on to create a larger ecosystem across as many available touchpoints as possible; by auctioning the islanders' outfits, staging take-overs of eBay's homepage and sharing wardrobes on social media.

Result

Satisfyingly, the partnership delivered for ITV, with ITV listed as the 'greenest' of the major broadcasters in a post-partnership survey. As for eBay, the results of the campaign speak for themselves.

Mirroring the move away from fast fashion that people saw on screen, viewers at home followed suit with eBay UK reporting over 1400 per cent more searches 'pre-loved fashion' on the marketplace during series nine, compared to series eight, as well as a 24 per cent increase in new circular businesses joining the online marketplace so far in 2023.

New research also found that one pre-loved item had been sold on the platform every second over the last year, with pre-loved fashion listings being up by almost 20 per cent year-on-year since the Love Island partnership launched – demonstrating the impact the partnership continues to have on consumer shopping behaviours.

Better still, ITV's Social Purpose Impact report estimates 2.7m young people are making more of an effort to shop sustainably having seen the Love Island and eBay partnership.

Advertising and the financial services industry

Financial institutions can be an important player in supporting genuine behaviour change. Banks have a tremendous position of responsibility, in what they choose to finance, and in the picture they can give to customers about sustainability of lifestyle through their financial data.

NatWest Group, a leading UK advertiser, was the first UK bank, and one of the largest banks globally at the time of writing, to have science-based targets validated by the Science Based Targets initiative (SBTi). It has a clear public purpose when it comes to climate change and its role in supporting the transition to a net zero economy. It states it wants to deliver a more sustainable economy and future for the customers and communities it serves. The targets underpin the first iteration of its climate transition plan with the aim of achieving its net zero climate ambition by 2050.

According to NatWest's 2022 climate-related disclosure report, its goals are:

- To at least halve the climate impact of its financing activity by 2030, against a 2019 baseline, and align with the 2015 Paris Agreement.
- To reduce carbon intensity of in-scope Assets under Management (AuM) by 50 per cent by 2030, against a 2019 baseline, and to move 70 per cent of in-scope AuM to a net-zero trajectory.
- To reduce emissions for its operational value chain by 50 per cent, against a 2019 baseline.

NatWest is also clear in the report about how it intends to achieve this. Supporting customer transition to net zero, it has a target to provide £100 billion sustainable financing between 1 July 2021 and the end of 2025. It aims to provide at least £10 billion in mortgage lending for residential properties with the highest (A and B) rated Energy Performance Certificates (EPC) between 1 January 2023 and the end of 2025, with the ambition to support those UK mortgage customers to increase their residential energy efficiency. Finally, it plans to incentivize purchasing of the most energy efficient homes with an ambition that 50 per cent of its mortgage portfolio has an EPC rating of C or above by 2030.

To help end the most harmful activities, NatWest is planning to phase-out of coal for UK and non-UK customers who have UK coal production, coal-fired generation and coal-related infrastructure by 1 October 2024, with a full global phase-out by 1 January 2030. It is also collaborating across industry to create products and services that help customers track their carbon impact.

And it is also focused on getting its own house in order, with annual targets for executive remuneration to reflect latest climate ambitions. Work will continue to integrate financial and non-financial risks arising from climate change into its enterprise-wide risk management framework (EWRMF). It has set a target to reduce own-operations emissions by 50 per cent by 2025, against a 2019 baseline, with plans to use only renewable electricity in its own global operations by 2025 (RE100) and improve energy productivity 40 per cent by 2025 against a 2015 baseline (EP100). Nat West also committed to installing electric vehicle charging infrastructure in 15 per cent of spaces by 2030 and upgrading its small fleet of around 100 vehicles to electric by 2025 (EV100).

NatWest supports hundreds of thousands SME customers in the UK with different finance options (Green Loans, Green Assets Finance, and flexible finance for Electric Vehicles), tailored grants and specialist mentoring advice. Its hero proposition is a free Carbon Planner tool to help businesses to track and reduce emissions, whatever sector they might be in. NatWest says that more than half of the UK's carbon reduction ambition could be delivered by UK businesses, and it wants to support other organizations in their emissions reduction.

As a bank to individual customers, to help explain what banking has to do with climate change, NatWest nudges customers towards climate-friendly actions that are good for their pocket and the planet with a carbon calculator in the personal banking app, launched in November 2021.

The outcomes so far? More than 20,000 customers have committed to action, with an average of 3.8 actions per customer. Actions are split into five everyday categories that any customers can relate to, these are shopping, transport, groceries, home and garden, and bills. Actions range from committing to meat-free Mondays or washing laundry at 30 degrees, up to more significant changes like switching out short-haul flights and buying pre-owned furniture. The most popular actions committed to are swapping to LED bulbs, washing clothes in cold water, not using a tumble dryer and turning down the heating thermostat. Over 18 months after launch, it continues to gain organic momentum. March, April, May 2023 have been its busiest months since launch for usage volumes.

NatWest's 'Climate Marketing Strategy: What's banking got to do with climate change?' during 2021 and 2022 was a winner in the 2022 Campaign Ad Net Zero Awards, for best example in the finance sector. The programme had four goals:

- Inspire – a rallying cry to signal our role and our commitment, creating a clear connection between banking and the climate crisis.
- Educate – a programme of content to demystify COP26 and build our credibility as a climate changemaker.
- Reward – win-win climate friendly choices that are good for pocket and planet.
- Empower – knowledge and tools for customers to track and reduce carbon emissions.

What were the results? Paid and organic views of 1.2 million of the hero film 'what has banking got to do with climate change?' resulting in a 10 per cent increase in average monthly usage of the carbon tracker in the banking app, 380,000 visits (Jan–April 2022) to the climate change hub, versus 147,000 in 2021, with a 425 per cent increase from search (Jan–April 2022 vs 21). All this led to a 1 per cent uplift (12MR) in NatWest's consumer brand association with 'helps address climate change'.

The key take-aways for the team at NatWest reinforce what we have seen earlier in the research studies:

- Make it local and personal – make climate action relevant to everyday actions.
- Make it simple – no scientific jargon.
- Make it win-win – connect climate action to cost savings.
- Make it social – make people feel part of a movement.

It should be noted that the NatWest team is a strong advocate for decarbonizing its own advertising supply chain, across ad production and ad distribution. It is taking steps to achieve this goal, as an active supporter of Ad Net Zero and AdGreen, working with agencies on a Climate Charter to embed all the principles of sustainable production and media. They track media spend emissions and offset annually through its bank-wide mechanisms.

The NatWest marketing team are testing sustainable media planning options: can they use only media partners with a product or service that offers a climate-friendly solution, and partners signed up to the IPA Climate Charter? They are working with Good-Loop on digital and Pureti Paint on out of home advertising. That's a photocatalytic coating that can be applied to print or exterior surfaces that reacts with UV light and local air pollutants to neutralize NOx gasses (smog) and VOC (volatile organic compounds) in the air.

What's clear as we review NatWest's programme is just how much thought and careful consideration is required in executing a strategy like this. To be a good corporate player, to demonstrate how you are shifting your own business to net zero and to evidence how you are helping your customers, whether they are a business owner or a member of the public, to do the same. We can see here how it is a good thing when a big business is given the room, especially in a difficult sector, to communicate its progress, how that business then has a credible position to help so many other companies do the same.

There is a risk, and this isn't just the case for NatWest, that the strongest voice of protest shuts out any opportunity to report and share progress or talk about what good looks like in advertising and marketing campaigns. It's a tightrope but one that advertisers like NatWest must continue to walk with effective sustainable advertising and marketing campaigns, however uncomfortable that might be for the marketing teams and their advertising partners. It must be done for the full potential of a net zero economy to be realized as quickly as possible.

Food, fashion and finance: summary

Our review of food, fashion and finance underlines how much of a significant role marketing and advertising can have in supporting the promotion of more sustainable products, services and behaviours across many different aspects of the way we live. But they can also become part of the problem perpetuating unsustainable business models which over-stimulate consumption. There are countless opportunities for sustainable nudges, contextual reframing and education that this industry can collectively make happen. Whatever the brief you are working on, there will be an opportunity to encourage a more sustainable outcome – it is this system change that we want to champion across every aspect of the work we do as an industry.

References

2022, Quorn Deli - So Tasty Why Choose The Alternative? 2022 TV Ad.

2023, ITV case study. *Information provided by ITV Sales.*

2023, NatWest case study. *Information provided by NatWest sustainability and marketing teams.*

2023, Quorn Deli - So Tasty Why Choose The Alternative? 2023 TV Ad.

2023, Tesco case study. *Information provided by Tesco sustainability and marketing teams.*

Boker Lund, T; Hiltje Hielkema, M. (2022) *Journal of Environmental Psychology: A "vegetarian curry stew" or just a "curry stew"? - The effect of neutral labeling of vegetarian dishes on food choice among meat-reducers and non-reducers.* Elsevier. October 2022. Available at: https://www.sciencedirect.com/science/article/pii/S0272494422001220 (archived at https://perma.cc/H4NE-YMPX)

Buxton, A. (2023) *Italy Makes Moves To Crack Down On Plant-Based Meat Labels.* Plant Based News. March 2023. Available at: https://plantbasednews.org/culture/law-and-politics/italy-vegan-meat-labeling/ (archived at https://perma.cc/385Q-JJQM)

Carrington, D. (2023) *Meatball from long-extinct mammoth created by food firm.* The Guardian. March 2023. Available at: https://www.theguardian.com/environment/2023/mar/28/meatball-mammoth-created-cultivated-meat-firm (archived at https://perma.cc/3QDH-Z282)

Channel 4. (2023) *Channel 4 and Vinted sign trailblazing multi-platform partnership.* [Online] Available at: https://www.channel4.com/press/news/channel-4-and-vinted-sign-trailblazing-multi-platform-partnership (archived at https://perma.cc/6AUP-5TKX)

Chrysanthou, A; Wildenberg, L. (2023) *Fast fashion, fast growth: have we given up on sustainable shopping?* The Times. Available at: https://www.thetimes.co.uk/article/fast-fashion-second-hand-sustainable-shopping-uk-2023-kxcljbsnb (archived at https://perma.cc/SE3Y-TNFP) [Accessed August 2023]

Fleming, A. (2022) *What is lab-grown meat? How it's made, environmental impact and more.* BBC Science Focus. June 2022. Available at: https://www.sciencefocus.com/science/what-is-lab-grown-meat-a-scientist-explains-the-taste-production-and-safety-of-artificial-foods (archived at https://perma.cc/HW8F-XSJB) [Accessed August 2023]

Good Food Institute. (2023) *Market Research.* Available at: https://gfi.org/marketresearch/ (archived at https://perma.cc/RW4C-RBV5)

Grand View Research. (2023) *Plant-based Meat Market Size, Share & Trends Analysis Report By Source (Soy, Pea, Wheat), By Product (Burgers, Sausages, Patties), By Type, By End-user, By Storage, By Region, And Segment Forecasts, 2023 – 2030.* Available at: https://www.grandviewresearch.com/industry-analysis/plant-based-meat-market (archived at https://perma.cc/3H2V-5DYA)]

Kunst, A. (2023) *Leading meat substitute brands ranked by brand awareness in the United Kingdom as of July 2023.* Statista. August 2023. Available at: https://www.statista.com/statistics/1309957/most-well-known-meat-substitute-brands-in-the-uk/ (archived at https://perma.cc/XJS5-WG5G)

Oxfam. (2023) *Get Involved: Second Hand September.* [Online] Available at: https://www.oxfam.org.uk/get-involved/second-hand-september/ (archived at https://perma.cc/VDE4-GZMW)

Schofield, B. (2023) *Is it payback time for the rags trade?* The Times. [Online] Available at: https://www.thetimes.co.uk/article/is-it-payback-time-for-the-rags-trade-fmjvv93dm (archived at https://perma.cc/3QN5-FSD4)

The Business research Company. (2023) *Fast Fashion Global Market Report 2023.* Research and Markets. February 2023. Available at: https://www.researchandmarkets.com/reports/5735360/fast-fashion-global-market-report?gclid=Cj0KCQjw6KunBhDxARIsAKFUGs-q-pQESfGdZof12d2HKjZgA3EP6zx8KwbDVb69iwR4ivKLUfGOHP4aAt2SEALw_wcB (archived at https://perma.cc/DFT6-5ZQV)

UN Environment Programme. (2023) *The Sustainable Fashion Communication Playbook.* Available at: https://www.unep.org/interactives/sustainable-fashion-communication-playbook/ (archived at https://perma.cc/WEP2-5VTL)

WRAP. (2021) *Wasting Food Feeds Climate Change.* WRAP. February 2021. Available at: https://wrap.org.uk/media-centre/press-releases/wasting-food-feeds-climate-change-food-waste-action-week-launches-help (archived at https://perma.cc/9HJG-P372) [Accessed August 2023]

WRAP. (2023) *Transforming the food system.* Available at: https://wrap.org.uk/taking-action/food-drink (archived at https://perma.cc/46LL-Y497)

14

Measuring the industry's impact

What should we measure in a sustainable advertising industry and how?

The question of measuring advertising's impact is one which has long challenged those in the industry to prove their work's value. Over 100 years ago, John Wanamaker, the department store pioneer, is credited with the quip, 'Half the money I spend on advertising is wasted; the trouble is I don't know which half.' That said, there have been tremendous advances in defining this value, linked to sales of products and services, perhaps best evidenced by the world-renowned IPA's Effectiveness Awards. Much has been written too about advertising's impact: 'Advertising's Big Questions' series by the UK advertising think tank, Credos, has published studies on growth, how advertising supports competition and innovation and how it operates in a mature market.

Now, though, we have an extra dimension and an added imperative, the impact of the industry on global GHGs and climate change. Thinking about how we measure advertising's carbon emissions, its contributions to climate change and the work it does in support of a net zero economy is rich with different points of view. We're going to try and unpick those and consider all perspectives to help provide some clarity in an area that will fast evolve over the next few years. Measurement is required for a variety of uses. And that can be part of the issue, as what satisfies one use can be too forensic, time-consuming, expensive, or insufficiently detailed for other uses.

The main demands for emissions measurement are setting definitions for net zero goals and the reduction plans that follow, investor risk profiling of companies, providing data to management to define strategies and to make everyday commercial decisions. You can see immediately how these may require different levels of standardization, accuracy and verification.

Part of the measurement challenge falls within the sectors of the industry: marketing teams, agencies, production companies, tech platforms and media owners. Or from the perspective of an advertising plan, the carbon emissions that come from creation, production and distribution. We've covered all of this in detail earlier in the book, each with their own chapter, plus examples of the types of measurements and reporting that is available. We could say that these emissions are from within the industry envelope.

At the time of writing there is no exact quantification of those emissions; estimates vary often due to the definition of the envelope, but it's fair to say that it's a sizeable footprint which must be measured and ultimately reduced. As AdGreen (Chapter 4) and the Media framework developed with GARM (Chapter 7) mature, these data sets will help to put a more accurate figure on it. The advertising industry needs to get its own house in order when it comes to tracking, reporting and reducing the carbon emissions from the way it works. This will be a fundamental requirement of all businesses that operate in a sustainable advertising industry to have any credibility helping other businesses do the same.

A global classification of distinct types of emissions came in with the 2001 Greenhouse Gas Protocol, introducing what we now know as scopes 1 and 2 – the direct emissions of businesses, and their indirect emissions in scope 3. SBTi was set up in 2014 (a partnership between CDP (formerly known as Carbon Disclosure Project), the United Nations Global Compact, World Resources Institute (WRI) and the World Wide Fund for Nature (WWF)) to help companies adopt climate targets in line with best-practice, and with science. Best practice today requires all companies to set targets and work to reduce emissions in their indirect emissions, scope 3.

How scope 3 is defined for companies in each sector of advertising is the industry's next big challenge. Without standardized definitions for what's included in scope 3, management, investors, clients and customers will find it hard to understand and compare data for similar companies. Many involved are proposing that standard scope 3 definitions for each sector should be arrived at by working as an industry in a pre-competitive way, holding true to the belief that this will be the quickest and most effective way to establish a measurement framework that all players recognize. This will then support effective and fair competition to deliver business success on a reducing carbon footprint. As it stands companies can make their own scope 3 definitions for their business.

For any one company operating in one sector of the industry, part of their scope 3 will fall inside the industry's envelope of emissions up or down the value chain. Any advertiser (and their partners) should be able to see the carbon emissions involved in the end-to-end process of their advertising campaign. With that information, they can make planning decisions to reduce that, or make decisions which allow them to trade carbon credits with other parts of their business or wider. Decisions will be made for advertising campaigns just like they have always been with a budget, a target audience, a cost-per-engagement metric, but in a world that supports a net zero economy, with a carbon metric too. So, any scope 3 definition should surely include as a minimum, indirect emissions that fall inside the envelope of the industry. For an agency this would include the indirect emissions from production and distribution of campaigns.

The next big question for all companies in the advertising industry is how much of the indirect emissions outside the envelope of the advertising industry should be included in their responsibility to reduce. How far does this responsibility extend into the footprint of clients, or how far into people's consumption habits and behaviours?

This area is highly complex with a range of views from across the profession. All voices and views should be recognized as the industry debates its role at the heart of a sustainable future. However, one thing to note is that climate experts are systematically helping every industry work this out, and marketing and advertising need to work with them, rather than on their own.

So, how exactly should advertising work out its real-world impact and account for that in each campaign that the industry delivers? Can it even be done?

Introducing the concept of Ecoeffectiveness

One of the original concepts to tackle this measurement challenge was something called Ecoeffectiveness. This was first raised by Caroline Davison, Managing Partner and Sustainability Lead at Elvis and Ben Essen, Global Chief Strategy Officer at Iris, during the Institute of Practitioners of Advertising's Global Effworks event in October 2020. For context, EffWorks is a reservoir of learning, research and debate established by the IPA with a host of industry partners. It has the ambition to provide the marketing industry with resources and tools to change its culture and realize the potential of truly accountable and effective marketing. Caroline and Ben presented a session titled Ecoeffectiveness: the missing measure in the climate crisis and asked whether there is a 'missing measure' in the industry's examination of advertising effectiveness to date – analysing and tracking the carbon impact of the work (IPA, 2020).

Their premise was that for more than 40 years, effectiveness studies have developed an almost scientific understanding of how advertising drives growth, profit and other key business metrics. But many major brands are now committed to delivering against a new metric: reducing greenhouse gas emissions to net zero. Therefore, if net zero is a key business target, then emissions become a key effectiveness metric. Caroline and Ben argued this sets an unprecedented 21st century challenge for advertising, for which there was no effectiveness data, frameworks, or insights to learn from: how to increase profitability while reducing emissions to net zero?

To answer this question, they launched a new methodology to establish 'Ecoeffectiveness' – the missing measure that, if society is to keep global temperature increases to within 1.5 degrees, must be a key element of all effectiveness cases going forward. Organizations were invited to calculate and report the incremental uplift in greenhouse gas emissions associated with all sales attributable to advertising.

The method incorporated three key elements:

1 Honest reporting of the incremental uplift in greenhouse gas emissions from the sales driven by advertising – to create a core data set and help measure improvements

2 The 'Return on CO_2e' (the revenue generated for every tonne of CO_2 equivalent emitted) – to provide a consistent approach that allows for comparison across sectors and campaigns

3 Levers of Ecoeffectiveness – a model for identifying where the headroom exists and what methods can be used to reduce impact while maintaining profitability.

The methodology was launched using data from the 2018 IPA Effectiveness winners, with a focus on the Grand Prix winning case from Audi. Caroline and Ben suggested reducing emissions while maintaining profitability will be the defining effectiveness challenge of the coming decades and shared their work as open source, inviting industry professionals to join the development of the tools and dataset.

Next up: 'advertised emissions'

A year later, Ecoeffectiveness had evolved into a new metric – 'Advertised Emissions' – which was presented at COP26 in Glasgow (2021) by econometrics consultancy, magic numbers, and the Purpose Disruptors, a group of advertising professionals organized to help stimulate positive climate action.

The researchers collected data on advertising spend in 19 UK sectors and applied average revenue returned of circa £6.30 per £1 spent on advertising to produce an estimate of the value created for businesses in each of the 19 sectors. On this basis, they argued nearly £90 billion worth of products were sold because of advertising in 2019 – 4 per cent of the UK's GDP (Purpose Disruptors, 2021). The researchers concluded this meant significant knock-on effects for global warming because incremental sales mean advertisers make more products and services, and their suppliers make more, and their suppliers too, with every step involving more emissions of greenhouse gases. Once they'd added all this up, they presented the challenge to advertising that it was responsible for +28 per cent on the annual carbon footprint of every single person in the UK – 186 million tonnes of greenhouse gases, or the equivalent of running 47 coal-fired power plants all year round.

The researchers also projected forward to 2030 and illustrated what they believed would be happening, should there be no reduction in this metric, suggesting it would contribute more than 270 million tonnes in the UK annually. Most emissions would be from high ad spend categories, with strong returns on investment, and carbon intensive production and supply chains, namely:

- Retail (from supermarkets to high street chains)
- Technology and electronics
- Transport and tourism
- Leisure and entertainment.

The researchers (Purpose Disruptors, 2021) concluded marketers needed to concentrate on four areas:

1 Help clients transition to cleaner production processes and supply chains by engineering the demand for the products they produce

2 Accelerate acceptance and adoption of new models where products are used for longer before being disposed of

3 Support, promote, and energize low or zero-carbon brands and industries whose business model is geared to serving a 1.5-degree world

4 Reduce or even remove spending that supports rare brands and sectors whose production is high carbon with no hope of transitioning to a cleaner production process.

The goal was bold – to put an 'Advertised Emissions' calculator on the desk of every marketer in the world.

Academia's view

The UK advertising industry's trade bodies, the Advertising Association, the IPA and ISBA, reviewed the research and asked the Saïd Business School at Oxford University to consider how best to help establish a metric that could work for all parts of the industry – advertisers, agencies, media owners and tech companies. Professor Felipe Thomaz, of Saïd Business School, published an academic paper for peer review in January 2023, and presented its findings in June 2023 at Cannes Lions.

Thomaz's approach set out how the advertising industry could integrate both its own emissions (Advertising Emissions) and the consequences of its advertising work (Advertised Emissions) into a single management framework. This could then guide future consumption towards both commercial value and carbon reduction, while minimizing capital and carbon budgets.

The report considered what other industries are doing to define their equivalent of Advertised Emissions. The first model, 'Financed Emissions', assigns greenhouse gas (GHG) ownership proportional to investment in a company or project with two goals: funding disclosure and measuring risk exposure from decarbonization and transition economy. However, suggesting 'Advertised Emissions' can be measured and attributed to advertising in the same way created 'a very dangerous and false equivalence'. Thomaz explained this is because advertising does not involve any share or value in the product or service that is sold. It is also difficult to determine the exact percentage of lift in sales directly attributable to an advertising campaign, adding further complications to accurate attribution of GHG emissions.

The 'Advertised Emissions' model presented in Glasgow (2021) by the Purpose Disruptors, similarly to 'Financed Emissions', connects advertising exposure to an increase in demand and in turn an increase in manufacturing, without a factor for substitution, where one purchase is displacing another. It then presents the challenge that all associated manufacturing, transport, usage and product lifetime emissions are linked back to the advertising ecosystem. Thomaz argued assigning the multi-stage and multi-dimensional costs of the economy to advertising is an accounting mistake that will create a bad system of incentives in a net zero economy, warning that it was 'a coarse measure leading to bad sustainability/conservation consequences'.

The second model was 'Facilitated Emissions', also being explored by the finance industry, which is being developed to capture the emissions contributions of the advisory parts of their industry. This shares similarities with the services provided by the advertising industry, as well as other business advisory services like management consulting, legal services, and accountancy. However, he recognized no methodology has yet been developed, and discussions still focus on issues of double counting and attribution – those same challenges faced by the advertising industry for years.

Remember, this does not mean the emissions from the consumption that advertising is part of stimulating are not being accounted for. Advertisers are already accountable for these. All face their own challenges in measuring and managing these scope 3 emissions, both 'upstream' from the suppliers used to deliver their products or services, and 'downstream' from the emissions that result from their use.

Thomaz also outlined how once tCO_2e is used for measurement or reporting, it becomes a cost, used as a competitive advantage, passed, or absorbed across the supply chain, targeted for cost reduction and traded against other costs such as monetary and time costs. As such, any careless or incomplete consideration of advertising's carbon cost could lead to simplistic or disproportionate devaluation of advertising. If the advertising 'cost' (monetary plus carbon) is too high, commercial performance would suffer accordingly.

Professor Thomaz's recommended approach begins with the GHG Protocol Life Stage to measure the carbon footprint of advertising, considering advertising's entire lifecycle through creation, production and media distribution. In addition, he adds the measurement and accounting of carbon arising from consumption or consumer behaviours in response to ads, including competitive forces and measurement.

Thomaz's paper proposes adoption of a more precise set of definitions around the indirect GHG impact of advertising, namely:

- **Consumption emissions** – the carbon emissions connected to the **use** of products and services as well as their disposal
- **Advertised emissions** – consumption emissions attributable to the **influence of an advertisement**

- **Incremental advertised emissions** – the novel and **differential (positive or negative) consumption emissions** attributable to an advertisement
- **Displaced advertised emissions** – existing **consumption emissions that shifted** from one unique entity (organization/brand/product/region) to another, due to the influence of an advertisement.

Professor Thomaz makes the case that not all the choices made to consume are made because of advertising, which is why he proposes that Advertised Emissions are a subset of Consumption Emissions. And that within Advertised Emissions it is the incremental (positive or negative) and displaced emissions that advertising companies would include in their scope 3. He suggests that joint consideration of more detailed aspects of advertised emissions opens a traditional market playbook that could lead to positive sustainability outcomes.

For example, he asked the industry to consider how to drive positive cannibalization, where a more sustainable new product replaces an older one with higher consumption emissions. This lowers environmental impact relative to the previous status quo and where margins or cash profit are higher, business, and environmental interests align. As such, incrementality and displacement matter significantly in creating the right market incentives.

However, to have the most effective measurement results, Professor Thomaz argued that attribution is crucial for proper management of emissions in the advertising industry and its impact beyond. He recommended the use of testing (and The Behavioural Response Function model) to help measure the likelihood of various groups taking certain actions, such as making a purchase or engaging in sustainability practices. If that can be done through testing, the extent to which advertising can help support a behaviour change towards a more sustainable outcome could be proven and this could be brought together into a framework. This would provide a carbon portfolio approach through a simpler overview of a firm's advertising and advertised emissions and their trade-offs. In this framework, the carbon equivalent cost of advertising activities (advertising emissions) and the behavioural consequences of those initiatives (advertised emissions) are combined to create a cost/benefit analysis and plotted against each other to evaluate the overall impact of a firm.

Professor Thomaz concluded that new approaches are needed to capture the details present in advertising and carbon accounting. He highlighted the difficulties with attribution as a significant issue and barrier to proper management of the advertising industry's impact and the carbon consequences of its actions. He recommended a detailed measure of advertising emissions, down to the minutiae inside each channel. He also argues that appropriate attribution is crucial in managing the interplay between advertising and advertised emissions and that there remains an enormous amount of improvement possible in how to implement these models, and he suggests possible ways forward to do that.

To summarize: we have a real challenge defining just how much consumption advertising is and isn't responsible for. To take full responsibility for all emissions from consumption, and the full supply chain of the brands that the advertising industry is working for, will cause many problems for the industry, its investors, and how it functions in a net zero economy, including in the carbon accounting sphere. But, to take no responsibility for the impact of the industry's work, and not connect how and where advertising is increasing or reducing consumption emissions is just as wrong, and it would ignore the role of the industry in support of achieving a net zero economy.

Here's the but... while Professor Thomaz's logic is very clear and hard to refute, we are not yet there in the practical execution. Taking 'Advertising Emissions' first, the good news is that GHG measurement in operations and production, as we say in earlier chapters, is well advanced. Work on standard definitions for carbon calculations in media is underway at time of writing, although there might be a risk of break-down or splintering, signs are encouraging. But for 'advertised emissions' the data set is not there to accurately attribute the incremental or displaced sales impacts of all advertising. Campaigns, even for the same brands, have different uplift. A group of companies working in a sector could share assumptions or commission the kind of research that Thomaz suggests. Maybe AI and big data in combination will be able to calculate some norms based on anonymized but sector specific models? Work needs to be done to most accurately calculate the next iteration of 'advertised emissions' fully accounting for attribution and substitution.

Monitoring advertising work for its alignment with a net zero goal

PwC was commissioned by the UK advertising industry's trade bodies, the Advertising Association, the IPA and ISBA, to tackle the challenge of how best to support the advertising industry's transition into a net zero economy.

In their report, they acknowledge that advertising can contribute to potentially unsustainable and carbon intensive consumption because a free-market, consumer-driven economy may not always allocate resources in the best way to tackle climate change. But they recognize the positive economic contribution that advertising makes as part of a free-market, consumer-driven economy. Advertising can usefully support the transition to a low carbon economy, in their view, particularly leveraging control on messaging and creative content and its influence on consumer behaviour, with responsibility shared across the industry.

However, they observe that advertising faces measurement challenges and that defining scope 3 emissions is not a straightforward task, especially any method to include emissions from the sales uplift generated by advertising campaigns. Even with perfect data, is it right to hold advertising accountable for 100 per cent of the emissions that result from the uplift in sales, they ask, without accounting for attribution and substitution.

The authors recommend turning the focus from 'attribution and baseline measurement' to 'monitoring the evolution of advertising driven carbon consumption over time', which could be a more effective way to drive progress at the company (brand and agency) level. They propose 'a monitoring and decision-making framework to help advertising companies and brands monitor the carbon intensity of their portfolios in a credible way'. The framework would ideally be linked to emerging environmental classification systems, such as the EU taxonomy and the Competition and Markets Authority (CMA)' Green Claims Code. PwC also argues it will have the most likely success of industry-wide adoption if the framework is led by brands, because they are the ones with the most data and information to support the framework.

What kind of objective data sets might be available to inform such a monitoring system which provide a clear view of what is being promoted, when, and how sustainable that is? Such a monitoring approach is already in development by major commercial media owners which need to demonstrate how much of their revenue is linked to the Paris Agreement by investors. As we've seen earlier in this book. Versions of this framework are now in development.

The first example to provide an immediate and credible way to assess businesses is the Net Zero Tracker (2023), a collaboration between four organizations. The Energy & Climate Intelligence Unit (ECIU) is a non-profit organization supporting informed debate on energy and climate change issues in the UK, the Data-Driven EnviroLab (DDL) is an interdisciplinary research lab headed by Dr Angel Hsu and based at the University of North Carolina-Chapel Hill. The NewClimate Institute, is a non-profit institute established in 2014 which supports research and implementation of action against climate change around the globe, covering the topics including international climate negotiations, tracking climate action, climate and development, climate finance and carbon market mechanisms. Oxford Net Zero is an interdisciplinary research initiative based at the University of Oxford, building on 15 years of research on climate neutrality.

The goal of the Net Zero Tracker is to increase transparency and accountability of net zero targets pledged by nations, states and regions, cities, and companies. The team behind it collect data on targets and on factors that indicate the integrity of those targets — essentially, how serious the entity setting the target is about meaningfully cutting its net emissions to zero. They have published data on the 2000 largest companies in the world, many of them leading advertisers. This kind of broad-based assessment of the ambition, credibility and transparency of a firm's own sustainability objectives can be the basis for decision-making on what businesses that advertising businesses choose to work with. It doesn't do this at a product or service portfolio level though.

Another way of looking at which sectors of the economy need what type of advertising support is to consider them, industry-by-industry. The Transition Pathway Initiative Global Climate Transition Centre (TPI Centre), an independent, authoritative source of research and data on the progress of the financial and corporate world in transitioning to a low-carbon economy, has launched a tool to do exactly that. Its online tool allows you to look at industries like the airline industry and see how fast it is progressing along to net zero, rating companies in the sector from Level 0 (unaware) to Level 4 (Strategic assessment) – the further the company along that rating, the better. At the time of writing the TPI Centre asses that 41 per cent of the companies are at Level 4. A big advertiser like Ryanair is assessed to be at Level 2 (Building capacity). This type of rating within an industry's progress to look at which companies are where along the pathway could prove to be a useful indicator of what and how companies should be supported by the advertising industry for a more sustainable future.

In other words, if it's not feasible to track the exact sales uplift of campaigns and attribute differential or displaced carbon emissions to those campaigns, advertisers and their agencies can collect data that rates the sustainability of different companies, products and services. This can be used to ensure that more sustainable version of products and services are being advertised and demonstrate a change in the GHG footprint of an agency or media owner's client portfolio over time. There are increasingly more trackers being created as the emphasis switches from pledges to delivery.

Tracking net zero – a useful overview

The team behind the previously mentioned Net Zero Tracker published its *Net Zero Stocktake 2023* in June 2023, assessing the status and trends of net zero target setting for countries, sub-national governments, and companies. Key points to note in the team's findings when it comes to companies specifically was that the momentum to set net zero targets continues at speed, but there was still a significant share of corporates lacking any emission reduction target. There were also limited signs of robustness in the setting of these targets and no major producer company had committed to phasing out fossil fuels.

Looking closer, 929 companies from the Forbes 2000 list had set net zero targets, doubling the number in two and a half years (Net Zero Tracker, 2023). Total annual revenue covered by net zero targets was now $26.4 trillion, but the Net Zero Tracker team (and others) highlighted that many company emission targets were of questionable quality.

This scrutiny of target setting and being 100 per cent clear what is meant by this and what is expected year-on-year is now the focus. To help, the team published a chart entitled *What Does 'Good Net Zero' Look Like?* – a review of where there is agreement on definitions of the targets across the emerging voluntary global standards.

Connecting the Chief Sustainability Officer with the Chief Marketing Officer

As sustainability efforts of companies continue to grow, many Chief Sustainability Officers are turning their attention beyond their immediate issues to look at their footprint in marketing and advertising. It can only be beneficial to connect efforts in our industry with those experts, especially in the definition of emissions when it comes to marketing and advertising. We spoke to Bill Wescott, Managing Partner at Brain Oxygen LLC about this.

Why do you think it is so important for the chief sustainability officer to connect and collaborate with the chief marketing officer?

The attention of the C-suite on sustainability and particularly climate issues has been so focused on the physical supply chain, that the marketing and advertising activities have been completely overlooked from an operational emissions perspective. The only time that marketing comes to mind typically is with regard to communicating product sustainability attributes, not on the emissions from marketing and advertising operations. In talking with many Chief Sustainability Officers and top climate experts in leading brands, I discovered none of them have thought about these emissions, but all of them committed to reaching out to the CMOs to get the conversation started.

In the absence of this internal support, the marketing function and their value chain partners started to take actions independent of the greenhouse gas accounting systems, standards and best practices that have been developed over the last two decades. Vendors with proprietary, black box 'carbon calculators' selling opaque offsets at many times their market value stepped in to take advantage of the lack of knowledge of buyers who were eager to take some sort of tangible action. In addition to the clear inefficiencies of reinventing the wheel, the real concern is that all the energy and resources spent in these efforts would be rejected in the end by the climate experts in the brands as they would not be able to use the emissions estimates in their official summaries that have to be third-party verified against existing standards. I was surprised at this 'Wild West' environment as in my world it is self-evident that serious companies don't make claims or accept claims from others that have not been verified by a reputable third party.

Facilitating CSO-CMO collaborations to accelerate real climate action in the ad sector is now a key focus of mine as it can quickly clear the air of confusion so the parties can focus on meaningful improvements.

How can an improved collaboration between these two areas of a business help the marketing function, with its own operations, and through the way it communicates about the pipeline of more sustainable products and services?

The first major benefit of this collaboration for the marketing function is an increase in the speed and efficiency that comes with alignment with the rest of their company's climate actions. The marketing function can use its leverage to align its value chain with the same climate systems used by the rest of the world. As product offerings become more sustainable via new business models (e.g., circular economy approaches to selling services instead of goods; reducing use of plastics, toxics, limited natural resources), consumers and other stakeholders will be delighted to know that the means of communicating these attributes are also sustainable.

What do you think will be the ultimate benefits of putting sustainability and marketing on the same dashboard for campaign planning, execution and evaluation?

> The marketing function and operations are really just an application of the philosophy of scope 3 to understand the climate impacts along the entire value chain, quantify and verify them so they can be reported to all stakeholders. This process enables the development of approaches that can then reduce these emissions to the maximum extent possible. These functions deserve to receive the same attention and follow the same standards as every other function on the sustainability dashboard of serious brands.

Measuring the industry's impact: summary

We're going to end this chapter based on what we know at the point in time of writing. That there is an ongoing debate about what to measure and/or monitor and how.

The absolute starting point is for every organization involved in the advertising eco-system to set and report on a science-based target for tCO_2e reduction near-term and a date to hit zero, in line with the best practice being advocated in this area for scopes 1, 2 and 3. We should expect this of every company we come into contact with, whether they are in our supply chain or whether they are a client. We hope that best-practice scope definitions for our specific sectors, such as SBTi Guidance, will be created, and have the highest expectations of every company to follow those. They will need to find the line through best methodology in theory, and ability to measure in practice. Once defined, they will be the standard for every company participating in a net zero advertising industry.

A quick and effective route through the decades-old conundrum of just how effective advertising is for sales is to make a concerted effort to get sustainability metrics alongside advertising metrics in the way advertising campaigns are created, developed, delivered, and evaluated. The more we try and obviously connect these two aspects of the business, the more we will be confident of producing work that supports a business to be successful in a net zero economy. There is no magic formula to apply, this is campaign by campaign work.

What does this mean? It means that we should always try and identify the sustainability intent in the brief for a campaign alongside the commercial goal. What is the sustainability problem being solved through the work and then how have the results of the campaign helped to address that? And make sure to factor in the emissions from the operations, production, and distribution of said ad campaign as standard in the campaign planning and evaluation.

Matt is reminded of a conversation he had at an event with an ad sales leader at a major media owner. The sales exec was recalling an idea from an award-winning agency for a new oven chips brand campaign which was going to feature details about its new more sustainable potato. His view was the audience they represented 'really wouldn't give a stuff about that, what they wanted to know as whether these new chips would be ready for the family in 18-20 minutes and be a delicious treat for the kids'. What he did say was that his media could help them make those 'more sustainable' chips famous and secure market share from competitors. By doing so, this campaign could help that sector take another step towards a net zero economy. It would be useful to have visibility of that 'more sustainable' option as a metric in the campaign brief and the evaluation, but it probably wouldn't be too much of a factor in the ad itself.

This discussion encapsulates a vital point about the transition to a sustainable future. Sometimes there will be a completely new product, one that is more sustainable and displaces the existing products in the market. EVs are one such example. Most of the time though, there will be smaller, more incremental changes. Sometimes overtly communicated, like the plant-based burger, the more sustainable potato variety, or the plant-based detergent that washes as well at low temperatures. There will be many more almost invisible to the end customer, like more recycled materials in the packaging, less water and energy in the manufacturing, greater end of life recyclability. Advertising will play a role in some, but many changes will be taking place anyway as businesses of all kinds decarbonize their operations. In the end the acid test will be 'has the amount of advertising for the most sustainable products gone up, has the amount of advertising for unsustainable products reduced to zero, and are most products advertised more sustainable than they were before?'. This can be assessed for an advertiser, agency, production company or media owner, which is why we also focus on the 'transition big picture', highlighted in this chapter through the Net Zero Tracker, the TPI Center, and the importance of connecting the Chief Sustainability Officer with the Chief Marketing Officer. That, and the active tracking of each company's own path to net zero, including responsible, appropriate, measurable standards for scope 3 through the public setting and reporting of science-based targets.

References

2023, Interview with Bill Westcott, Managing Partner at Brain Oxygen LLC, the WRI/WBSCD Greenhouse Gas Protocol subgroup leader on boundaries (which led to the creation of scope 3), and climate science advisor at *Ad Net Zero*.

2023, PwC, *Advertising-driven carbon consumption*. (Preview copy accessed August 2023)

Credos. (2023) *Advertising's Big Questions: Does advertising grow markets?* Advertising Association. June 2023. Available at: https://adassoc.org.uk/ credos-category/ad-big-qs/ (archived at https://perma.cc/43TM-GHBY)

Davison, C; Essen B. (2020) *Ecoeffectiveness*: *The missing measure in the climate crisis*. IPA. January 2022. [Online] Available at: https://ipa.co.uk/effworks/ effworksglobal-2020/ecoeffectiveness-the-missing-measure-in-the-climate-crisis (archived at https://perma.cc/VK9J-6F47)

Dr Thomaz, F. (2023) *Ad Net Zero. Conceptual Framework for Integrating Advertising and Advertised Emissions*. Elsevier. January 2023. Available at: https://papers.ssrn.com/sol3/papers.cfm?abstract_id=4337355 (archived at https://perma.cc/QD3E-AER9)

IPA. (2023) *Effectiveness Awards*. [Online] Available at: https://ipa.co.uk/awards-events/effectiveness-awards (archived at https://perma.cc/TLW6-HN72)

Net Zero Tracker. (2023) *Home*. [Online] Available at: https://zerotracker.net/ (archived at https://perma.cc/MGM6-HWBW)

Net Zero Tracker. (2023) *Net Zero Stocktake 2023 Report*. [Online] Available at: https://zerotracker.net/analysis/net-zero-stocktake-2023 (archived at https:// perma.cc/P359-H4ND)

Purpose Disruptors. (2023) *Advertised Emissions*. [Online] Available at: https:// www.purposedisruptors.org/advertised-emissions (archived at https://perma.cc/ QWT7-QPZM)

Quote Research. (2022) *One-Half the Money I Spend for Advertising Is Wasted, But I Have Never Been Able To Decide Which Half*. Quote Investigator. April 2022. [Online] Available at: https://quoteinvestigator.com/2022/04/11/ advertising/ (archived at https://perma.cc/EX8C-D8FY) [Accessed August 2023]

Science Based Targets. (2023) *Home*. [Online] Available at: https:// sciencebasedtargets.org/ (archived at https://perma.cc/54UF-LECS)

Transition Pathway Initiative. (2023) *The Transition Pathway Initiative Global Climate Transition Centre*. [Online] Available at: https://www. transitionpathwayinitiative.org/ (archived at https://perma.cc/7256-WKBD)

15

A rewarding profession and career

Research by UK advertising thinktank, Credos, commissioned during the development of Ad Net Zero, identified real concerns among advertising professionals about climate change. It found that 71 per cent of UK ad professionals were worried about the negative impact of the industry on the environment while 91 per cent agreed that knowing their organization was taking climate action would improve their job satisfaction (Credos, 2020).

During the research and writing of this book, we have come into contact with many people from across the industry and spoken at length about the challenges and opportunities in creating a truly sustainable advertising industry. Many people are frustrated with the slow pace of change, while others are finding ways to deploy their skills on more sustainable projects and defining new standards and ways of working. Some people are anxious about what might be coming, and others are energized and challenged by the opportunities in the belief that their professional skills align with their personal purpose to make a difference.

This sits at the heart of *Sustainable Advertising* – harnessing the connection between the strategic, creative and technical skills possessed by hundreds of thousands of advertising and marketing professionals around the world and the objective of helping to secure a sustainable future for us all. Doing meaningful work, there is true fulfilment in seeing the combined power of sustainable and commercial results. As Seb frequently reminds us, this puts pressure on advertisers to come forward with briefs and business models underlying them which seamlessly integrate business and sustainability strategies. While there is much that agencies can do in process and advice, the heavy lifting needs to start with advertisers and media owners to commit to transforming the sustainability of their core businesses.

What are the main impediments? Beliefs that there is a choice or trade-off between business success and environmental success come near the top of that list. How could anyone be in any doubt that the long-term success measure is a planet in balance where people can live well, and the economy can thrive? Actually, this takes reflection, awareness of the facts, conversations, and the time to make sense of it all, ask questions and find credible answers. This is about how leaders are developed in business and society more widely, and how everyone learns and is prepared for their role. And then there is the *think-do gap*. What holds us back even once we are clear about the situation? This is another critical topic for leadership development; of which more later.

Helping people unlock the motivating connection between advertising and sustainability

Training and people development are key, of that there is no doubt, to make the type of system change we are aiming for to make our industry a sustainable one. This change can be led by the learning and development programmes of the major players and their learning and development providers across the industry, as they invest in the skills we will need for a sustainable future.

The following is an example of just this taking place at one of the major agency groups, Dentsu. It has recently launched a dedicated learning and development programme on sustainability to upskill employees globally, including accredited training from the Cambridge Institute of Sustainability Leadership. This is specifically about putting team members through an eight-week online training course called Sustainable Media, Marketing and Creative. The Dentsu team is not alone in this approach. More and more brands are investing in educating their people on sustainability, for example Chanel, a major brand advertiser, is investing £3 million in sustainability training with Cambridge Institute of Sustainability Leadership (edie, 2021).

This type of training is necessary as, according to the World Federation of Advertisers (WFA, 2021), only 10 per cent of marketing teams have the sustainability skills they need and 7 per cent of board members are climate competent. Speaking with the dentsu team, the motivation for training as widely as possible is two-fold. Firstly, the increasing amount of legislation around greenwashing means employers need to upskill creatives and marketers to know enough to be aware of potential pitfalls and avoid unintentional greenwashing. Secondly, the more confident a team is in their sustainability knowledge, the more likely they are to confidently communicate a brand's sustainability story, and so less likely to 'greenhush'.

Training courses about sustainability and advertising will grow in importance and profile over the coming years. The Ad Net Zero Training Course is an entry-level course which anyone can take online, requiring around 6–8 hours of your time to complete. More than 1,500 advertising professionals have completed that training at the time of writing and there are now UK, Global and US versions of the training available for people to access (Ad Net Zero, 2023). The #ChangeTheBrief approach we wrote about in Chapter 11 includes detailed, tailored training for teams across all kinds of advertising and marketing services businesses.

Inspiring people towards a new way of life

How to stay focused on the goal of a sustainable future is tricky when many other business priorities vie for leadership attention, as well as your own personal feelings about climate change. The following is an interview by Matt with Anna Lungley, dentsu Chief Sustainability Officer, international markets, about her approach in her role at the global agency group.

The climate crisis can seem all-encompassing – how do you keep a clear focus for dentsu's drive through its work to support a more sustainable way of life around the world?

> Strategy is about choices – it's as much about what you don't choose to do, as what you do choose to do. With 69,000 employees working across 146 markets, we have unlimited opportunities within our ecosystem to create a better future. But we understand that the true value we create is our ability to shape human and societal behaviour. That's why we have made Sustainable Development Goal 12 (Sustainable Consumption and Production) our priority and embedded this into the heart of our 2030 Sustainability Strategy. We are on a mission to inspire people everywhere to a new way of living and we try hard not to get distracted. There are times when distractions are necessary – for example, humanitarian response to the war in Ukraine. But you won't see us activate around every calendar event. We know where we can make the biggest difference and we work hard to stay focused.

What is the best example of sustainable economy in action that you can point to? An example that people can draw from, both in terms of learning

of how it is being achieved, but also in terms of belief that a sustainable future is possible?

> I don't believe a perfect case study exists yet, but you don't need to look far to find hope. I live in a village in Gloucestershire where people have embraced sustainable and inclusive living. Cafes are vegan, shops are plastic free, air source heat pumps and solar panels are the norm. People embrace low impact lifestyles. This change has been driven at community level, but it has inspired local entrepreneurs to start new business models, for example Stroud Brewery and Ecotricity. Even the local football team is vegan (Forest Green), and they recycle the water from their pitch. I think what is special here is that people feel deeply connected to the land – to nature – and know that together we thrive.

What does success look like for you – what will a sustainable advertising industry be delivering for people around the world?

> Success will ultimately be defined by a wholesale societal shift towards a more sustainable, inclusive, and low carbon lifestyle. This will be driven by consumer demand but will be inspired and enabled by the creative industries. As advertisers and marketers, we can make plant-based food, electric vehicles and recycling irresistible. We can make ethical banking and green pensions the only choice. By placing the needs of people and society at the heart of our design processes, we can accelerate the net zero transition.

Can you share how you motivate people within dentsu to make changes to be more sustainable? And how does this translate into the work the teams then do for your clients?

> We understand that our people are at different stages in their own sustainability journey. Most want to act in a way that is more sustainable, but they don't always know how. If you start small, for example protecting nature through beach clean ups, or repair cafes, then people start to connect the dots. They bring that insight and understanding back to their client work. At Dentsu, our annual One Day for Change volunteering event has created thousands of advocates who are passionate about building a more sustainable world.

Closing the organizational intention-action gap: Give marketers the mandate to innovate

In Matt's conversation with Dominic Powers, Dentsu APAC Chief Growth Officer, Dominic built on the theme that Seb refers to about the leadership role of advertisers.

With their significant influence on consumption behaviours, marketers hold the key to accelerating progress on the demand-side of the climate change solution and have the potential to be generational change agents. However, there is a fundamental disconnect between business' declared sustainability commitments and marketing departments' ability to achieve those goals. To mirror the oft-quoted consumer intention-action gap, we've termed this 'the organizational intention-action gap'.

The 'gap' is that despite business' intent to drive more sustainable consumption, their marketing departments – the all-important bridge between them and their customers – are not being given the tools nor the jurisdiction to play a central role in this endeavour.

Dentsu x Kantar's recent 'Marketing A Better Future study' found that marketing functions lag behind other divisions in contributing to their companies' sustainability agendas. Only one in three (34 per cent) marketing teams were 'executing against their sustainability plans and measuring progress' compared to 46 per cent in supply chain, and 51 per cent in corporate strategy.

More fundamentally, marketers' potential to create deep change is stymied by the imperative to generate growth quarter-on-quarter – growth regardless of its impact on the planet or on our collective well-being.

Some 38 per cent of the marketers surveyed 'have been challenged by the business' on the impact of their sustainability efforts, and 31 per cent 'want to do something about it but there's a lack of budget'. A sizable 25 per cent say 'internal stakeholders resist the move because the P&L and bonus will be challenged.

To enable marketing departments to fulfil their logical role as generational change agents and actually fuel growth that is consistent with positive planetary outcomes, businesses must make a radical corporate mindset shift.

The emphasis on constricting quarterly growth KPIs must be eased, and marketing departments must be given room to shape the sort of consumer preference-led innovation that can generate new, sustainable consumption behaviours at scale.

The good news is doing so will support evolving business models and long-term business resilience. A win for business and a win for the planet. Who wouldn't want that?

Dominic is making two important points. Firstly, that focus needs to be put on the knowledge-base and readiness of marketers to innovate sustainably. Secondly, that another critical part of training people to perform is the reward and incentivization framework: nothing teaches you what people want more than what they pay for. Aligning incentives is one way companies can close the think–do gap and make their intentions crystal clear. That's why many of the leading companies have sustainability metrics in their long-term incentive programmes for top execs and beyond. Conversely, nothing sends a clearer signal than when sustainability metrics are not in the incentive programme.

Use your company's sustainability credentials to attract the best talent

Grace Blue, the global executive search firm, joined Ad Net Zero in summer 2022, becoming the first talent-based company to embed sustainability so visibly this way in its business. It did this in recognition that increasing scrutiny will be placed by both employers and employees on their respective sustainability credentials, expertise, and net zero transition plans. This is making climate action a critical factor in where and how people choose which companies with which to build their careers.

To further build on this, Grace Blue formed its own sustainability team. The aim of the sustainability team was to educate its team, clients, and candidates on positive changes to the way it works with partners, encouraging best practice in sustainable ad operations, promoting sustainable behaviour change as a core skills requirement of leadership talent and facilitating knowledge-share across its leadership network of clients and candidates.

Matt spoke with Sarah Skinner, CEO EMEA and Global MD, Grace Blue, about how the issue of sustainability was shaping talent recruitment for employers in the marketing and advertising sector.

> Pressure is coming from talent – and is one that we anticipate will continue to grow. Where employer brands demonstrate a positive commitment and action around sustainability, that can make a business more attractive. At more junior levels, and for up and coming talent this is becoming a more important area they look for in businesses. It's worth recognizing too that the pressure is coming from the end consumer – talent will want to work more on accounts that can demonstrate a positive contribution to climate action.

From an employer perspective, we are seeing growth in briefs for NED work where candidates are needed that can demonstrate contribution to and impact on ESG, which has become a key criterion for boards. An increasing question we are starting to hear at the leadership level is "sustainability is important, but I have no direct experience in this – how do I gain this?".

Going forward, businesses need to practice what they preach - commitment to sustainability and real behaviour change are different. The latter is what is most important, and it needs to be championed across an organization including the C suite.

This shift in employee expectations isn't unique to Grace Blue's experiences. In Spring 2023, Matt spoke at an event for AdForm and had a follow-up conversation with recruitment consultants who specialized in the adtech space. They shared how an employer had been surprised when recruiting for a graduate role that 8 of the 10 candidates had asked to see the company's sustainability policy and plans. This is going to become standard for talent entering our industry – any company looking to recruit the best and brightest new stars will make sure that what they are doing in this area gives them advantage against their competitors.

So, what's your motivation to help make *sustainable advertising* a reality?

Tim Munden, former Chief Learning and Development Officer of Unilever, HR professional for more than 30 years, and now director of leadership development company, Kairon, talked to Matt about why it is beneficial when the organization's purpose and the individuals' purpose align. He explained that all the research shows that people motivated by purpose are generally happier, more productive, and more effective. Tim put in place the purpose training at Unilever which helped employees to identify and articulate what was important to them and how that could align with their work. Tim and Matt discussed how achieving this alignment of purpose might help to accelerate the sustainable and net zero economy, through the work people do in the advertising industry. Tim suggested considering a simple framework of questions as you reflect on how your role and the contribution you make can help to address the concerns and questions that most motivate you. This reflection can take many forms: some people like to reflect alone, while others need to hear what they think by speaking to others. And it may take a bit of time over several sessions.

- What do you love?
- What concerns you? And why?
- How do you build your experiences to put you in the place where you can do something about this?
- What will you do at work to answer your purpose?
- How will you respond to things that happen to you in the workplace day-to-day? Which things might get in the way?

A rewarding profession and career: summary

As we bring this chapter to a close, we hope every reader of this book can find an opportunity to deploy their talents in a way which is in support of a positive, sustainable outcome, speeds up the reality of *Sustainable Advertising*, and aligns with their personal purpose. For those that can achieve this, the personal rewards are abundantly clear.

Keep asking employers about their plans for sustainability, check they are fully embedded in their business strategy, and manifest again in their incentive programmes. Take the time to learn and train, and be aware of the think-do gap, which is far from unusual when tackling difficult challenges.

Anyone in a leadership, management, or mentoring position should look to encourage these reflections on alignment of purpose in the people they are responsible for. Anyone entering the industry should actively seek this in every role they consider.

References

2023, Interview with Anna Lungley, Chief Sustainability Officer, dentsu.

2023, Interview with Dominic Powers, Chief Growth Officer, dentsu APAC.

2023, Interview with Sarah Skinner, CEO EMEA and Global MD, Grace Blue Partnership.

2023, Interview with Tim Munden, Director, Kairon.

Ad Net Zero. (2020) *Ad Net Zero Report, Credos research*. [Online] Available at: https://adnetzero.com/ (archived at https://perma.cc/D3LU-DKP4)

Grace Blue Partnership. (2023) *Sustainability*. [Online] Available at: https://graceblue.com/sustainability/ (archived at https://perma.cc/99XE-SLK7)

16

Start your change journey here

Sustainable Advertising Handbook

Over the chapters of this book, we have attempted to do three things: share a vision; set out a practical plan and framework; and provide case studies from across the industry to show what can be achieved. It is a handbook primarily to help you play your vital role in transforming the economy, and the way we all live today.

A vision

Beginning with the end in mind, we shared a vision for a vigorous and thriving advertising industry that has stepped up to play a critical role in advancing a more sustainable economy in the shadow of the climate crisis, to engage citizens with products and services that are better for them and better for the planet. This attracts the brightest and the best into advertising by connecting to their sense of purpose. Leading companies in the industry can become beacons for giving more than they take by solving the biggest challenges, not creating them.

This vision stands in stark contrast with the alternative for our industry – a future where governments, encouraged by citizens, seek to curtail the scope and power of advertising to limit its harmful effects, on human health, wellbeing and climate. Doing nothing is not an option.

The growth of the green economy, triggered by innovation and new services, is the biggest opportunity in a generation for advertisers, advertising agencies and the whole industry. The case for a rapid transition to sustainable advertising is indisputable – if you've read this far, then hopefully you agree!

A practical action plan

We have laid out a practical plan to make the industry run more sustainably and tread most lightly on the resources of the planet in the way it works every day. A plan that will need to be activated by the industry, by individual companies, and by you, in whatever role you have in making and distributing advertising.

The 5 Actions give clarity and structure for actions. The tools that we have featured here give you access to shared standards and framework definitions, essential for conversations to flow across the industry where everyone is speaking the same language. These tools also provide benchmarks and allow companies to collect and compare their own data with them, which in turn create action plan agendas. The tools will only get better, enhanced by the network effect of widespread adoption, and become more useful as they are more used across the world.

Insights and examples

We have shared case studies of the best thinking we have come across, the best actions and the best campaigns to show what is possible and inspire more work. Collected in one place are many examples of behaviour-changing work that have helped citizens choose the best products and services for their needs. We especially thank those contributors who had the courage to share what did not work, or at least what turned out differently from the outcomes they expected. Our goal in sharing them is to inspire scale acceleration of better products and services: to make the big brands better and the better brands bigger, quickly. Put together, these need to scale up to decarbonize everyday life and disconnect value creation from greenhouse gas emission and nature depletion.

Join in

If you share our vision, help make it happen. Whatever your role, you can make a difference in adopting sustainable advertising ways of working. Get your team to join in. Sign up your company. Reflect it in your strategy. Transfer that strategy systematically into actions with owners. And most importantly, work up and down your supply chain, to require where you can, and request or choose alternatives where you cannot, that the whole value chain moves towards sustainable advertising. To make that tangible and concrete, here is our 16-point to do list to mobilize your company.

16 Steps to mobilize your company

1 Summon your courage. Ask for a review of the strategy (for your brand, department, division, or company) ensuring that climate change, bio-diversity loss and the circular economy are fully embedded in the risks and opportunities as well as in the choices you are making on where to play and how to win. Does your strategy fully consider all your stakeholders, and will it succeed commercially by solving some of society's challenges rather than create them?

2 After a future-proofed strategy, every company needs a climate action plan with science-based targets in line with the Paris Agreement – this should be published publicly and progress reported annually. Where possible your results should be aggregated with others in the industry to help keep track on the industry's progress to net zero. Ask your company about this plan and insist on one being developed if it is not yet in place. Once that is in place, insist that everyone up and down your supply chain does the same – this applies to your clients and to your partners across the advertising eco-system.

3 Train everyone in your company on the issue of climate change and the fundamental points of making our advertising industry more sustainable. Help them to understand the language, the developments in policies and regulations which will impact the way we work and the context for all these things that are happening.

4 Avoid greenwashing at all costs. There is absolutely no excuse for greenwashing, however unintentional it might be. Train yourself and your teams on all the rules that are in place around promoting environmental claims. Every ad that breaks the rules is a step backwards when it comes to the industry's work being trusted to promote a sustainable future. Stay up to date on these rules and principles too because they will change over time.

5 Implement practical action within your operations now to reduce GHG (Greenhouse Gas) emissions, starting with a switch to renewable energy suppliers and significant reduction of business flights as these are the two biggest causes of emissions.

6 Put in place a process to track, measure, report and reduce the emissions involved in the production of your advertising. Make the most of the knowledge and tools available from initiatives like AdGreen and Green The Bid.

7 Take immediate action to implement the recommendations by the WFA/ GARM and IAB Tech Lab to decarbonize your media plans – there are quick wins which can have a significant impact on reducing GHG emissions caused by the distribution of advertising. Get ready to engage with a global data framework.

8 Stay up to date on the practical steps being taken by media and tech companies in the supply chain to decarbonize their operations. Develop a framework which allows you to reward and invest in those leading the way (while maintaining the full effectiveness of your media plan). Consider how your ad investment can facilitate a more rapid transition by your most important media partners.

9 If you run any type of advertising industry awards scheme, include sustainability criteria around the operations, production and distribution of the work, and around the objective and evaluation of the campaign's success. No work can be deemed creatively excellent in a sustainable advertising industry without this evidence supporting every award entry. Declaring winners but not making this type of information publicly available will simply not be credible.

10 If you run any type of advertising industry event, consider all the ways you can reduce the environmental impact without reducing the quality for your attendees (in-person and online). Make sure you access knowledge and tools from the likes of isla which specialize in helping event teams decarbonize all kinds of events. Wasteful events will rightly become targets for those critical of the advertising industry.

11 Familiarize yourself with, and stay on top of, the critical geopolitical developments around climate action – these will shape the industries, markets, and future client companies that the advertising industry serves.

12 Be clear in your mind about where the big citizen behaviour changes are required to support a sustainable future: around energy, travel and

transport, food consumption/waste, consumables, fast fashion. How do brands and even adjacent sectors like financial services help people make better, more sustainable choices? 'Ask what role does the business I am producing work for have in this, and how we can support and encourage rapid scale behaviour change in a responsible way?'

13 Understand the levers of sustainable behaviour change – how to motivate citizens at scale to do things in support of a sustainable future. Understand the value of insights that identify the moment of change and the most crucial factors in landing the change. Consider the effectiveness of campaigns with positive framing, how to highlight the personal benefits and how sustainability messaging figures best alongside other key factors such as pricing and ease of access to the better, more sustainable choice.

14 Learn from others – keep connected to experts in climate science, nature, or circularity to help your understanding stay current. Regularly look for best practice and the work that is being recognized as good by the industry. Ask yourself how you can go one better than your competitors. Compete and innovate to inspire the fastest possible progress for a sustainable future.

15 Work to ensure every campaign is measured across two key parameters – its behaviour impact or commercial success (as it always has been) but, in addition, its sustainability success (with a series of new metrics in play). Ask: am I helping to make the big brands better and the better brands bigger? Is my work solving more challenges than it's creating? The best work should be rewarded for its net positive impact, alongside the sales it achieves. Take the time for those conversations between client and agency to change the brief and align on the metrics of success.

16 Secure the best talent. Create a talent strategy based on the insight that the best people are motivated to work on campaigns where success includes a sustainable outcome. Any business not evidently pursuing this objective will be a second-choice employer to a competitor that evidently addresses the needs of all its stakeholders. Bring your incentive scheme into line with commercial and sustainability metrics.

Start your change journey here: summary

This is a pivotal moment for the advertising industry – we have a unique role to play in helping to meet the challenge of climate change and biodiversity loss. Our industry needs your help to deliver the actions that are needed, not just to shift this industry to a sustainable footing, but to help all other parts of the economy and society around the world to do the same.

A *Sustainable Advertising* industry will be a better form of our industry, better equipped to support a sustainable future on this planet – do not underestimate the importance of the action and the impact you can have with the work you do. It's difficult to imagine the world tolerating a version of our industry which fails to meet this challenge.

We end this book with a call-to-action to you, the reader. You are a *Sustainable Advertising* change-maker. Take the resources we have laid out and put them into practice now, in every way that you can. Be part of the change, help to ensure advertising is a net positive force for good, and use your energy and talents to build a sustainable future for us all.

If you'd like to continue the conversation we've started in this book, please get in touch. www.sustainableadvertising.uk

INDEX

Note: Page numbers in *italics* refer to tables or figures.

Looking for another book?

Explore our award-winning
books from global business
experts in Marketing and Sales

Scan the code to browse

www.koganpage.com/marketing

Also from Kogan Page

ISBN: 9781398604049

ISBN: 9781398609839

ISBN: 9781789668247

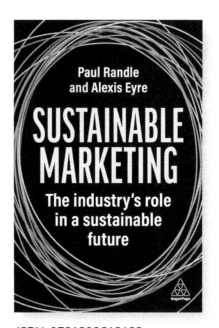

ISBN: 9781398613133

Printed in the USA
CPSIA information can be obtained
at www.ICGtesting.com
JSHW050008170524
63287JS00004B/90